ALSO BY JOHN MAN

*The Survival of Jan Little*
*Atlas of the Year 1000*
*Gobi*
*Alpha Beta*
*The Gutenberg Revolution*
*Genghis Khan*
*Attila the Hun*
*Kublai Khan*
*The Terracotta Army*
*The Great Wall*
*Xanadu*
*Samurai*
*The Mongol Empire*
*Saladin*
*Amazons*
*Barbarians at the Wall*

JOHN MAN

# CONQUERING THE NORTH

## China, Russia, Mongolia: 2,000 Years of Conflict

**A Oneworld Book**

First published in the United Kingdom, Republic of Ireland
and Australia by Oneworld Publications Ltd, 2025


A CIP record for this title is available from the British Library

ISBN 978-0-86154-960-3
eISBN 978-0-86154-961-0

Typeset by Geethik Technologies
Printed and bound in Great Britain by Clays Ltd, Elcograf S.p.A.



The authorised representative in the EEA is eucomply OÜ,
Pärnu mnt 139b–14, 11317 Tallinn, Estonia
(email: hello@eucompliancepartner.com / phone: +33757690241)

Oneworld Publications Ltd
10 Bloomsbury Street
London WC1B 3SR
England

# CONTENTS

**Genghis or Chinggis?**

'Genghis' is traditional in English, and incorrect. It's time to use his name in Mongolian, Chinggis. Appendix III explains why.

**A note on subjects covered previously**

This book revises and condenses several chapters in *Genghis Khan, The Terracotta Army, Barbarians at the Wall, The Great Wall* and *Xanadu*. Chapter 9 on the Treaty of Nerchinsk is a revised version of an article published in the *Journal of the Royal Asiatic Society China* in 2020 (Vol. 8, No. 1).

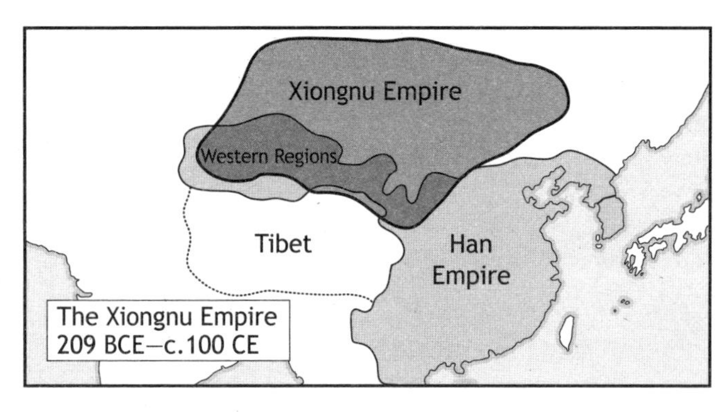
Xiongnu Empire
Western Regions
Tibet
Han Empire
The Xiongnu Empire
209 BCE–c.100 CE

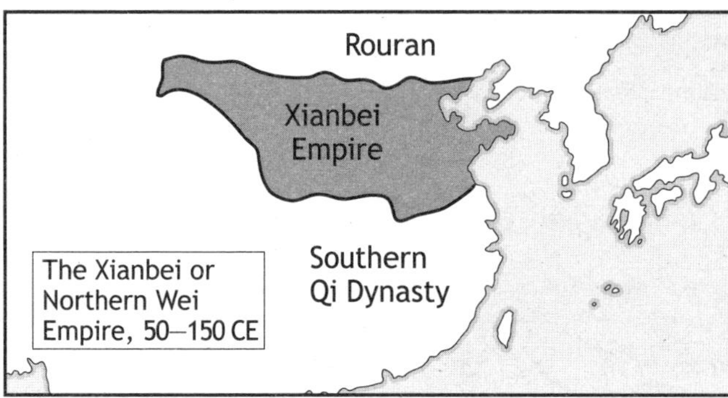
Rouran
Xianbei Empire
Southern Qi Dynasty
The Xianbei or Northern Wei Empire, 50–150 CE

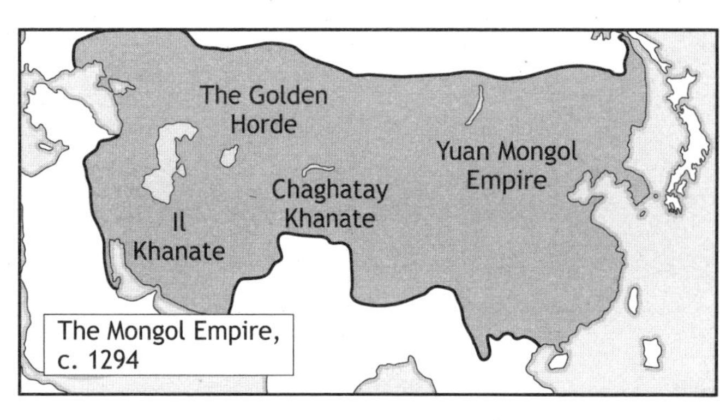
The Golden Horde
Yuan Mongol Empire
Chaghatay Khanate
Il Khanate
The Mongol Empire, c. 1294

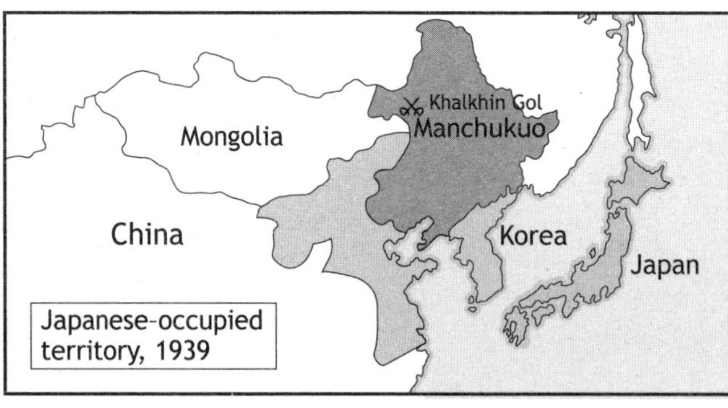
Khalkhin Gol
Manchukuo
Mongolia
China
Korea
Japan
Japanese-occupied territory, 1939

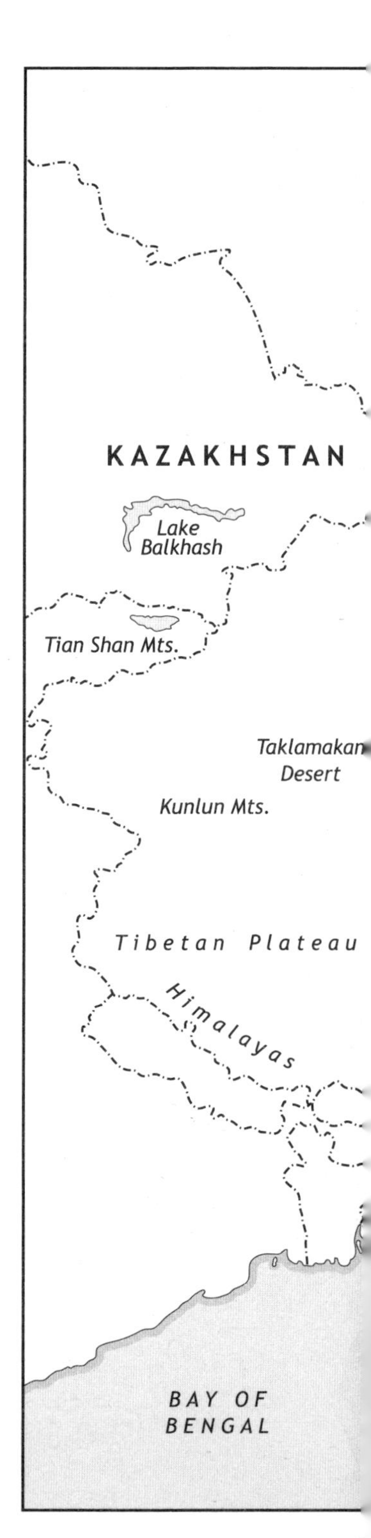
KAZAKHSTAN
Lake Balkhash
Tian Shan Mts.
Taklamakan Desert
Kunlun Mts.
Tibetan Plateau
Himalayas
BAY OF BENGAL

Russo-Chinese border, Treaty of Nerchinsk, 1689
Territory Gained by Russia from China, 1858
Territory Gained by Russia from China, 1860
Great Wall of China
RUSSIA
Lake Baikal
Noyon Uul
Gol Mod 2
Gol Mod 1
Burkhan Khaldun
Ulaanbaatar
Ga Xian Cave
Khalkhin Gol
MONGOLIA
INNER MONGOLIA
Gobi Desert
Shang-du (Xanadu)
Vladivostok
NORTH KOREA
SOUTH KOREA
Ordos
Beijing
Yellow River
Luoyang
Xi'an
JAPAN
CHINA
PACIFIC OCEAN

# Preface

The Gobi Desert, on Mongolia's southern border: sand, gravel and gnarled saxaul bushes.

I was travelling in a Ukrainian 4x4 with my guide, Erdene, and the driver Byamba. We stopped at a tent for the night, expecting and receiving hospitality from the herdsman and his family, as is normal in rural Mongolia. In the morning, I was outside with Erdene, 'looking after our horses', as the Mongolians say; taking a piss in other words. The sun was not yet up. But across a grey infinity was a wonderful sight, a saw-tooth of fire floating in the twilit sky. It was, as I realised later, the snows of the Tian Shan mountains rising above the horizon and set aflame by the unrisen sun. I was amazed and puzzled.

'What,' I asked, 'is *that*?'

Erdene glanced up. 'China,' he said. 'Very dangerous.'

China proper lay two hundred kilometres away, the other side of the Great Wall, that ancient division between settled and nomad, but for centuries the Wall has been no division at all. Once China had included all Mongolia, and even now it flowed almost to our feet. The fear that Mongolians have of their vast neighbour is a major theme of this book. Another is the ancient fear felt in China for the rapacious northern 'barbarians' and a much more modern feeling that the Mongolians and other northern minorities are, or should be, part of China. The minorities are right to be nervous. China, mainly in the form of the dominant Han (ethnic Chinese), is so supreme, its population so overwhelming, its economy so hungry, that it cannot help but dominate, flowing northwards like the waves of an incoming tide, advancing, retreating, advancing again, beyond the Great Wall, on to the grasslands and deserts of Central Asia, and further. Russia, too, should be nervous, for China has claims – established in a seventeenth-century treaty – to chunks of Siberia and Manchuria. If these claims are ever made, the world will face a crisis rivalling that posed by a Chinese invasion of Taiwan.

This is a big subject. A definitive history of all non-Chinese peoples and empires beyond the Wall would take more lifetimes than I have available.[1] I have chosen subjects from areas I know best to illustrate the main theme of China's erratic northward expansion over two millennia. Many of the stories resonate today, which allows me to include experiences gathered over twenty-five years of travel in independent Mongolia and Inner Mongolia, now part of China.

The Yellow River southbound on the eastern edge of Ordos.

# PRELUDE

# The Making of the Borderlands

## A Swim in Silt

AS THE YELLOW RIVER SWEEPS CLEAR OF THE TIBETAN highlands, it makes a bend to the left and heads north. It is not a pretty river at this point – patchy fields on the west bank, low hills of semi-desert on the other, and between them a 500-metre-wide slurry carried from the roof of the world, Tibet, three thousand kilometres to the west. This is the siltiest river in the world, notorious for its power to flood and destroy. It runs on north, is diverted east and then south by mountain ranges, its silt acting like a chainsaw, cutting away at cliffs, until, with a sharp left turn, it resumes its course across the fertile, silt-rich lowlands of central and eastern China. For centuries, the burden of silt dumped barriers of sediment, which at unpredictable intervals diverted the river into new channels, drowning untold lowlands and untold victims in catastrophic floods. Chinese scientists have estimated the amount of silt involved. Before the building of dams, the river carried around 1.5 billion tonnes a year – a quarter the weight of London.[1]

The first time I stood by its muddy side, I saw a chance to learn about its silt first-hand, by total immersion. It was high summer, the current sluggish. There was a bridge a kilometre upstream and a collection of

108 Buddhist stupas marked a gentle rise back from the bank, but no one was around. The nearest city, Yinchuan, was far off. My companion, a Mongolian teacher and old friend named Jorigt, was appalled by my idea.

'Do not do this thing,' he said as I stripped off.

Mongolians live in land-locked regions. They are often nervous of water.

'Oh, come on, Jorigt,' I said. 'It's shallow. I can swim. What could go wrong?'

I waded in through mud until the water swirled round my waist. The current picked up, but there was no danger. I took a breath, ducked into the murk, opened my eyes and saw absolutely nothing but a pale light filtering through the silt. It was like being wrapped in a liquid blanket. I stood, ankle-deep in mud, dripping silt, and gave Jorigt a wave, to show him that to duck beneath the opaque waters of a notoriously destructive river was no big deal, not here, not at this time of year.

'You're crazy,' he said as I waded ashore. 'What would I do if you drowned?'

I shrugged off his worry. I had what I wanted, a baptism at the point where the Yellow River starts on its rectangular sweep around this section of our subject. The box made by the Great Bend, as it is called, encloses Ordos, a slab of ancient grassland, desert and semi-desert. The name, used by its Mongolian inhabitants from the seventeenth century, means 'palace-tents', after the shrine of tents that once, it is said, held the remains of Mongolia's greatest hero, Chinggis Khan. You may not know that you know of Ordos, but you do, sort of. It is the only Mongolian word to have a version of itself in English – a Mongol-Turkic root produced *ordos* in Mongolian and (via Turkic) 'horde' in English, as in a 'horde of nomads', or the Golden Horde, which was the Mongol-controlled region of southern Russia for three centuries.

It's hard to grasp the scale and emptiness of these plateaus and eroded semi-deserts, let alone the surrounding landscapes. Ordos, with a population of two million, is almost three-quarters the size of England, but only one of twelve subdivisions of Inner Mongolia, a region of grasslands, deserts, mountains and forests that would fill most of western Europe. Scale, though, is not the point. Ordos plays a role in history far greater than the size of its population would suggest.

It is a geographical anomaly. Embraced by the Great Bend of the Yellow River, Ordos should be part of the rest of China. But in terms of climate and culture, it belongs north of the river, as part of the grasslands that flow all across Eurasia to the *puszta* of Hungary. Three thousand years ago, when it was much lusher than today, Ordos was home to tough horsemen, the precursors of the Mongols. Then the Chinese seized it, after which it became a shuttlecock, disputed by both sides, slowly and erratically colonised by China. When the area came under the control of Beijing, it became a league (or province) called Ikh Juu* (Mongolian for 'Great Monastery'), another reference to the shrine of Chinggis Khan. Only in 2001 did the Great Monastery formally become Ordos (E-Er-Duo-Si / 鄂尔多斯) in Chinese, which is also the name of its capital. So it's formally Chinese, but retains its Mongol roots.

Today, farmers plough its south, villages have become cities, mines tear out its guts. To understand its essence – its shape, its subterranean wealth, its nomadic traditions – demands that we delve deep into its past.

## OF SWAMPS, FERNS AND THE GREAT BEND

If you could go looking for Ordos 350 million years ago, you would have a hard time finding it. The world then was an unrecognisable scattering of continents and mini-continents left over from the break-up of the super-continent known to geologists as Gondwana. One of these bits was the future China. It had broken away from Gondwana 200 million years earlier and, like all the other continental fragments, was being

* In 'Ikh' the *kh* is pronounced like the *ch* in *loch*. An alternative transliteration is *Yeke*, which is from the ancient vertical script used in Inner Mongolia. The language has moved on, but the script hasn't.

carried by a conveyor belt of molten rock surging up from deep inside the earth. 'Ordos' rode on the front of 'China' as it migrated westwards, very slowly – continents move at about 1.5 centimetres per year – but it adds up, given enough time: 1,500 kilometres in 100 million years. Some 335 million years ago, the scattered continents drifted together to create another super-continent, Pangaea (from the Greek, meaning 'Land Everywhere').

For much of this time, the region that would become Ordos was a bog. The low-lying land was covered with trees, not like today's, but ferns, which had been evolving over millions of years to be tall and strong. When they died, they turned into stagnant swamps. You would have expected them to rot away, as fallen trees normally do today. But they didn't. Scientists argue about why not. One theory is that the micro-fauna that rot trees had not yet evolved. Another widely accepted view is that, as the lakes continued to come and go, each inundation covered the fallen trees with sediment, protecting them from decay and fungi. Fern-trees fell on fern-trees, swamp flattened swamp, for tens of millions of years. Protected from decay by ever-thickening blankets of sediment, the fallen trees turned to peat, and then coal, a process that in Ordos occurred mainly in the Jurassic Period (200–145 million years ago).

Coal, coal and more coal, in layers that go down some 350 metres, making up one-sixth of China's coal reserves. You would not believe the amount of coal there is under Ordos's dusty surface, until you see blue trailer-trucks nose-to-tail, hauling the guts of Ordos eastwards over the Yellow River to feed China's insatiable hunger. The coal roads are arteries, the economy's lifeblood, and its poison. The arteries, like the economy itself, clog with pollution. Too often, Beijing and other great cities of the east turn into cauldrons of murk, some of it swept in from the sandy Gobi, but much of it from yet another million cars and the smoke coughed out by coal-fired power-stations. It won't go on. China is making huge investments in wind-power. In decades to come, what's left of Ordos's coal will remain buried.

Ordos's coal deposits long pre-date the Yellow River and its great three-sided, 1,300-kilometre Great Bend (sometimes called the Ordos Loop). This, more than any other feature, defines Ordos. The river owes its course to mountain ranges, which guide it in ninety-degree turns north, east and south, before it joins another great river, the Wei, and veers again eastwards to start its final thousand-kilometre course to the sea. But when dinosaurs were roaming Ordos, there was no Yellow River, and the mountains that guide it today did not exist. What is now Tibet was not the Roof of the World but a floor.

Come forward in time to about fifty million years ago. The dinosaurs have been gone for sixteen million years. The continents are now vaguely recognisable, except that there is no Central Asia. It is under the warm waters of a great inland sea, the Tethys. To the west of Ordos is a lowland plain bordering the Tethys. But change is coming. All this while, for some hundred million years, a small continental plate that would become India has been drifting north.

Some fifty million years ago, India hit Asia. The two continents buckled, along a front of 3,400 kilometres, forcing rocks upwards and downwards in a crumple-zone that spread some 2,000 kilometres inland. The Tethys slowly drained away, becoming a series of puddles – the Mediterranean, the Black Sea, the Caspian, the Aral. Great new mountain ranges pushed up: the Hindu Kush, the Himalayas, the Tian Shan, the Altai.

While this was happening, there was indeed a river flowing from the forming hills to the west of Ordos. It was an early version of the Yellow River. But it did not flow around Ordos. At Lanzhou, where the river turns north today, it went straight on, into the valley of what is now the Wei. Vast tectonic forces were creating geological wrinkles across all Central Asia, building new, small ranges like the Helan Shan, running north from the Lanzhou area, the Yin mountains running east–west and the north–south Lüliang mountains. By chance, as you see from the map, these three made the rectangular box-like shape that exists today.

Pressures were growing in what was the upper Wei. Silt, folding and uplift combined to dam the river, separating the two systems by two hundred kilometres. The water chose a new course, northwards, constrained by the Helan Shan to the west. Some 650 kilometres later, it ran up against the Yin mountains. After a hesitation in lowlands between the two ranges, the waters found their way along the southern flanks of the Yin until they encountered the Lüliangs and veered south, scouring away the underlying strata. Today, as for the last five million years or so, the Yellow River finally rejoins its old course, with the Wei as its major tributary.

That's how its course arose, defining Ordos with a shape that Chinese see as the character *ji* 几. This meaningless coincidence seems to Chinese like an expression of some deep truth, namely that Ordos and the upper Yellow River have always been Chinese. Well, no. Far from it, as we'll see.

## AN X-RAY OF ORDOS

To see what silt and water can do, head east from Ordos City, towards the bridge that carries the G18 expressway across the Yellow River into Shanxi. If before the bridge you turn right, you have a chance to look under the soft skin of Ordos and examine her bones. Head south and then east over side roads until, quite suddenly, you fall off the edge of the world. The road winds down, along with an endless line of trucks battering the already battered road beneath a craggy rock face. Far below, past many hairpin bends and crossed by an ancient bridge, runs the green water of the Yellow River. *Green?* It was the unlikely colour of an unripe plum. Something seemed to have captured the yellow silt that gave the river its name.

Across we went, with truck nudging truck like a herd of restless bulls. A winding rise took us out of the shadows on to rolling hills, where farmers spread their newly harvested crops on the road to be winnowed by passing cars. Within minutes, we were looking down on an immense vista, from a place which – a notice announced – was called Heaven and Earth Bend. A walkway punctuated by statues and pagodas led along a cliff, where a concrete winged bull hauled a concrete plough. A notice explained that the bull prevents the ghost of the river from 'making trouble'.

No trouble was visible from this vantage point. Our clifftop fell away to a clutter of terraces, their crops harvested to leave a stubble of autumnal brown. Beyond, was the edge of Ordos, its surface of low hills cut away by the river in two great curves, making an S-shape as smooth and neat as the teardrops of the yin-and-yang Daoist symbol, which converts all opposites into harmony. That day, with the river's bends emerging from distant haze, nothing could have been more harmonious.

But this was a heaven's-eye view. To see deeper into Ordos – to feel the power of the silty water – you need to get up close.

The road wound onwards and downwards, past terraces of sorghum, around gullies, past hills capped by beacon towers, outposts of the Great Wall. A few minutes' drive brought us to a charming village, Old Cattle Bend, that looked like both an artists' colony and a tourist camp. But this was autumn, and there were few people to disturb the peace. Houses were made of old wood and the local slate. An antique wooden doorway, draped with banners pleading for prosperity, hid a stone-walled courtyard. There was even a delightful little outside theatre.

The paved path and some rough steps led down to the river bank, where a red-and-white speedboat waited to take out-of-season tourists closer to Ordos's foundations. We put on cumbersome lifejackets, held tight, zoomed off downstream and across the river towards cliffs and steep, grass-covered slopes which ended in sudden drops, like feet sliced off at the toes by the river. The light-grey cliffs, towering over us, showed the power of the silty water. They were stacks of strata, hundreds of them, the fossilised sediments laid down at the bottom of lakes, making a pile like rocky documents hinting at a narrative stretching back 350 million years. Some were as thin as sheets of paper, some as thick as a book, a few as solid as encyclopaedias. And that was just what was on view above the waterline. Those layers were as nothing compared to the libraries that lay hidden beneath the river, for the strata, including layers of coal, go down for hundreds of metres.

Hair flying, we retraced on still waters the twisting road we had just taken by car. The reason for the calmness came into view: a huge dam, Wanjiazhai, 'Ten Thousand Households' – one hundred metres high, holding back waters eighteen metres deep, as the boatman shouted. Below the water were thirty to forty metres of sediment, the residue of what used to flow downstream. Now this section of the river, like every other section, was tamed. That's why the Yellow River, stripped of its yellow silt, is as green as an unripe plum below the dam.

## THE EASTERN GRASSLANDS EMERGE

Ordos is just a small part of our subject, which is China's northern border with Mongolia and Russia, four thousand miles of it, from the deserts of Xinjiang, along the sandy and gravelly wastes of the Gobi, over the grassland and forests of the north-east and descending to the edge of North Korea. The border has emerged and vanished and shifted many times during the last two thousand years. Today's China has settled into a surly acceptance that a limit has been reached, for the moment anyway.

In the far north-east is a region named after its two biggest lakes, Hulun and Buir. Hulunbuir is another of those vast areas with few inhabitants, wonderful natural expanses – grasslands in the west, the forest of the Khingan mountains in the east – and a past full of very un-Chinese peoples who have seen their homelands eaten up by the ever-hungry culture to the south.

The road northwards into Hulunbuir leads uphill into a wilderness of rough lava, where firs fight for a foothold in small pockets of soil. Hot springs show that underground the earth is still settling after some enormous volcanic outburst. This is the Arxan National Forest Park, newly opened for tourists, with camping spots and walkways over a tortured landscape. Side roads lead to lakes, lava tubes, fumaroles and caves. Pale in the distance rises a peak with a dip in the top – the crater of an extinct volcano that holds the Tianchi Crater Lake, capped by firs, like a jewel set in green satin. It was from this peak and others that the lava poured, for millennia, hardening into the rubble on view as you cross the provincial border into Hulunbuir.

The park testifies to the forces that made today's grasslands and forested mountains. As China-to-be inched towards the rest of Eurasia, it squeezed away much of the ocean between them. Around 270 million years ago, they met, thrusting up a crumple-zone of mountain ranges, including the Urals and the Khingan, leaving a remnant of the former ocean.

After gathering breath for a hundred million years, the continental plates shifted again, eating up the last bit of ocean, rebuilding the old worn-down ranges and forcing up new young peaks. Volcanoes blasted through the earth's distorted crust, like steam bursting through the top of a pie in a hot oven. In Ordos, as in other parts of the world, dinosaurs roamed, while here lava flowed over hundreds of thousands of square kilometres, the vestiges of which you see today in the Arxan National Forest Park. The lowlands, previously covered by oceans, became huge plains overlying a complex of rocky arcs running south-west to north-east across north China and Mongolia. On geological maps, colourful minerals look like a swirling palette freshly squeezed from gigantic tubes.

The road winds down to Chai He, the first town inside Hulunbuir. We had been driving for over three hours along a fine new road. Newly wealthy China is good at new roads, linking these remote places. We had seen perhaps a dozen cars and no settlements except buildings marking a few scenic spots. Otherwise, nothing but rolling, tree-clad hills, the pristine home for bear and elk. Now, at last, we entered the lowlands named after Hulunbuir's best-known minority, the Ewenki, whose story I will tell in due course.

In the far south-west of the province, just before the broad and slow-moving River Kherlen, a track leads into grasslands – so dry when I was there that it was almost desert – climbs into low hills, past rocks that poke through the skin of soil like the bones of the earth, and at last, over a rise, ends in a charming hidden valley: a little winding river, well-watered pasture and a mass of vast, smooth boulders tumbled together to make a cliff and a hill.

This is the local geopark, a memorial to the last ice age, as my guide Ying Bai explained. She was a young Daur, a Mongol subgroup. For tens of thousands of years, north-east China had been locked in ice, the ground permanently frozen. By about twelve thousand years ago, the ice in the northern parts of Russia, Europe and America was on the retreat, and the frozen island of ice centred on Hulunbuir and the Khingan mountains melted. The two lakes, Hulun and Buir, are remnants of that meltwater. That was when the geopark emerged roughly in its present form.

It's a pretty spot. On our right, as we walk down over the grass, stand two willows, both doing well, alongside a third tree, this one a desiccated skeleton. Visitors, seeing the green-leaved trees as symbols of enduring love, have wrapped blue silk scarves round their trunks and hauled rocks around them, turning them into the centrepieces of a nature-worshipper's shrine.

There's water and pasture, enough for a small family to live here, according to a story told by Ying Bai. Once, there was a Mongolian wrestler called Ishgin, who lived here in the 1930s and 1940s, before going to Mongolia. So strong was he that when he went off to Mongolia, he put a whole tent on his back and set his mother on the top. 'His name is interesting,' Alatan, my Mongolian-Chinese companion, put in. '*Ishig* is a young goat in the first year of life, very weak. They called him Ishgin Bökh, "The Strength of a Young Goat", as a nickname, a joke.' Anyway, went on Ying Bai, he came back, and set himself up here – in a cave up there in the rocks – as a sort of a Robin Hood, attacking rich men and officers and giving what he stole to the poor. His noble efforts were rewarded with death in prison.

'They call his home Cave Rock,' she said. 'Come and see it.'

It was an easy climb over the ice-rounded boulders, moulded together as neatly as lumps of dough by millennia of rain, snow, frost and sun. Swallows swooped and twittered above, hunting unseen insects. At the highest spot, two massive stones, one overlapping the other, formed a roof, as in a Stone Age tomb, except they had not been placed by people but dumped by ice. Underneath yawned the cave, not a comfortable place, because the 'floor' sloped at a steep angle. But with enough animal skins Ishgin could have survived a winter or two.

Down below, where the little river swirled around the base of the cliff, visitors had climbed a couple of metres to shove silk scarves into a rocky cleft. I supposed they were honouring Ishgin's memory and, perhaps, the rocks themselves, which marked the slow changes as the soon-to-be grasslands shrugged off the mantle of ice.

Time passed, ice vanished, grasslands grew, rivers formed. In many official buildings in Hulunbuir, you see a glorious high-angle panorama of a river wandering along a grassy valley. The river, the Mergel, is only about thirty kilometres north of the capital Hailar, which makes the Mergel valley the second most popular destination for tourists in Hulunbuir (the main one being Manzhouli on the Russian border, which has casinos, night clubs and leggy Russian pole-dancers). One summer's day, I joined the grasslanders. The driver turned off the expressway on to a narrow concrete road, abandoned the road for a track, forded a shallow river and climbed steeply over well-worn mud to a ridge.

And there was the famous view: the Mergel below, twisting its way over pasture as green as the lawn of an English stately home, sheep and horses grazing, but not a herder or a tent in sight, and all laid out under a blue sky and bright sun. Sometimes on the grasslands, mosquitoes and flies pester, but there were none. It could not have been more perfect. This was nature at its most pristine, untouched by human beings, just like the panorama I had seen in Hailar, the river as motionless as a well-fed snake.

The vision lasted a few seconds only. There was movement. Light flickered on ripples. The water was flowing from left to right, eating away its green banks. A tongue of land stood clear as the water swung round a corner, cutting a low cliff. Other bends told of a slow-motion dance between water and earth, as with any other meandering river. Every now and then, the current had cut through a corner, and left a gently curving lake, which over the years had filled with earth and become again part of the grassland. Grassy furrows showed where the river had once flowed, and narrow spits of land where the water would cut through in the not-too-distant future. How boring a straight river would have been, or even a succession of regular curves. It was the irregularity, those hints of past changes and changes to come, of a narrative working itself out over centuries, that created a scene more beautiful than any print or poster.

I became aware of the others who had come to stare. We were lined up like the front row of a theatre gallery, with cars parked by the dozen on either side. Now the onlookers became as intriguing as the view, taking selfies, posing and smiling for friends. Up here, the mass of 4x4s had churned away the grass to leave bare earth. It seemed that to view one large well-preserved section of grassland it was necessary to ruin a smaller one.

How long would it last, people and nature in balance? It was already manufactured; prehistory restored to draw tourists in. Not long ago, there had been herders here, with their tents and telegraph poles – all gone now, to maintain the illusion of an unsullied landscape for the visitors. How to manage this artifice? I imagined a consumerist future: a paved road leading up here, a viewing platform, viewing times, tickets sold, perhaps more being charged for a front seat, all to see a river and a pasture kept timeless by laws and restrictions.

I had not seen the half of it. From this glorious view, we followed the track down to a road that led on along the valley, swinging back and forth, up and down. The valley itself is some eighty kilometres long, and the river, with its countless twists and turns, many times longer. The whole valley is one huge tourist site in the making, served by the newly paved road, already punctuated by encampments and food stalls. A side road leads to a luxury hotel, where you can get an air-conditioned bedroom overlooking the Mergel. All along the road, fences keep grazing sheep at bay, but leave plenty of room for cars.

We pulled into a huge car park, where canvas-roofed stalls offered food for tourists. 'Ice cream!' yelled a voice over a loudspeaker. 'Local yoghurt!' A sign read: 'Feed the sheep, twenty yuan a turn.' Twenty yuan for what? For grass, of which there were infinite amounts on the other side of the wire fence. Perhaps, I joked to Alatan, some enterprising businessman will bottle the Mergel air for visitors to take back to Beijing. More than likely, he rejoined: gasping Beijingers can in fact buy compressed air from Tibet.

The road dropped and ran closer to the river. I walked down to a bend where the slow-moving current revealed a gravelly beach. A lone fisherman stood like a statue further downstream. I dipped a hand into the water, feeling privileged, as if by some dreadful administrative error I had been allowed access to a priceless artefact. I imagined a future in which such an intrusion into such a carefully managed scene would be banned, unless I paid extra.

## THE COMING OF THE NOMADS

As the ice retreated, warmer climates across Eurasia gave rise to two new systems. The first was farming, which allowed for permanent settlements and larger, complex societies, typically based on major rivers. But the heart of Eurasia held another world that was no use to farmers – an ocean of grass stretching from the far east to Hungary, from the forests of Siberia down to the deserts of western China and

Ordos. This was the domain of gazelles and wild horses and wolves, until those on the borderlands developed another lifestyle entirely. In about 3500 BCE, some groups learned how to tame horses. With nothing but a bit and reins (neither saddles nor stirrups are necessities), horse-riders could herd horses, sheep, cattle, goats, camels, reindeer and yaks. To stay with your herds, all you needed was a tent (which evolved into today's warm, cool, wind-shouldering domes of felt) and a wagon to put it on. Grass, when processed by animals, became food, fuel, clothing and covers for your tent. This new grassland culture spread slowly during the first millennium BCE. Herders learned how to forge bronze and then iron for swords and arrowheads.

Pastoral nomads were also warriors. A tool used for hunting also served as a formidable weapon. The composite recurved bow is a half-circle combination of horn, wood, sinew and glue, which is strung by a strong arm bending it back on itself. It ranks with the Roman sword and the machine gun as a weapon that changed the world. Who first invented it and when is much debated, but by the time of the Trojan War, perhaps about 1250 BCE, it was the weapon of choice for hunters and mounted warriors across all Europe and Asia.

The power of this weapon was astonishing. At close range, say fifty to a hundred metres, the right sort of arrow with the right sort of head can pierce armour. The range was equally astonishing, as the earliest inscription in Mongol reveals. It was carved on a two-metre-high stone, probably in 1226. Found in 1818 in southern Siberia near today's Mongolian border, it was made when Chinggis Khan had just returned from a triumphant campaign in the Muslim world. He ordered a celebration during which his nephew Yesunge decided to display his legendary strength and skill. The stone records the extraordinary result: 'While Chinggis Khan was holding an assembly of Mongolian dignitaries... Yesunge hit a target at 335 alds.' An *ald* was the distance between a man's fingertips with arms outstretched, about 1.6 metres. So Yesunge's unspecified target – a tree, perhaps, or a tent – was some five hundred metres away.*

Horse-riders, armed with their powerful little bows, could gallop wherever there was grass and raid whoever happened to be in the way, like other nomads and merchant caravans and – on the edges of their world – villages and cities. Settled societies had no answer, because the horsemen appeared from nowhere and vanished like mist at dawn.

Arrowheads had their own sub-technology. Pastoral nomads had metallurgists, who knew how to smelt iron from rock, and smiths with the tools and skills to cast and forge. Bone served well enough for hunting, but warfare demanded points of metal – bronze or iron – with two or three fins, which would slot onto the arrow. Blacksmiths became crucial members of their societies – Chinggis Khan's birth-name was Temujin, given him by his father after he captured an enemy of that name, or possibly profession: it means 'blacksmith'.

In the mid-first millennium BCE, pastoral nomads established themselves from the borderlands of China to the Black Sea, where they became the distant neighbours of the Greeks. They were known then and now as 'Scythians', a vague term grouping untold numbers of clans and tribes that spanned all inner Asia. They get their name from a mythical Greek hero called Scythes, the son of the famously strong Hercules and the only one able to bend and string his father's bow. As Greek civilisation rose in the seventh and sixth centuries BCE, the Greeks knew about the 'Scythians' only from a distance. In the West, the Greek historian Herodotus is our major source. In about 460 BCE, he travelled to Olbia, then a thriving Greek frontier city on today's Ukrainian coast. From here, trading caravans run by Scythians set out

* Today, with modern materials and specially designed arrows, handheld bows can be made to fire three-quarters of a mile. The world record for a bow drawn purely by muscle-power is 1 mile 268 yards (1.8 kilometres), set by Harry Drake on Ivanpah Dry Lake, California, in 1971. Using his own specially designed bow, he lay on his back, pulling with both hands, with the bow braced by his feet.

for Central Asia and vanished into a void. 'I have never met anyone,' he wrote, 'who claims to have actually seen it.'

At the other end of Asia, the land that would become China was a mass of competing kingdoms. War followed war as each state struggled for survival and conquest. Over three hundred years, a hundred states whittled themselves down to seven, who were left to battle it out in the so-called Warring States period (about 481–221 BCE). Centuries of war to the east and south made little impression on the borderlands and their ancient ways.

But change was coming, kickstarted by the ambitious and ruthless man who forged the iron heart of a new empire.

The First Emperor's tomb mound (c.210 BCE), near Xi'an.

# PART I

# THE TALE OF THREE EMPIRES

*The story of China's erratic expansion northwards starts over two thousand years ago, before there was a China. Two antagonistic empires formed: one of farmers and cities, the core of today's nation; the other of nomadic herders on the northern grasslands. For almost three hundred years they were bitter enemies – one of the longest wars in history, and one of the least known to the outside world. Its end was unique: the total annihilation of this, the first nomad empire. It vanished, to be rediscovered only in recent decades. A third empire filled the void, also originally one of nomads, who, over the next three centuries, survived by settling down and adopting Chinese culture.*

A bers, *a mythical monster, on a plate found in a Xiongnu grave.*

CHAPTER 1

# FORGING UNITY, TWICE

## A MYSTERY IN MONGOLIA

IF YOU LEAVE THE CRAMMED STREETS AND TOXIC AIR OF THE Mongolian capital, Ulaanbaatar, and drive a hundred kilometres north along the only road, a track leads off to the right over the open steppe. Follow it towards the Russian border for half an hour, pitching like a dinghy in a swell over grassy dunes, and you pull at last into an area of pine-covered hills. Wander around. You will find yourself amid dozens of holes and trenches, all overgrown, like a long-abandoned battlefield. These are not shell-holes and dug-outs, but graves. The place, called Noyon Uul ('Royal Hills'), is a huge necropolis.

The site was discovered over a century ago, in the spring of 1913, by a Russian geologist named Andrei Ballod, surveying for a gold-mining company. Seeing that the mounds had been dug up some time in the past, he assumed they were old gold-workings, and ordered his team to excavate one. Almost four metres down, they hit a covering of wood and reeds. Underneath, lay a puzzling collection of objects – a jug, an axle-cap, bits of horse harnesses, pieces of gold and bronze. Ballod realised this was a burial mound. He sent some of the finds to the Imperial Russian Geographical Society's East Siberian branch in Irkutsk, describing them as 'The Ancient Tombs of Unknown People'. The Russian scientists were puzzled, but could do nothing, given the onset of war and revolution in both Russia and Mongolia.

Eleven years later, after Ballod's death, the famous Russian explorer Petr Kozlov arrived on his way to Tibet. He heard of the finds from a member of Ballod's team, and sent out a colleague, Sergei Kondratiev, to check out the site. Realising this was a major discovery, Kozlov changed his plans, joined the work and found that Noyon Uul covered almost twenty square kilometres, with 212 tumuli. The graves had been robbed, and had then become waterlogged and deep-frozen – luckily, because everything remaining had been deep-frozen as well.

Excavating eight mounds, Kozlov's team found sloping approaches to two-metre-high rooms made of pine logs, carpeted with embroidered wool or felt. Each contained a tomb of pine logs, and inside that a silk-lined larch-wood coffin. Every grave was a chaos of objects, some two thousand in all (most of them now in St Petersburg), tossed about among human and animal bones. These had been wealthy, cosmopolitan people. They valued handicrafts and foreign goods, some of which came from China, even Rome and Greece: patterned felt, lacquered wooden bottles, bronze pots, spoons of horn, knee-length underpants of wool and silk, bronze buckles, fur hats, jade decorations, golden jewellery, silver plates with yaks and deer in bas relief, felt carpets and tapestries embroidered with the heads of men and animals.

One summer a few years ago, I went to the site with two experts from Ulaanbaatar's Museum of Mongolian History – Odbaatar, weasel-slim and quiet-spoken, and his boss Gelegdorj Eregzen, whose dissertation was on Noyon Uul. Hidden by the trees and shrubs was a circular mound with a hole in its side. This was Kozlov's tomb No. 1, now looking like an overgrown well. Other mounds nearby were practically invisible. But within a kilometre, we stumbled on dozens, mostly only a metre or two high and ten metres apart. One, No. 24, was a crater six metres deep with an entrance road running into it – the result of excavations over recent years.

This cemetery was the first evidence of the earliest of many nomadic empires, and the greatest until the rise of the Mongols under Chinggis Khan over one thousand years later. It was this empire that set itself in opposition to China's newly formed core and caused China's first, and very expensive, surge northwards.

## IN ORDOS

At the time, no one knew who these people were or how they had arisen. We know a lot more now.

By about 500 BCE, many Scythian tribes had risen and fallen. Some left long-lasting remains, others vanished with hardly a trace, which was not the fate of two minor tribes living close to what we now call China.

Their homeland was Ordos, that region skirted by the Yellow River as it sweeps around the Great Bend. In 500 BCE, it was firmly in the hands of several tribes of nomadic herders, most notably two tribes called Di and Rong. Conditions were better then. According to recent archaeological evidence,[1] some eighty-five percent of Ordos was covered by forests and grassland as compared with only about nine percent today.[2] Those pastures were ideal for horse-riders and herders. Though they surely traded with their Chinese neighbours to the east and south, they looked mainly west and north to the grasslands, sharing with their peoples a way of life and a culture. We know something about them because of what they left beneath the soil.

One summer day in 1972, an old herdsman named Wang Shun was tending his flock in the semi-desert west of the region's capital, Ordos City, when a sudden storm shifted loose earth from a nearby slope. As the skies cleared, something glinted in the newly fallen soil. He dug, and found bits and pieces of gold, mixed in with bones. The storm had washed open a tomb, one of two, as later excavations revealed.

One of the 218 finds was a golden coronet with a separate golden skullcap topped by a turquoise-headed eagle. Despite not being bronze, it has since become the centrepiece of the Ordos Bronzes, the objects that define both the culture of Ordos and much of Scythian culture. It is the inspiration for Ordos City's Bronze Museum, which opened in 2015 to house the world's greatest collection of bronzes. The coronet is mirrored by the museum's design – circular, as the coronet is, with a blue domed roof, decorated with clouds, suggesting both the coronet's skullcap and the Mongolian deity, the Blue Sky.

The museum's curator, Wang Zhihao, introduced me to the collection, aided by Zhang Ziyang, deputy director of the Education Department. Mr Zhang was a fan of the imposing American ex-basketball player and rapper, Shaquille O'Neal, 'Shaq' to his admirers, which Mr Zhang had adapted into a pseudonym. He called himself 'Mr Shark'.

The coronet, of course, had pride of place, well-lit and glittering in its glass case. Up close, gold braid forms two semicircles – linked by horse-and-ram clasps – and above it another semicircle with a crouching tiger at either end completes the forehead section. On the separate skullcap stands the golden eagle with its turquoise head, which is attached to its body with gold wires, so that it would sway as the wearer moved. The skullcap itself is of four embossed sections, each holding a stylised wolf intertwined with a goat or ram. Dating probably from the third to second centuries BCE, it seems to assert the wealth and power of its owner.

As I gazed in awe, Mr Shark interjected: 'It's good, isn't? For a replica.'

'*What?*'

'Yes. The real one is in the museum in Hohhot.'

But why?

Mr Shark explained: Inner Mongolia's capital had the original long before the Bronze Museum was built, so they weren't about to give it up.

The bronzes themselves, only a few centimetres across, are mainly belt buckles, for belts proclaimed status, power, adulthood and identity. But the bronzes also include the tops of tent-poles, decorations for horse harnesses, daggers with decorated handles, mirrors and hooks.

A unique pair of weights were (perhaps) attached to a rope and thrown to entangle the legs of fleeing animals – a device otherwise unknown in Asia, but widely used in South America by Patagonian *gauchos* and as a weapon by the Incas.

The designs reflect a fascination with animals. Some are commonplace – horses, sheep, deer, birds – others less so: an eagle fighting a tiger for a goat, monsters of various sorts, warriors killing captives. Any of these may have a mirror-image double – the other half of the belt buckle. One odd mythological creature with a beak-like nose seems to have been unique to Ordos. A favourite motif was the tiger – as the golden coronet showed – often depicted eating a sheep or carrying a deer over its shoulder. Yet China had no tigers. The nearest ones, as today, were in the forests of Manchuria. Perhaps a tiger on your belt buckle was a statement of status and power.

Most of the bronzes come from graves, not just in Ordos but from hundreds of graves scattered across north China and inner Asia, even Iran. Specialists try to categorise the stylistic variants, tracking trade routes and dating them within their thousand-year span, between about 800 BCE and 200 CE. One cemetery alone, found in 1979 in Maoqinggou (Liangcheng County, Inner Mongolia, just east of Hohhot), had seventy-nine graves, with 229 bronze plaques, fairly evenly distributed between men and women (though elsewhere belt-plaques were mostly used by men). Many of these had Chinese characters on them, showing that China was not only an enemy but also a prime market.

A century ago, bronzes could be found lying about in the sand. Locals gathered them by the bucketful and sold them for a pittance. Only a few people, mostly foreigners, were interested in Chinese art and antiquities, which made the early twentieth century a golden age for foreign collectors of bronzes. As Mr Shark said ruefully, 'Some people might call this robbery.' But most of the recent finds are safe in in the museum. 'We have a collection of about ten thousand,' added Mr Wang. 'People still find them today.'

'What would one sell for?'

'Nothing,' said Mr Wang. 'It is illegal to sell them.'

But, as I discovered later, those rare bronzes that come up for auction fetch $600 and up. In 2015, one sold for €123,000.

## A NEW POWER ON THE GRASSLANDS

No one knows who made the bronzes. Carbon-14 dates of graves suggest that they were being made before 500 BCE, when pastoral nomadism began to develop. A reference in about 661 BCE mentions the Di and Rong, who had a reputation for violence. 'The Di and Rong are like wolves,' wrote an adviser to the state of Zhao, Guan Zhong. Fortunately for their neighbours, they lacked a charismatic leader to unify them. From the second half of the fourth century BCE, they were being conquered by, or absorbed into, a single tribe, who we can at last name as the Xiongnu (pronounced Shiung-noo).

We don't know what this new group called themselves in their unrecorded language, but another source suggests their name. In 313 BCE, a trader from Sogdia (in today's Uzbekistan and neighbouring countries) abandoned some letters – that is, strips of bamboo that were used to write on – in a tower near Dunhuang. The writer complains bitterly of the destruction caused by people he calls the *Xwn*, Hun. That is the core of their name in both Mongol and Chinese. In the Latin script versions of both languages, they are often simply 'Huns', implying that they were the ancestors of Attila's people who helped undermine the Roman Empire in the fifth century CE – an idea for which there is little evidence (see Appendix II).

The most common name reflects the Chinese version. To represent foreign names, Chinese chooses syllables that sound vaguely like the original. Since each syllable has many written signs, Chinese commonly select a character that suggests something suitable. 'Hun' in Chinese is represented by the sign 凶, that is transliterated in today's pinyin system as *xiōng*. Among other things, the sign means 'terrible, horrible, bad, fear-inducing'. Then, for some unknown reason, a Han-dynasty scribe added a second word with an ascending tone, *nú*, 奴, meaning 'slave'. 'Horrible slaves' – apparently that seemed a suitable name for the 'barbaric' northerners. Since China is the region's dominant culture, the new arrivals in Ordos are generally known as Xiongnu (or Hsiung-nu in the outmoded Wade-Giles transliteration).

That's what the historian Sima Qian called them, writing in the late second century BCE. Sima Qian, our major source, needs a diversion. Born around 145 BCE, he became the court's Grand Historian in his thirties, writing a monumental history, the *Shi Ji* (*Historical Records*), usually referred to in English as *The Records of the Grand Historian*. The books cover the whole history of China down to his own day. The history is a brilliant mix of oral and written sources, though he does not provide references, which makes him the top historian of ancient China. More than a historian, he is a wonderful teller of stories rich with anecdotes, personalities and dialogue. On one subject, he had a hidden agenda. He disapproved of the way his Emperor, Wu, dealt with the Xiongnu – by all-out war. This had been the policy of the First Emperor, China's unifier, the instigator of the Great Wall, his massive tomb mound and its guardians, the Terracotta Army. (More on both him and Wu later.) Sima Qian wished to criticise Wu, but could not, without courting death; so he attacked the First Emperor instead, giving him a very bad press, fleshed out with dramatic tales of dubious reliability. Much of what he says is backed by earlier sources, for all dynasties had their official histories, but some stories are well-spun, and a few are nothing more than hearsay or (in light of his Hollywood dialogue) pure fiction. The problem is that we cannot know which is which. Uncertainty permeates our story. It is the stuff of life, but that is not the same as truth.

Sima Qian's excesses are countered by another major source, written a thousand years later by Sima Guang (a remote descendant of Sima

Qian), who spent nineteen years with a team of researchers writing the monumental *Zizhi Tongjian* (*Mirror of Good Governance*) – 284 chapters, 354 volumes, covering almost 1,500 years from 403 BCE to 959 CE, and published in 1048. Very different from Sima Qian's biographical approach, Sima Guang's chronicle is chronological, more rigorous and much harder going.[3]

Neither of the Simas can say where the Xiongnu came from. No one can. In the words of Nicola Di Cosmo, of the Institute of Advanced Study, Princeton, 'After several decades of debates, questions relating to the ethnic and linguistic identity of the Xiongnu are still unanswered.' They migrated into Ordos from who-knows-where and somehow, by the late third century BCE, they had become a significant force. Their first proper mention comes in about 250 BCE. A few years later, they come into focus as they get their first named leader, Tumen. His title is *chanyu*, short for 'Chengli Gutu Chanyu', possibly meaning 'Heaven-sent Supreme Leader'.*

Not supreme yet. The Xiongnu owed allegiance both to the Dong and to the Yuezhi, a tribe ruling the west, in what is now Gansu. The Yuezhi are not well known, but they deserve better, because they play a major role in the Xiongnu story as well as the history of inner Asia. They probably migrated from southern Russia and settled in Gansu around 2000 BCE. Trading with China in jade and horses, they acquired their Chinese name, meaning 'Clan of the Moon', but what they called themselves is unknown.

Tumen, boss of the still insignificant Xiongnu, had a son named Modu,** who will soon take over the storyline. But not yet, because we must wait while Sima Qian gives him a motive to act. Tumen becomes infatuated with a new young wife with whom he has another son, and decides to replace Modu as his heir with his newborn. What is to be

---

* Perhaps, if their language was Turkic, 'chengli' equates to 'Tengri', the Turkic-Mongol god; and perhaps the 'chan-' of 'chanyu' sounded more like 'khan'.

** Or Modun, or various other transliterations. No telling which is correct.

done with Modu? A solution is at hand. To guarantee their security, and as a sign of submission, minor tribes often sent princes as hostages to dominant ones. So Tumen sends Modu off to the Yuezhi, where Sima Qian leaves him, seething with resentment against his father.

## MEANWHILE, IN 'CHINA'

It is 300 BCE, halfway through the Warring States period (403*–221 BCE): a hundred mini-states and city-states have fought themselves down to seven. The seven are at war, constantly. The obsession with war has equal and opposite obsessions: with peace, diplomacy, art, philosophy and poetry. Great thinkers struggled with great questions, the greatest thinker being Kong Fuzi, or Confucius in his Latinised name.

Dismayed by the evils of his world, he sought to redress them with a system of ethics and good government. Everyone should understand their place in society, from king to commoner, and fulfil their responsibilities to those above and below, living in accordance with the prime virtues: loyalty, piety, filial respect and benevolence. Act virtuously, he taught, and peace will follow.

But it didn't. Cynics asked: what was the point of rulers applying Confucian virtues if it did not lead to peace? Their answer was brutally pragmatic: none at all. For rulers, the only way to peace was to prepare for war, fight, win, then prepare for yet more war. This agenda received its most forceful expression from an ambitious young scholar named Shang. Lord Shang (Shang Yang) was born in the state of Wei, which dominated the middle Yellow River, probably around 400 BCE. For rulers, he argued, power is the only virtue. Ordinary people are lazy, greedy,

* Or sometime in the fifth century BCE. Sources disagree on the start date by several decades.

cowardly, treacherous, foolish and shifty, so the only way to rule them is to terrify, reward and punish them. This should be a universal Law, applied to everyone without distinction, an agenda from which it gets its name – Legalism. We don't call it that today, but it sounds strangely familiar. Shang Yang would approve of Machiavelli and modern autocrats. 'A weak people means a strong state,' wrote Shang. 'A strong state means a weak people.'

Wei's prime minister, Gongshu Cuo, feared what might happen if the young man took his persuasive ideas to a rival king. When the prime minister was on his death bed, he advised the king to keep Shang's loyalty by making him the next prime minister. If not, he said, 'Be sure to have him killed. Don't allow him to leave the state!' Claiming that Gongshu was 'Quite out of his mind', the king dismissed both ideas, with the very result that Gongshu had feared. Shang, unrewarded and very much alive, turned to the neighbouring state of Qin (pronounced Chin), which, under its king, Xiao, was emerging as the strongest of the warring rivals. When King Xiao died, Shang met a nasty end, 'tied to two chariots and torn apart'.[4] His ideas lived on in Han Fei, whose Legalism found ready acceptance in Qin. Here are three examples of his advice to would-be dictators on how to gain and hold power:

1. 'Where there are accomplishments, the ruler takes credit for their worth; where there are errors, the ministers are held responsible for the blame; hence the ruler's name never suffers.'
2. 'Be empty, still and idle, and from your place of darkness observe the defects of others. See but do not appear to see; listen but do not seem to listen; know but do not let it be known that you know.'
3. 'This is the way to listen to the words of others: be silent as though in a drunken stupor. Say to yourself: Lips! Teeth! Do not be the first to move… Let others say their piece – I will gain knowledge thereby.'

His policies worked. Qin turned itself into the hardest of the hard.

## A FORCE FOR NATIONAL UNITY

We are ready for the entry of the First Emperor, the man who would create a nation, confront the 'barbarians' and turn them from rivals into an existential menace.

This is the story as told by Sima Qian. In the neighbouring state, Zhao, lives a rich and ambitious merchant named Lü Buwei. He meets a minor Qin prince, Zichu, the son of a junior concubine of the heir to the Qin throne.[5] Zichu is not in line for succession – indeed, there is no line, because the crown prince's official wife is barren. He has been sent by Qin to be a hostage in the Zhao court, a common diplomatic ploy to show Qin's good intentions. Lü proposes a scheme to lever Zichu on to the Qin throne. He gives the prince some cash to buy some 'rare objects, trinkets and toys', which he takes to the Qin capital, Xianyang. He has his purchases delivered to the wife of the crown prince along with a letter proclaiming his admiration. Since she has no son, he says, she will need protection when the Emperor dies. She should have a stepson, who will become the crown prince's heir, and second in line to the throne. Eventually, when 'the one whom you call son becomes king, you need never fear any loss of position'. So it happens. Zichu becomes the princess's stepson and the crown prince's heir, with Lü as his tutor.

Now comes a dramatic incident, typical of Sima Qian and his flair for narrative. Lü has a very beautiful girlfriend. She becomes pregnant. Zichu sees her, falls in love and asks for her. Lü, whose whole future is now tied to Zichu, hands her over. In 259 BCE, she has a son, named Zheng. In due course, Zichu becomes king, the girlfriend his queen, Zheng the crown prince and Lü – the queen's ex-lover and Zheng's natural father – the prime minister. Five years later Zichu dies, leaving thirteen-year-old Zheng to succeed under the control of his patron and father, Lü.

Meanwhile, Lü and the beautiful queen reignite their relationship, but Lü, afraid of discovery, hatches another plot even more complicated than the previous one. In Sima Qian's words:

> The queen dowager did not cease her wanton behaviour. Lü Buwei began to fear that, if her conduct were ever brought to light, he himself would become involved with the scandal. He therefore searched about in secret until he found a man named Lao Ai who had an unusually large penis, and made him a servant in his household. Then, when an occasion arose, he had suggestive music performed and, instructing Lao Ai to stick his penis through the centre of a wheel made of paulownia wood, had him walk about with it, making certain that the report of this reached the ears of the queen dowager so as to excite her interest.

Perhaps Lao Ai and his attribute is nothing more than palace gossip. But Sima Qian, a master teller of tales, tells this one, not because it is true, but as a way to explain later events.

The queen asks to meet Lao Ai. But 'real' men are not allowed into the dowager empress's quarters. So Lü arranges for Lao Ai to be falsely accused of a crime for which the punishment is castration. The official in charge of castration is bribed to pretend to carry out the procedure, plucking out Lao Ai's beard and eyebrows to make him look like a eunuch. 'In this way,' says Sima Qian, 'he eventually came to wait on the queen, who carried on clandestine relations with him and grew to love him greatly.' Lao Ai acquires a retinue of a thousand retainers. The queen bears him two sons, half-brothers and possible rivals of the teenaged King Zheng, who is kept in the dark by his mentor, Lü Buwei, his mother's ex-lover and his real father. This is a disaster in the making.

In the ninth year of his reign (238 BCE), King Zheng discovers the truth. He orders an investigation. Lao Ai, panic-stricken, tries to start a revolt, but his followers desert him and he is quickly captured. So now the 22-year-old Emperor, Zheng, knows that he is the bastard son of his nominal father's mentor and that his mother is obsessed by a well-endowed and treacherous gigolo, all with the participation of the man to whom he owes his throne. He faces a choice: either to remain a puppet, controlled by his mother, her lover and his mentor; or he has to assert himself, by crushing the lot.

He chose suppression, for the details of which we are on firmer ground. Lao Ai was tied to four chariots, which were driven off in different directions. His associates and relatives were executed, as were the two boys, his half-brothers and the possible future rivals. Lao Ai's thousand hangers-on and four thousand noble families had their estates confiscated and were exiled, as was his mother and Lü Buwei, who committed suicide by drinking poison.

That left King Zheng, now aged twenty-four, betrayed and alone. His first reaction was uncontrolled anger. In the words of Sima Guang, the king issued a decree: 'Whoever even dares to utter a word regarding my mother, I will have him decapitated, quartered and his remains scattered in front of the palace as exhibits.' Twenty-seven people died for daring to utter a solitary remark about the king's mother.

What now? He had the answer, from Li Si, an ambitious Legalist, who had been advising the king throughout his teenage years. His advice, based on Han Fei and Shang: withdraw into a world of mystery, show no mercy and do only those things that increase power. The First Emperor* became power incarnate. Later portraits show him as an icon, bearded, bulky and wearing headgear with tassels dangling down to hide his semi-divine features, but Sima Qian makes him slit-eyed and pigeon-breasted, with a high pointed nose and also extremely scary: inscrutable, short-tempered, unpredictable.

The army, the key to his success, had no secret weapon. The same weapons were common to all the warring states – bows and arrows, halberds, swords, leather armour and crossbows. Far more powerful than an ordinary bow, the crossbow could be cocked, its string held by a bronze trigger, and held ready like a loaded rifle. Qin also had repeating crossbows, which had a magazine and could fire ten poisoned bolts in twenty seconds. Triggers are worth a comment. As Joseph Needham puts it in his monumental *Science and Civilisation in China* (Vol. 5, 30),

---

* The usual short form of his official title – Qin Shi Huang Di, the Qin First August Emperor.

they were 'among the greatest triumphs of ancient metallurgical and engineering practice in any civilisation'. Six precisely made pieces of bronze made the crossbow into the ancient equivalent of the Kalashnikov: mass-produced, easily dismantled, easily maintained.

Qin was a state-sized fighting machine. Its troops – tough, mobile, highly disciplined – could march fifty kilometres a day in leather armour, carrying weapons and provisions for three days. There was nothing new in any one element. It was the whole coordinated package that set the Qin army apart – the food supply, the recruitment, centralised control, communication, training, discipline. And a vision. For the first time in Chinese history, an army was dedicated not simply to victory in battle but to the conquest of territory, with each victory gathering more troops and more weapons. Once started – with the conquest of Han in 234 BCE – the Qin army snowballed from strength to strength. Of the conquests themselves, we have no details except their dates. In the course of thirteen years, Han, Zhao, Wei, Chu, Yan and Qi all fell, and in 221 BCE Qin and its six victims became the core of today's China, the 'middle kingdom' (*zhong guo*), which is what the nation is still called by its people and by other nations in nearby Asia.

But not by Westerners. Once unified from the borders of Tibet to the Pacific, from the edge of the Mongolian grasslands to the South China Sea, this region was gradually equated by many with its dominant power. Thus, as the name passed from language to language across Eurasia, did Qin become China, or its equivalent in numerous languages.

Now began a revolution involving all aspects of society. The old kingdoms gave way to three dozen centrally controlled commanderies, subdivided into several hundred prefectures. Each of the seven states had used different measures of area, widths of cartwheels, coins, weights, measures, styles of clothing and scripts. All were ditched for new ones imposed empire wide. Labour became available as never before – the newly conquered millions, the hundreds of thousands of soldiers freed from military service by peace. To keep them busy and avoid revolts, the Emperor set them to work on huge infrastructure projects: palaces, canals, dams, roads, the Emperor's tomb, the Great Wall.

One problem remained unsolved, one crucial area untaken: Ordos and its nomads. And to tackle them, to get his troops into and across Ordos, Qin would need a road of unprecedented scale to be constructed at unprecedented speed.

## THE STRAIGHT ROAD

Once again, the source for this extraordinary idea is Sima Qian, who tells us that Qin's 800-kilometre Straight Road, as it is known, was built to drive out the Xiongnu, seize Ordos and extend Qin's borders all the way to the Yellow River. I was intrigued. Surely, if the road had been suitable for carriages and battalions of soldiers, there would be remnants. Driving along Ordos's expressways, I brought up the subject with my companion, Alatan. Occasionally, we would be diverted on to earth roads by some new construction project, and we would wonder how many men with spades it would take to match these contingents of scrapers and trucks.

First, the facts, such as they are. The story starts in 214 BCE, seven years after unification. The First Emperor was becoming obsessed by the possibility of achieving immortality. One of the officers sent to discover the secrets of eternal life returned 'claiming that it had come to him from gods and spirits' that Qin would be destroyed by the barbarians of Ordos.

At this – as Sima Qian says in Chapter 88 of his *Shi Ji* – the Emperor ordered General Meng Tian to pre-empt any such possibility. Meng Tian, son of a famous father and brother of one of the Emperor's closest advisers, was the greatest general of his day. He was told to 'lead a force of 300,000 men and advance north, expelling the Rong and Di barbarians and taking control of the region south of the bend of the Yellow River'.

The Rong and Di, remember, were two of several subgroups coming together to become part of the Xiongnu. In another section, Sima Qian says that 'Meng Tian's might struck terror into the Xiongnu people' (with results that will become clear).

Sima Guang adds to Sima Qian's account, saying that Meng Tian 'made successive assaults against the Xiongnu tribes, recovering the territories south of the [Yellow] River… the armies of the frontier were engaged in a protracted war that lasted for more than a decade', after which 'they held sway in the lands of the Xiongnu'. By that time, Meng Tian was dead, in circumstances we will get to later.

Meng Tian's invasion would do more than counter the mounted archers. The deeper reasons lay in the Emperor's domestic needs and imperialist ambitions. Firstly, armies must be used. Idleness breeds boredom, a decline in morale, insubordination, even revolution. So, secondly, the First Emperor gave them huge and challenging tasks – take Ordos, and build, build, build. Thirdly, armies must be fed, so Qin needed new lands and new colonists. Ordos, once cleared of its nomads, offered prime new territory. Finally, though this is nowhere stated, it would have seemed vital to extend Qin to its 'natural' western and northern boundary on the Yellow River. It was as much a manifest destiny as young America's urge to expand all the way to the Pacific Ocean.

But conquest was not enough. Ordos was to be secured by the Great Wall, the grandest of the infrastructure projects. It supposedly ran from Lanzhou along the Yellow River and on to Liaodong on the Pacific, a distance of ten thousand *li* (about five thousand kilometres), which conforms with the usual name for the Wall, the Wan Li Chang Cheng (the 10,000-*li* Long Wall). Sima Qian is weak on detail. In one chapter he says the army numbered 300,000, elsewhere 100,000, and he does not specify the route. Archaeology is no help, at least so far. True, north of the Yellow River in the Yin mountains, a low wall winding over the hills has a big sign that names it 'The Great Wall of the Qin Dynasty'. It is no more than waist-high, a metre across, and made of slate. It's a tourist attraction, with nothing great about it, certainly nothing ancient.

Decaying bits of the Great Wall, the packed earth eroded into saw-teeth, are common across the southern Ordos, but they were built centuries later and have nothing to do with the Qin wall. We must be content with generalities. Outposts were constructed, says Sima Qian, and 'convicts transported in to populate the new districts'.

The first task was to expel the nomads, an act we would now term 'ethnic cleansing'. Tumen, still the chanyu of the Xiongnu in Ordos, had no chance against the massed forces of Qin. He led his people across the Yellow River, to safety north of the Gobi, in the grasslands of central Mongolia, to wait until the time was ripe for revenge and booty-hunting.

For Qin, victory was just the start. If the frontier was to be held, troops had to remain there, be relieved regularly and be supplied with food, clothing, tents, mounts and weapons. Let's say it took a few years of preparation, and that the army needed to be in camp by the autumn of 214 BCE, since Qin leaders would not have wished to go on campaigning in the winter with no basecamps.

So the First Emperor had good reason to demand a road. And we know it was a good one, because Sima Qian travelled along it a century after it was built. 'I have travelled to the northern border,' he wrote. 'And returned by the Straight Road. As I went along, I saw the outposts of the Great Wall which Meng Tian constructed for the Qin. He cut through the mountains and filled up the valleys, opening up a direct road. Truly he made free with the strength of the common people!' Sima Qian told some tall stories, but here his eyewitness testimony sounds convincing. Shouldn't there be something concrete to see – or at least the Qin equivalent of concrete?

It was also built very fast. Meng Tian's military orders came through in 214 BCE, and thereafter work continued only for another four years at most, because in 210 BCE Meng Tian became a victim of the revolution that ended the Qin dynasty. A road 740 kilometres long (to be exact), from the First Emperor's capital Xianyang to the Yellow River, built in four years? Was this really possible? And if so, how?

A few kilometres north of Ordos City there is a tourist attraction called the Qin Straight Road. This would surely answer my questions. Approaching over ridges and eroded ravines, we turned into a site that looked like a film set for a Great Wall movie. A tiled car park fringed a mock fortress with a raised terrace, six metres above the ground, supporting a statue of the First Emperor in his carriage, its four horses rearing as if about to leap into a void. The place was abandoned. The three of us – me, my guide 'Water' Xu and the driver – were the only ones there. Weeds poked through the tiles. There wasn't even a ticket office. Someone had had an idea that had not worked.

It was obvious why not. There was no road. A bare spot revealed eroded, gravelly earth, with no hint of paving. A faint path of flattened grass led to a shoulder-high white boulder, on which three characters, cut into the rock and painted red, proclaimed this was the 'Qin Straight Road'. Well, no, it wasn't. Beyond the rock, the faint path showed that a few curious visitors had been drawn to check the stone's claim. After a hundred metres the path dropped into a ravine, with no sign of any road over the rolling grass beyond.

So much for my fantasies. I needed to rethink. Perhaps today's engineers could throw light on the problems and solutions of 2,200 or so years ago. Who better to help than an expert in road building? I contacted the boss of the Oriental Holding Group, which built many of the major roads and expressways across the Ordos. His name was Ding Ding, which to my English ears sounded like a charming tintinnabulation. We met in Beijing's elegant Kunlun Hotel, with a discreet orchestral version of Elvis Presley's 'Love Me Tender' to accompany the coffee. I asked him to imagine himself as Meng Tian, commissioned by the First Emperor to conquer and occupy Ordos by building the Straight Road. How would he do it?

He certainly had experience to address the problem, not that modern roadbuilding should be compared to Qin roadbuilding. In 2002, he started work on the road between Dongsheng (part of Ordos City) and Kangbashi, the new town to the south. Back then, I recalled, those thirty kilometres had been a battleground of potholes, which at one point had vanished under an overflowing river. Soon after that, the government decided to turn the road from two rough lanes into four good ones, which, said Mr Ding, 'we did in one year'. Two years later, it was too busy, 'So in 2009 the government said, "Let's double it again!" So now it's an eight-lane expressway.'

'You're a modern Meng Tian,' I said.

He demurred. 'Building roads across the desert is not very difficult' – made even less difficult in Meng Tian's case by the fact that Ordos back then was a lot greener than it is now.

What would have been involved?

Mr Ding became thoughtful. First, a survey: to map hills, ravines and ridges to bridge and cut through. Fifty five-man teams could survey fifteen kilometres each in the course of a summer, but work on the road would need to start before the surveyors had finished in order not to lose time.

'The Qin Emperor standardised the width of chariots,' said Mr Ding. 'So Meng Tian would need to ensure the road was wide enough without being too wide, and firm enough without being too slow to build. I think perhaps crushed stones, like gravel, would make a good surface.'

How many men would it take to build 740 kilometres of hard-packed road in four years? As a rule of thumb, one man with a spade can shift about 3.5 cubic metres or five tonnes per day, but only in conjunction with several two-man teams carrying slings on poles to cart the earth away. Sima Qian's disparate figures – 300,000 or 100,000 – are not much of a guide. That doesn't matter, because the numbers needed to make the road are much smaller than that.

In very round figures: a road 740 kilometres long, four metres wide (enough for two carriages to pass), and (say) half a metre deep would mean 1.5 million cubic metres of earth to dig up, combine with gravel and then replace: about 3 million cubic metres to be shifted. There were no wheelbarrows yet; the first illustration of one dates from the early second century CE. Assume one worker with a spade fills a sling carried by two sling-carriers. If three workers can remove 3.5 cubic metres per day, and if they can replace it in the same amount of time, the job can be done with 4,500 workers in 571 days – 1.5 years, in round figures. That's working flat out, eight hours a day, seven days a week. Double the time for bad weather, winter and engineering works, like cutting descents into ravines, filling in the gullies at the bottom and making wooden bridges. That is still only three years. And if things went wrong – a plague, say, or assaults by nomads – Meng Tian knew he had a potential workforce of millions as back-up.

## DEATHS, CONSPIRACIES AND REVOLUTION

Qin control of the northern frontier was brought to a sudden end by interlinked dramas: the Emperor's death, a bizarre plot, several other deaths, plus the collapse of the dynasty, all vividly told by Sima Qian.

At the end of 211 BCE, the Emperor was on a tour of the east. His son and heir, Fusu, had been seconded to Meng Tian in Ordos. With the Emperor were nine ministers and a vast entourage in four-horse chariots, with unknown numbers of troops and replacement horses. This mass included three crucial characters: Li Si, chancellor; Huhai, one of the Emperor's younger sons; and Zhao Gao, transport chief and Huhai's tutor. Suddenly, at a place called Sand Hill on the flat and river-rich expanses of southern Hebei, the Emperor fell ill with some unspecified disease, and was dead in a week.

Zhao Gao foresaw imminent disaster: if Fusu became the next Emperor, Zhao Gao himself would be out of a job, or exiled, or dead. So he devised a conspiracy – which Sima Qian called the Sand Hill Plot – to withhold news of the Emperor's death, fake accusations of treachery by Fusu and Meng Tian, demand that they commit suicide, arrange for Huhai to become Emperor and, ultimately, secure his position for life.

Two weeks later, on receipt of the letter, Fusu accepted it at face value and committed suicide. Meng Tian, however, said he needed to know the order was genuine. So the messenger had the general and his entourage arrested, and told the conspirators that all was well: Fusu dead, Meng Tian in jail. Huhai came to the throne as the Second Emperor, with Zhao Gao as his top adviser.

But very quickly the new regime unravelled. Huhai was weak, utterly dependent on Zhao Gao. 'The chief ministers are unsubmissive,' he complained. 'What can I do?' Zhao Gao told him to unleash a reign of terror. Six princes were put to death, three others fell on their own swords, ten princesses were torn apart. Fear spread to the population at large. Meng Tian, proclaiming himself guilty of the unlikely crime of 'cutting through the veins of the earth' with his construction projects, committed suicide. The empire collapsed into civil war. The Second Emperor himself committed suicide. Qin fell, and in 202 BCE a new dynasty – Han – began a reign that would last four hundred years (with a brief, bizarre interregnum we will get to in the next chapter).

## ON THE GRASSLANDS, ANOTHER EMPIRE FORMS

By then, to the west, a different sort of regime had formed. Again, Sima Qian is our guide. He does not say where he got his information but, as always, he tells a good story, this time about how the Xiongnu began to build an empire. The lead character is Tumen's son, Modu. When we last heard of him, he was a resentful hostage with the Yuezhi.

This is Sima Qian's version of how the Xiongnu Empire began:

The prince stages a dramatic escape, stealing a horse to gallop home. His father is impressed by his bravery, gives him a generous reception, and bestows him with his own troops. But he does not reinstate him as heir, and Modu plans revenge. To ensure the loyalty of every one of his soldiers, he drills them into total obedience. 'Shoot wherever you see my arrow strike!' he orders. 'Anyone who fails to shoot will be cut down!' Then he takes his band hunting. Every animal he aims at becomes a target for his men. He takes aim at one of his best horses. The horse dies in a hail of arrows. But some soldiers hesitate, and they are executed.

Next, he takes aim at his father's 'favourite' wife. (I did say this is folklore.) She dies, and so do those who waver. Then Modu shoots at one of his father's finest horses. More arrows, another death, and this time there are no waverers. Now Modu knows all his men can be trusted. Finally, 'on a hunting expedition, he shot a whistling arrow at his father and every one of his followers aimed their arrows in the same direction and shot the chief dead', filling him so full of arrows that there was no room for not even a single arrow more. Finally, Modu secured absolute power by going 'on a bloodletting rampage', killing his stepmother, her son – Tumen's heir and his own half-brother – and all those he suspected of opposing him.

Is there any truth in the stories? Very little. 'Tumen' means nothing in Chinese, but in Mongolian it means 'Ten Thousand'. It is both a military unit and a common name. There are lots of Tumens in Mongolia today, and the Tumen River marks North Korea's frontier with Russia. But a single name is no evidence of anything much. The whole story of Tumen and his son is just too good to be true. As Nikolai Kradin, of the Russian Academy of Sciences, Far Eastern Branch, Vladivostok, points out,[6] 'historical events and elements of fantasy are mixed'. It is as if the origins of Xiongnu power had already been turned into an epic by bards, and then told to Sima Qian. Is it really credible that the plot to murder Tumen should unfold in public? That it involves the killing of both a beloved wife and a beloved horse? That events unfold in threes, a common device in folklore? Perhaps Tumen is no more than a symbolic character, an Everyman from whom Modu seizes power.

But perhaps folklore is also used, as it often is, to capture a truth – that in 209 BCE, one year after the death of the First Emperor, Modu became the new chanyu of the Xiongnu, and began to turn himself from a tribal chief into the ruler of an empire.

Seeing a threat in Modu's ambitions, the nearby tribe to the east, the Dong, to whom the Xiongnu owe allegiance, demand a sign of submission. They ask for a stallion that belongs to Tumen. Modu's advisers are horrified, but Modu complies. Next, the Dong demand one of Modu's wives. Again, the advisers object. Again, Modu refuses to break the peace: 'Why bother losing our accord over a woman?' Finally, the Dong king demands a bit of wasteland measuring a thousand *li* (five hundred kilometres) from north to south. This time his advisers say, 'Yes, the wasteland is useless to us. Give it to them.' At this, Modu flies into a towering rage: 'Land is the essence of our nation! How could we possibly cede it?' He strikes like lightning against the complacent Dong, who are overwhelmed.

And so the empire begins.

It would last some three hundred years, which is a tribute to Modu's drive, intelligence and leadership skills. He imported or devised a new system of government. His rule depended on pairs of officials who were designated 'left' and 'right', the left being the senior one and the chanyu's heir. The system stopped the chanyu becoming oppressive, and stopped those below him turning into warlords. Beneath the two Wise Kings of the Left and Right were twenty-four 'great chiefs'. The army was organised on the long-established 'decimal' system, in which households, or rather the men, were grouped into ten-thousands, thousands, hundreds and tens. Modu's vision and authority built, from notoriously fickle elements, a confederacy powerful enough to challenge the new dynasty that had sprung up south of the Gobi.

China unified, and so did the nomads. Was this a coincidence? Or cause and effect? That idea was proposed by the great Mongolist Owen Lattimore in the 1940s, and accepted recently by – among others – Thomas Barfield, professor of anthropology at Boston University. He argues that the Xiongnu and later nomadic empires centred on Mongolia – over a dozen in the course of the next 1,500 years – were 'shadow empires' that arose 'as secondary phenomena in response to imperial expansion by the Chinese'. It's a controversial hypothesis, but, in the case of the

Xiongnu, it seems more than coincidence that both empires arose one after the other, both with charismatic leaders.

Events and personalities feed an old controversy. Those who believe that great events are caused by great historical forces would argue that the two empires would have arisen anyway – China unified by forces evolving in the Warring States, the Xiongnu unified by the need to fight and loot China. Those who argue that history is the product of great leaders point to the two dominant characters of the late third century BCE, without whom (they argue) the two empires would never have come into existence. Whether you conclude that China inspired the Xiongnu or the First Emperor inspired Modu, it's hard to deny that there was in fact a cause and an effect at play.

And with yet more consequences: one of which was rivalry and warfare for almost three hundred years, which, with China's victory, would lead on to her expansion westwards into today's Xinjiang and northwards into today's Inner Mongolia.

## ADDRESSING THE XIONGNU QUESTION

How could China deal with its new rival?

One idea was bribery. The Xiongnu would be paid to behave. The two empires, Han Dynasty China and Xiongnu, signed a treaty in 198 BCE – the so-called Peace and Kinship (*he qin* 和亲) Treaty – which would supposedly mark the beginning of a new world order in Asia. The Xiongnu and their chanyu were recognised as equal to the Han Chinese and their Emperor. Han would send a princess for each new chanyu, the idea being that the offspring would be relatives of the Chinese royal household – and who among them would attack their own family? Along with the princesses would flow gifts of silk, cloth, grain, chariots, mirrors, jewels and many other luxury items. An unnamed beauty was sent off to the chanyu's tent-capital, travelling in style in a carriage, with staff and outriders, presumably along the road built by Meng Tian. This policy had an additional aim: it would subvert the Xiongnu, undermine their warlike spirit with good food and luxuries, seduce their allies away from them and cause the Xiongnu to defect in ever-increasing numbers.

The treaty remained on the books, sometimes observed, sometimes not, but it never really worked for very long. Thirty years later, a leading scholar, Chao Cuo, together with a co-author Jia Yi, came up with two other suggestions. Chao was one of the great men of his age – severe, outspoken, austere and inflexible, according to the sources, but with such a formidable intellect that he was nicknamed 'the Wisdom Bag', a reference to the sealed bundle of secret instructions that generals carried with them on campaign. He would come to a bad end fifteen years later, when the Emperor blamed him for looming unrest and had him cut in two at the waist. But at the time he was riding high, and his proposals would eventually, after a delay of another thirty years, be put into effect.

The Peace and Kinship Treaty, Chao argued, needed to be scrapped. The army was a disaster. Generals were inept, soldiers undisciplined, war-drum signals meaningless and weapons so ineffective that 'one might as well fight with one's bare hands'. And the Xiongnu, being barbarians, were just too tough. 'When trudging over craggy mountains and fording rapids… the Xiongnu are most proficient with their riding and archery skills. During thunderstorms and torrential rain, the Xiongnu warriors persevere and continue to fight on in the most adverse conditions despite hunger and thirst.'

He proposed two new policies.

Firstly, to 'use barbarians to fight barbarians'. There were several groups in the Han Empire who lived and fought like the Xiongnu. They should be enlisted, armed and used as border guards.

Secondly, in a recommendation that sounds like a draft for modern China's policy in Tibet and Xinjiang, he said that the government should send civilians to colonise the border regions, providing them with protected settlements; in short, settlers by the million, state-funded, over decades. They should receive official titles, tax relief, clothing allowances and food until they could look after themselves. 'This is a lasting strategy,' Chao Cuo concluded. 'And the benefits will be enduring.'

Chao Cuo urged instant action, because he was sure that the Xiongnu would attack whenever there was a hint that the Peace and Kinship Treaty was at risk. So it proved. In the winter of 166 BCE they invaded, with 140,000 horsemen – well, lots anyway – some of whom galloped to within eighty kilometres of the capital, Chang'an, before retreating over the border long before the Emperor's troops could reach them.

So it went on, with the Xiongnu growing ever stronger. In 162 BCE, they delivered a death blow to their old enemies, the Yuezhi. Sima Qian records: 'The chanyu killed the king of the Yuezhi and made his skull into a drinking cup,' the common way for steppe dwellers to proclaim victory over a rival. The Yuezhi's unnamed new khan authorised a momentous decision: get out, or die. Cut off from on three sides, they had only one line of retreat – north-west. Imagine several hundred thousand with their herds and a myriad of horses moving almost two thousand kilometres, seeking to put a safe distance between themselves and the Xiongnu. They had no idea that they were starting on a far more momentous migration, as we shall see.

In the same year, the Emperor and the chanyu renewed the Peace and Kinship Treaty. Nothing changed. Records mention thirty thousand Xiongnu here, another thirty thousand there, smoke-signals sent along the Great Wall from beacon tower to beacon tower, the capital 'reverberating with shock', generals appointed, imperial inspections made, armies mobilised and sent to the frontier, only to find the Xiongnu long gone.

To cap it all, the Xiongnu showed no sign of being undermined by their newfound wealth. The ruling class built a rich life for themselves in northern Mongolia and southern Siberia. They held more land than ever: having expelled the Yuezhi, they now controlled a number of little kingdoms, thirty-six in all, in the far west.

## THE KEY TO XIONGNU SUCCESS

How was it possible for a million 'barbarians' to make themselves a match for the world's foremost culture, numbering some sixty million? Simply having a charismatic founder and political stability is not enough of an explanation.

True, stability was important. It was guaranteed by a system of succession, which worked well from Modu's time for 150 years and ten heirs. Each chanyu chose his heir, the Wise King of the Left. This system avoided the possibility of a child-king, always a problem in China, where a young heir was under the control of his mother or a top adviser, opening the way to power struggles and civil war. To start with, sons succeeded fathers, and later brothers succeeded brothers. Subsidiary families, intermarrying with the chanyus, had a vested interest in preserving the status quo. The system had only a few hiccups, but created no civil wars, because wealth and security depended on relations with China.

The real secret – the economic foundation for their empire – was the exploitation of China. The Xiongnu had worked out how to run a vast protection racket. They were master blackmailers. They had to be, because in steppe societies there was no other way to accumulate wealth. In China, power and wealth depended on grain surpluses and taxation and an enduring bureaucracy and countless other elements of a complex society; on the steppe, in the past, power and wealth had depended on animals, which might vanish overnight in a blizzard or a raid, and on loyal chiefs who might suddenly become disloyal and vanish over the horizon. Now, lasting success meant extracting wealth from China by raiding or trading or receiving 'gifts'. That was the chanyu's purpose in life – to do whatever it took to lever wealth from China.

What did Xiongnu success mean, exactly? Not enough for everyone to get a share, but enough to fund a lavish lifestyle for the top people. The grain sent from China would have fed about 140 people for a year, or 700 people if it was an addition to the normal Xiongnu diet.[7] They had food enough anyway, as Mongolia does today, because the steppes produce meat way beyond what the population can eat. Drink, though, was a different matter. They had their *koumiss* (which is a mildly fermented mares' milk), but Chinese grain-based 'wine' gets you drunker quicker. The Chinese sent the Xiongnu about 200,000 litres of the stuff every year, enough for a thousand feasts of two hundred guests each. The aim, as Nikolai Kradin says, was to turn the nomads into drunkards.[8]

Then there was the real wealth: silk. Sericulture – the cultivation of silkworms – was older than China itself, and used not only for clothes and furnishings but also as currency to pay salaries and taxes. Silk was common as paper is to us, and indeed used as such. Coming in rolls or 'bolts', the Xiongnu received almost a hundred kilometres of it every year (ten thousand bolts, each just short of ten metres long and just over fifty centimetres wide, weighing about 2.4 kilos). It sounds a lot, but China produced silk in prodigious amounts: in 301 CE, the court recorded that the treasury stored four million bolts (almost ten thousand tonnes, approaching forty thousand kilometres, enough to circle the earth at the equator). On average, every year, China dispensed to the Xiongnu just 0.0025% of its silk-based wealth. If that bought peace, which it sometimes did, it was a good investment.

This was not, as the Chinese court seemed to believe, to feed the chanyus' greed. Most of it went to subordinates in displays of generosity that bought their loyalty. Far from undermining the Xiongnu, the luxuries in fact strengthened the political system, guaranteeing that when the gifts ran low, there would be more raids followed by more demands.

One general, Li Guang, was said to be in 'almost daily skirmishes with the Xiongnu'. Li Guang is worth a diversion, because he will play a significant role in Han–Xiongnu relations later and because there is a good story told about him. He was the most famous general of his day, tall, strong, 'with arms like an orangutan', and a noted archer. Also, he was the most popular, because he 'disseminated rewards to his followers, and while his army was on the move, he lived in their quarters, ate their food and shared their congenial and arduous moments'. Sima Qian liked him: 'I met the general in person. He had a mild manner and was most approachable. He was like a commoner, not particularly proficient with words.'[9] Li Guang's men 'are relaxed and contented, and they would die for him' – which is just as well, considering how the following incident played out.

It is 144 BCE: the Xiongnu enter through the Yanmen ('Wild Goose') Pass, the main entry through a section of the Great Wall that runs through north Shanxi. Surrounded by the towering Heng and Wutai mountains, it gives way 150 kilometres further south to the rich plains of central China.

Wild Goose Pass is a haunted place. I was there once, on a drab autumn day with my Mongolian-Chinese friend Jorigt. We drove uphill on a back road, hemmed in by coal trucks keen to avoid motorway tolls, through a village guarded by beacon towers and up past a baffling maze of walls and terraces and fields towards misty hills. A wild area of ravines and boulders and dripping trees led to a dead-end at a stream. An abandoned bridge had been turned into a drying floor for a shaggy mat of cornstalks. Beyond lay a rough track. Up we went, through slowly swirling mist, into a stone-built village. It seemed abandoned, until two damp camels with drooping humps proved it wasn't. Further on, a small house turned out to be a guide-hut with – to our surprise – a guide, Miss She Yifeng. Apparently this was a major tourist attraction in summer, the most important pass in Shanxi. Two hundred people a day came here, she said. We had missed the summer season, but she was still on duty. She led the way steeply upwards into deepening fog, until a wall loomed up with an arch at its base. A memorial recalled that a predecessor fortress had stopped the Jürchens of Manchuria. Though this wall and fortress was more recent, in strategic terms nothing much seemed to have changed in a thousand years.

The story continues. The Xiongnu gallop on to the Yellow River, 140 kilometres beyond low hills where farmers had made terraces and cave-houses, as they still do today. A few days later, a eunuch leading a recce group from a contingent of a hundred commanded by General Li Guang is spotted by three Xiongnu riders. The three Xiongnu circle the eunuch's force, picking the Chinese off until the eunuch is the sole survivor. He gallops back to base with the news. At this, Li Guang leads his hundred men out to track down the three Xiongnu.

Suddenly Li Guang and his contingent stumble on a whole army of several thousand mounted Xiongnu. Li Guang's men are extremely nervous, 'their faces turning a deadly pallor, eager to make a run for their lives'. But Li Guang keeps his nerve. The Xiongnu know all about ambushes. If they see us flee, he says, they'll come after us, and we're doomed. If we stay cool, they will fear an ambush, and not attack. So, he orders 'resume normal marching formation'. When they get closer to the wary Xiongnu, he tells his men, 'Dismount and undo your saddles!' His men protest. 'They expect us to run away,' Li Guang insists. 'If we show them we have no intention of fleeing, they will be more convinced than ever that there is something afoot.' The Xiongnu blink. By dawn, they are gone, and Li Guang leads his men safely home.

But a bold move by one general was not a victory. It could not go on like this. As one official wrote to the Emperor, the natural order of things – the Emperor at the top, the vassals below – had been turned on its head. 'Hanging upside down like this is something beyond comprehension.'

*When extended west, the Great Wall completed the defences that were supposed to keep out the 'northern barbarians'. Some eroded sections survive, like this bit in eastern Ordos.*

## CHAPTER 2

# A WAR TO END THE WAR

### WARLORD AND WAR-EMPEROR

THE MAN WHO GRASPED THIS NETTLE WAS EMPEROR WU (141–87 BCE). Wu was a monarch of genius – autocrat, statesman, strategist, artist – with a reign long enough to follow through on his long-term plan. Starting as a fifteen-year-old, his fifty-three years on the throne was unmatched for 1,800 years. His despotic ways mirrored those of the First Emperor, and his achievements – laws, institutions and conquests – would mark China from then on, especially in the north-west. Five decades of war would not quite break the Xiongnu, but they would prepare the ground for victory.

His answer to the Xiongnu menace was to set the boundaries of China wider, and to escalate the rumbling rivalry into a full-scale war. But this would take time to prepare.

First, he needed allies – tribes to the west, beyond the Xiongnu – so that he could open a war on two fronts. No one had yet penetrated the expanses of Central Asia, but there was at least one tribe which would surely hate the Xiongnu: the Yuezhi, expelled by the Xiongnu from Gansu three decades previously and now somewhere deep in the heart of Asia. Where exactly no one knew, but once contacted, the tribe would surely make a valuable ally.

In 138 BCE, Wu sent off a hundred-strong expedition headed by a man noted for his strength, generosity and charismatic leadership, Zhang Qian, who was to become one of the nation's most romantic figures, a hero of exploration. He set out with instructions to persuade the Yuezhi to return, become allies of the Han Empire and help destroy the Xiongnu.

This highly dubious venture foundered almost at once when Zhang was captured by the Xiongnu. This event began a series of adventures which turned him into a sort of Chinese version of Lewis and Clark, the explorers who crossed the United States in the early nineteenth century. As an eminent official with no immediate hostile intent, he was treated well by the Xiongnu – perhaps also because he had a Xiongnu companion, Ganfu – and stayed with them for ten years, taking a local wife. Then he escaped, with his wife and Xiongnu companion, and resumed his journey westwards.

Two thousand kilometres further on, he found the Yuezhi, who were in today's Tajikistan on a long migration to north-west India, and had no interest in going to war with their old enemies, the Xiongnu; it would mean returning over the Pamir and Tian Shan mountains, not to mention the Taklamakan Desert and the Lop Desert. Instead of going home with this bad news, Zhang continued his explorations, visiting many of the great cities of Central Asia, even picking up information about India and the Eastern Roman Empire, before finally returning home after an absence of thirteen years, having lost all his entourage except his Xiongnu wife and the faithful Ganfu.

After Zhang Qian vanished into the wilderness, and without any barbarian allies to protect him, Emperor Wu tried diplomacy, but with no luck. A new Peace and Kinship Treaty, moribund for fifteen years, instantly fell victim to another invasion. Wu accepted that war was inevitable. Except not yet, because war was ruinous, high risk and, above all, ineffective unless the total destruction of the Xiongnu could be guaranteed. It would take more years before Wu could find the strength of mind and the resources to commit to all-out war against the Xiongnu.

Meanwhile, attacks and counterattacks continued. In 127 BCE, a campaign into the Great Bend of the Yellow River re-took lands once conquered, and then lost, by Qin, thus 're-establishing the old border that Meng Tian had created in Qin times, and the river was fixed as the border'.

Two years later, Zhang Qian returned with a treasure trove of information about peoples and established trade routes that would change his country's history, turning attention westwards to realms of which the Chinese had had no previous inkling – thirty-six in the Western Regions alone – all leading like stepping stones along what would eventually be called the Silk Road, to India. Wu was happy to learn that, in military terms, these thirty-six powers were 'feeble at best'. So, given a decent army, 'all the lands within the realms of the four seas and all the people therein would be under the beneficence of Han'. In particular, Zhang told of wonderful horses raised in Fergana, the fertile valley of what is now eastern Uzbekistan. Tall, standing at sixteen hands, these 'celestial horses' – or 'blood-sweating' horses, as they were known, from the pin-prick wounds in their flesh caused by local parasites – were just what Wu needed to strengthen his cavalry.

Such tempting prospects – equine and otherwise – would inspire China's conquest of Central Asia and in effect determine its modern borders. From the seeds planted by Zhang sprang both the great trade routes joining China and the West, and their defence: the Great Wall's western extension.

The years after Zhang's return saw a catalogue of Xiongnu assaults: a provincial boss killed and a thousand captives taken in one raid; another thousand in a second; more thousands in a third, fourth and fifth; a full-scale invasion across the Gobi that took fifteen thousand prisoners (again, definitely a lot anyway); a counterattack; a counter-counterattack, with many more prisoners taken and unlikely numbers killed on both sides.

This was not the kind of 'stability' Wu could tolerate. No Emperor of a unified China could claim the Mandate of Heaven and at the same time put up with a 'barbarian' neighbour who saw himself as an equal, and who was liable to launch raids whenever he felt like it. The only answer was to set the boundaries of China ever wider. In the words of Owen Lattimore, Wu needed 'a closed economy, a self-sufficient world, and an absolute Frontier'. It was in pursuit of this absolute goal that Wu escalated the rumbling rivalry into full-scale war.

He had to grapple with two problems. The first was the grasslands of Mongolia, which started just north of the Yellow River and ran eastwards and northwards, fading into the wastelands of the Gobi and picking up again to the north. The other problem was the oasis states – the thirty-six mini-kingdoms ruled by the Xiongnu – of the Central Asian badlands, which lay westwards. In strategic terms, the two were very different. The Gobi and the steppe could not be conquered and held; the oasis kingdoms could. Once the Chinese had taken them, they could run them like their own cities, whereas nomads could benefit from them only by giving up nomadism. The war aim that Wu adopted, therefore, was to 'cut off the right arm' of the nomads (this being the west, since the dominant direction for the nomads was southwards) – i.e. to pick off the tribal kingdoms one by one and garrison them in order to deny them to the Xiongnu. With the Western Regions in Chinese hands, it would be possible to invade and destroy the Xiongnu.

There were two keys to success. The first was Ordos, newly reoccupied in 127 BCE. The second, starting only 150 kilometres west of Ordos, was the narrow stretch of land running westwards through what would later be named Gansu. The Gansu Corridor (as it became known later), also known as the Hexi (*hé xī* / 河西, 'river-west', i.e. west of the Yellow River) Corridor, is another geopolitical keystone, crucial to understanding China's relations with Inner Asia. The Corridor is hemmed in by the Qilian mountains to the south and deserts to the north, with icy rivers from the Qilian's snowy heights forming fine pastures down the middle. It was through this bottleneck, only some twenty-five kilometres across at its narrowest point, through which nomads galloped to invade northern China from the west. From now on, Chinese Emperors imbibed a great truth with their mothers' milk: whoever wishes to rule China must rule the Gansu Corridor.

To close off this open frontier, Wu had only one option: total, all-or-nothing commitment to a range of tactics, all interlinked, all leading step by very expensive strategic step to an extension of the Great Wall. He had the manpower (a population of sixty million, a million-strong conscript army, some ten to thirteen million available for forced labour). He had the firepower. He needed horses by the tens of thousands, and these would have to be raised in China, or bought. There had to be an enduring relationship with the oasis kingdoms to the west, which meant great expenditure on gifts, especially silk, and on garrisons, which would have to be fed, which meant sending in colonists to grow grain, and on fortresses, and overnight places, and houses, and lookout points, and an administrative apparatus to supervise the whole operation. This was the iron logic that drove Wu's decision to conquer the west.

In 121 BCE, Han attacked in the far west and the centre (Dingxiang, the region adjoining the Yellow River where it turns south near Hohhot), two vast invasions, each with fifty thousand cavalrymen and 'several hundred thousand' infantry, complete with baggage trains and fodder.

The two commanders of these two invasions demand our attention. Commander-in-chief and commander of the central force was Wei Qing. In command of the western force was Huo Qubing. The two – especially the young Huo – are about to play vital roles in the story of the Xiongnu wars.

The most remarkable thing about Huo was that he was just nineteen, and this is all the more remarkable because of his unusual origins. He was the product of a series of scandalous events in the palace of Princess Pingyang, the elder sister of the Emperor. This is the story in brief, without names:

A servant girl in the princess's palace had a baby girl. The husband died. The mother had two affairs and produced two more children, a boy and a girl. The first-born girl became a song-and-dance entertainer, the other two grew up as servants. Eventually, the princess put on a show for her brother the Emperor, who was unhappy with his empress, a women eight years his senior and childless, which, to his embarrassment, was blamed on *his* impotence – bad news for him, given that he was young and politically weak. During the show, the first-born girl caught his eye, and then his heart. He took her into his palace, along with her half-brother to act as a stable boy. The empress was bitterly jealous, made the girl's life a misery and ensured she was employed as a maid, not a concubine. A year later, depressed, the girl applied to leave the palace. By chance, the Emperor saw her tearfully waiting her turn to leave. By now, he had gained in authority. Re-smitten, he told her to stay, took her to bed, made her pregnant and thus proved his virility. The bitter empress sought revenge by kidnapping the pregnant girl's half-brother, who was saved by friends. When the Emperor heard of the incident, he demoted the empress, made the girl his No. 1 consort and the half-brother his chief-of-staff. Meanwhile, the other girl, the half-sister, produced another illegitimate child, a boy.

Now to add the names. All the main characters belonged to a single family, named Wei. The Emperor's pregnant concubine, Wei Zifu, became Empress Zifu, and remained the Emperor's consort for the next forty-nine years. The ex-stable boy half-brother, Wei Qing, became one of the two most famous generals of his generation. The son of the other sister, Wei Shaoer, was named Huo Qubing, who as a teenager was taken under the wing of his uncle General Wei Qing. At the age of seventeen this 'exemplary horseman and archer'[1] made a name for himself fighting the Xiongnu, which is why, two years later, he was leading an army on his own account with the poetic rank of Agile Cavalry General, and was well on his way to matching his uncle in fame.

The 121 BCE campaign westwards marked a turning point, because Huo Qubing was aiming to clear the way through the Gansu Corridor. He 'trampled five Xiongnu vassal kingdoms', marched on for five hundred kilometres, captured a Xiongnu chancellor and several commanders, and killed or enslaved 8,900 Xiongnu. He returned with his prisoners to rich rewards and a towering reputation that, two years later, would win him a special place in the history of the Xiongnu wars.

## The Black Water fortress

You have to get up close to sense the events of two thousand years ago. My guide, Xu Zhao Yu, or Michael, as he called himself, was the best guide in Gansu. He told me so, several times, and – owing to his immense store of historical information – I was inclined to believe him.

We headed north-west out of Zhangye, which guards the Gansu bottleneck, to a site that was important in the struggle between the Xiongnu and China. Autumnal corn lay drying in the fields and the radio blared pop songs – No. 1 at the time was 'Ta bu jidao': 'She doesn't know (I love her)'. We turned down a farm track, and Michael led the way through fields of chilli peppers and corn. Ahead loomed a sand dune, dotted with camel thorn and red willow bushes, above which rose an earthen wall. This, Michael explained, was once a Xiongnu fortress-city, their advance base, dominating the Gansu Corridor. We climbed, and the full structure came into view – eroded walls making a huge square, 250 of my paces on each side, with the stub of a guard tower in the north-east corner.

A river used to run through here, Michael explained. He was talking about the Black Water (Hei Shui) – the Edsen Gol, the Lord's River, as it is in Mongolian – which flowed from the heights of the Qilian mountains, and still does, though with a different course. The Xiongnu must have thought they were there for keeps: fine farmland, their own river, a stranglehold on trade through the Corridor. But they had reckoned without Emperor Wu and his brilliant young general Huo Qubing.

Huo at once saw the weakness of the Xiongnu position: there were no defences right across the Corridor, and the fortress was utterly dependent on its water supply. So he diverted the river, isolated the fortress, destroyed it and then moved on into territory once occupied by a tribe called the Wusun, before the Xiongnu kicked them out. (We'll hear more about them later.)

Emperor Wu was so delighted with the victory that he sent Huo a huge flagon of wine, which caught up with him in a town 150 kilometres further on. Huo said that it was his soldiers, not he himself, who deserved the wine, so he poured it into a spring to share it with all his men. The town was renamed to proclaim his generosity: Jiuquan, meaning 'Wine Spring'.

Huo went on to follow the Black Water northwards to what was then Lake Juyan, part of a vast and well-watered delta where the river vanished into the desert. It has all changed now. Lake Juyan has been a dusty plain since the mid-twentieth century, though the lake's last remnant still appears on maps as Lake Gaxun. In Huo's day, the lake lapped a fine city, which bore the same name as the lake. The chanyu, down but by no means out, escaped, returning to his tent-city 750 kilometres to the north, in the heart of Mongolia. As a result, wrote Sima Guang, the whole region from the Gansu Corridor into the Taklamakan Desert 'had become a no-man's-land, in which there were no Xiongnu to be seen'.

Wu offered Huo Qubing a mansion to settle down in, to which Huo replied: 'The Xiongnu have not yet been wiped out. How can I settle and start a family?' He died on his return in 117 BCE, aged just twenty-four, supposedly after drinking water from wells the Xiongnu had poisoned by dumping dead animals in them.

His grave, fifty kilometres west of today's Xi'an (the modern name for the old capital Chang'an), confers on him unprecedented honours. Emperor Wu had Huo's tomb-mound raised close by his own, itself a considerable accolade. In addition, the tomb became the focus for something entirely new in Chinese art: monumental rock sculpture. As the historian of Chinese carving Ann Paludan points out, Huo's tomb is the first example of stone animals of the kind that line the approaches to later imperial tombs.

Set out in the pavilions and arcades around Huo's forty-metre tomb-mound are seventeen lumps of roughly carved boulders weighing many tonnes each, all made of granite quarried from the Qilian mountains some five hundred kilometres away. The mound is swathed in firs today, but originally the statues were scattered over the bare flanks. Mostly of animals – fish, tiger, elephant, boar, frog, ox, horse – they seem unfinished, as if each subject is struggling to escape from a rocky embrace. One statue is of particular importance. Usually described as 'a horse trampling a barbarian', it seems to be an obvious symbol of Huo's achievements. But that idea comes from the man who first described the statue in 1914, the French ethnographer and art historian Victor Segalen. In fact, there is no trampling going on. These imposing 3.8 tonnes of granite portray a horse simply straddling a heavily bearded 'barbarian', holding a bow in his left hand and an arrow in the other. Perhaps the horse and the barbarian are in some sort of formal relationship, superior and inferior, a portrayal of an ideal, now that the inhabitants of the Western Regions had been brought inside the empire.

But there's another memorial to the scale of Huo Qubing's victory: the ruins of the Black Water fortress – desolation incarnate. Sand had piled up against the walls and flowed down the inside. At the south-east corner, a dune had risen higher than the walls. I climbed it, and saw that someone in authority had made an attempt to recall the significance of the place with a little pavilion and a plaque: 'Ancient Ruined City of Black Water'. But it was not its history that was recalled. 'This is the most mysterious sand dune in history,' it announced in Chinese and poetic English. 'It is shaped like a big whale. No matter how the wind blows, it has not moved in two thousand years. It is as if it is waiting for something. Who can solve the problem, and say why it is still here?'

So much for the western campaign. What of the other one, in the centre, north of the Yellow River? It had had its successes, mixed with disasters.

It was plagued by disputes, because the eminent, elderly, feisty, loose cannon that was Li Guang, veteran of seventy battles against the Xiongnu, demanded a chance to finish them off once and for all. But because of his age and perceived unreliability, he was granted only a sideshow, leading his own contingent apart from the main force. That one, the main force, was under the command of Wei Qing, who in 119 BCE headed north across the Gobi and ran directly into Chanyu Ichise and his army. Wei Qing formed a laager with armoured wagons, Wild West fashion. There were charges and counter charges, 'carnage and slaughtering' (in Sima Guang's words) until late afternoon, when a vicious dust-storm struck: 'sand, gravel, pebbles and stones were sucked into the sky, pelting against the faces of the warriors… it became almost pitch black, so that the warriors could not distinguish friend from foe'. Then, as the storm passed, Wei Qing ordered a two-pronged assault, driving Ichise to clamber into 'a carriage drawn by six mules' and escape to his tent-city capital several hundred kilometres to the north-west. 'Shocked to the core,' the Xiongnu scattered, while Wei Qing led a taskforce in a night-time pursuit of the chanyu. Come the dawn, 'they looked to the horizon. It was a desolate wilderness with no Xiongnu in sight.' Arriving at a Xiongnu fortress, Wei Qing's men raided the stores, trashed the place, then returned to Chang'an.

Li Guang, meanwhile, had lost his way, and, on returning, was arraigned before a military court. He was a model of decorum. Getting lost was all his own fault, he said, 'my subordinates are not guilty of any blunder'. He was over sixty now, he went on, and 'simply could not bear to face these petty bureaucrats'. Saying which, 'he drew his sword and slit his own throat'. All his men 'wept bitterly' at the news, as did civilians young and old.

## THE WALL GOES WEST

Military victory was not enough. Something had to fix the frontier, define what was China and what wasn't. That something was, of course, the Wall. Wu picked up where the First Emperor had left off. In the centre and east, old walls were repaired, and sections linked. In the west, new bits of the Wall arose, running from Lanzhou northwards then west over the border of what is now Xinjiang, and on for a thousand kilometres into wilderness. Now the remnants are saw-toothed from erosion and earth-grey, but back then the Wall was a brilliant line of white – yes, whitewashed, which is why the Mongolians still call it the White Wall. To build and man it, four new administrative areas sprang up, with two, Gan and Su, straddling the narrow mid-section. Eventually, once joined, the two gave their names to the province, Gansu, with its odd thigh-bone shape, 1,500 kilometres long, fat at either end with the extremely narrow Gansu Corridor in the middle.

Wu's push west was based on a neat theoretical model. The border-lands would be colonised. The colonists would make deserts bloom, and feed themselves, and provide labour for an extension of the Great Wall, which would protect the soldiers, traders, farmers and administrators. The far western oasis kingdoms would fall into line, as China proved itself the dominant power. Silks would be sent, and horses would be received. China would not only be unified, she would be secure at last and eventually, surely, richer than ever. What greater legacy could an Emperor leave?

This, the influx of 119 BCE and afterwards, was the real beginning of the modern Wall as the defining symbol of China, the one running all the way from the western deserts to the Pacific. It became a subculture, a 'long city', which is the alternative meaning of its Chinese name, indeed several 'long cities', given its many branches and doublings. Soldier-farmers began to arrive by the hundred thousand, supplementing volunteers, conscripts and convicts. Families followed, making an estimated 1.5 to 2 million settlers, all being provided with land, animals and seeds. Silk began to flow westwards in prodigious amounts to buy the loyalty of the oasis kingdoms – the beginning of the trade network we now know as the Silk Road, an exercise in empire-building that would reach out far beyond the Great Wall, driven by the need to outflank the Xiongnu. It was an empire inspired by strategic need, founded by force, underpinned by bribery, secured by colonists and traders, and guaranteed by government.

And there could be no turning back. Princesses could not be abandoned and treaties broken, or the Xiongnu would be back in an instant.

By 111 BCE, ten vast caravans a year, each the size of a small city on the move, were rolling west, the beginning of an economic offensive that would soon carry westwards every year anything up to eighteen thousand rolls of silk and some three to four *billion* coins, about thirty percent of the national cash income, perhaps seven percent of the empire's total revenue. In 105 BCE, another princess was dispatched to the chief of the Wusun, two thousand kilometres westward in the Ili valley, in present-day Kazakhstan. Other tribes surrendered to military expeditions. Loulan, for instance – once the western corner post of the Xiongnu Empire – got a new, pro-Chinese king, complete with a concubine from Emperor Wu's harem, a carriage, wagonloads of gifts and an armed guard.

Further west, a Chinese force drove into the Fergana valley, in a region known as Dayuan, over two thousand kilometres from Chang'an, aiming to capture enough 'blood-sweating horses' to start a breeding programme, and to shock vacillating states into submission. In the first approach, all the Han envoys were killed, leaving Emperor Wu 'seething with rage too fearful to behold'. His response was: more of the same, much more. An army of 60,000 headed both an invasion and a migration: 100,000 cattle, 30,000 warhorses and 180,000 settlers started to arrive to build new farming communities along the Gansu Corridor and up the Black Water.

Even so, it took another two campaigns and two years to assert the royal will on Dayuan. A forty-day siege of the capital ended after engineers diverted the river on which the city depended. 'In a state of complete bedlam,' the inhabitants of the capital revolted, killed their king, sued for peace and handed over 'a few score' of those infamous blood-sweating horses. Wu got his way: Dayuan cowed, the Western Region kingdoms stunned into compliance, the Xiongnu held in check, potential allies bribed and scared into allegiance, blood-sweating horses delivered. (Though no one heard of them again; perhaps in the end there was nothing special about them after all.)

## LI LING'S LAST STAND

Yet the raids continued, worse than ever. In 99 BCE, another campaign ended in a total and very famous catastrophe. A force of five thousand men with wagonloads of food and arrows struck northwards across the Gobi and into the Mongolian heartland, aiming perhaps to entice the Xiongnu into a frontal assault against Han's repeating crossbows. It was led by Li Ling, grandson of the late and much-lamented Li Guang, with all his forebear's bravado. It was not a big force, but Li Ling was confident, even arrogant: his warriors, armed with crossbows, with 500,000 arrows in their wagons, were 'great fighters, specialists and swordsmen. Their strength is so great they could kill a tiger bare-handed, and when they shoot they never miss.' He was short of horses, but said it didn't matter, because his infantrymen were supreme. Besides, it was autumn, the best weather for marching. He planned to be back before winter, stopping off at a Han border fortress in the south Gobi to rest his soon-to-be-victorious troops.[2]

The fortress, called Shouxiang in Chinese and Bayan Bulag ('Rich Spring') in Mongolian, was near the present-day town of Nomgon. It still has a rich spring, though its surroundings are much grimmer now than they were two thousand years ago, when the guards could grow their own crops. Russian and Mongolian archaeologists, who excavated it in 2009, identified the fortress from bronze crossbow triggers, which the Chinese used but the Xiongnu did not. This confirmed the written accounts that mentioned the crossbows, and also confirmed that the Han had a forward base within what should have been Xiongnu territory. Not just one: there is another 180 kilometres to the east – due east, exactly, the same latitude to within 0.03 of a degree. It was a great location, for back then it was on an island in a river. Its local name is Mangasin Khuree, the Ogre's Circle, an insulting reference, perhaps, to the Han soldiers who manned this square base, which is about 150 metres per side, and guarded by a circular wall, 3.7 kilometres around.[3]

What happened next turned into one of the best-known incidents in Chinese military history, a sort of Custer's Last Stand, with tragedy for some, embarrassment for the Emperor and which triggered his renewed determination to end the menace of the Xiongnu for ever.

A month's march and 250 kilometres into the Gobi, Li Ling's force was in mountains – probably the Gurvan Saikhan ('Three Beauties') range – when they found themselves surrounded by thirty thousand Xiongnu horsemen. Li Ling laagered his wagons, and readied the crossbows. Stunned by losses, the Xiongnu commander sent for reinforcements, another eighty thousand according to Sima Guang. Outnumbered twenty to one, Li Ling staged a fighting retreat into a valley. 'The enemy was lodged in the hills, surrounding him on all sides and shooting arrows like drops of rain,' according to the *Han Shu*. With only half their number still alive, the surviving Chinese, with few arrows left, fled into a narrow defile, while the Xiongnu fired down on them and rolled boulders to block their path. Days passed, arrows ran low, death for all seemed the only outcome when – in Sima Qian's vivid words – 'Li Ling with one cry gave courage to his army, so that every man raised himself up and wept. Washed in blood and choked with tears, they stretched out their empty bows and warded off the bare blades of the foe.' Finally, one night, Li Ling ordered his men to disperse in small groups, each with some food and a chunk of ice for water. They were fifty kilometres from the border. Perhaps a few would make it. Li Ling himself galloped clear, only to be hunted down and forced to surrender. Just four hundred of his men made it to relative safety, back over the Gobi's coarse gravel and tussocky dunes.

Li Ling lived on with the Xiongnu for another twenty-five years, too ashamed to return home. Eventually, he accepted his privileged position and served his captors as a commander. A later chanyu, Hulugu (97–85 BCE) gave a daughter to him in marriage. Having rebutted an offer of reconciliation from the Han court, Li Ling died of natural causes in 74 BCE.

*Terracotta Army soldiers: the chariots, archers and infantry (pictured) buried to fight for the First Emperor in the spirit world.*

# CHAPTER 3

# THE ANNIHILATION OF THE XIONGNU

## GOING, GOING, BUT NOT YET GONE

THE LOSS OF THE WESTERN REGIONS WAS THE BEGINNING OF the end for the Xiongnu. Between Han and Xiongnu, envoys came and went, talking about talks about reviving the Peace and Kinship Treaty. But with the Xiongnu on the back foot, and with no hope of them regaining the crucial Gansu Corridor, Han could afford to ignore the pressure. From the settled oasis communities of the west, the Xiongnu had derived grain, iron weapons, taxes and manpower. Their rulers now worked to make themselves independent. From the early 70s BCE, former Xiongnu vassals turned against them. One of them, Wuhuan, in the north-east of present-day China, was shattered by a Han invasion. To have a vassal destroyed by Han might once have galvanised the Xiongnu. Now it stunned them into inaction. The once great empire was in a slow but steady decline.

For the Xiongnu, decline spelled an end to more than political and economic control. It broke their spirit. For almost two centuries, they had taken what they wanted. They had become rich. What happened to all the wealth – the silks, the carriages, the ceramics? Scattered, given away, wasted, buried. They might have invested it in cities, roads and institutions as grand as those of their Chinese enemies. Instead, there is almost nothing. There are graves, but for the first 150 years of empire there was nothing much in them – until, suddenly, they increased in size and wealth. That is the mystery at the heart of Xiongnu studies. Something changed. This chapter looks at the nature of that change, and seeks to explain it.

For over a decade after Wu's death in 87 BCE, Han was in no shape to reinforce Wu's warrior policies. His young heir died in 74 BCE, aged twenty-one, leaving as empress dowager a fourteen-year-old wife. Under the guidance of the regent, Huo Guang, the throne went to Wu's grandson, Liu He, who – according to Sima Guang – proved to be 'totally debauched, a hedonist, given to a life of utter and excessive dissipation'. Liu was the sort of man who arrived from his estate with 'young women concealed in the baggage carriages for his sensual pleasure'. When they were discovered, he said he knew nothing about them and had those who had hidden them executed. Moreover, he refused to undertake the rituals of mourning, saying he had a sore throat and could not weep. In brief, he would obviously be a disaster as Emperor.

A month after the coronation, the regent Huo Guang summoned the ministers, announced that Liu was wantonly debauched and proposed that he should be impeached instantly. The young empress dowager, wearing her imperial tiara, enthroned in state and flanked by hundreds of guards, summoned Liu He, accused him of a string of crimes – ignoring rituals, using the Treasury as his personal cashbox, having an affair with one of the dead Emperor's concubines and many more. He was then deposed and banished to his former estates, becoming the only Emperor in Chinese history to be, in effect, fired. His replacement was a virtually unknown great-grandson of Emperor Wu, an eighteen-year-old named Liu Bingyi, who was reportedly erudite, austere, parsimonious, gentle, benevolent and in all ways thoroughly filial.

In 71 BCE, now restabilised, Han joined with the Wusun to attack the Xiongnu again, capturing '40,000' people and '700,000' animals, all in quotes to inject a hint of scepticism, but there was no denying that the blow was devastating. Xiongnu weakness inspired further uprisings by vassal states, more deaths in battle, more livestock lost, yet more deaths through famine, chaos, anarchy, and in response only frantic, hopeless efforts by the Xiongnu to re-establish the terms of the Peace and Kinship Treaty.

As the Xiongnu declined, Han rose. To stamp his authority on the west, the Emperor ordered the construction of a new fortress-city just north of the Taklamakan, declared the whole Western Region a protectorate embracing all thirty-six mini-kingdoms, and proclaimed 'that the entire region was again open to travellers'.

Take the Wusun, the people who had been forced from Gansu by the Xiongnu some seventy years before and who had settled in the Ili valley on the border of present-day Kazakhstan and China. When a string of crises threatened anarchy, the chaos was sorted out by a remarkable woman called Feng Liao, the companion of one of those princesses sent by the Emperor to marry a 'barbarian' king. Lady Feng 'could read and write', looked after the princess's accounts and 'the people respected and trusted her fondly'. Known now as 'China's first official female diplomat', she negotiated with local chiefs and the Han government. Summoned to report directly to the Emperor, she was sent back 'as the official Han envoy in a brocade-adorned imperial carriage, clad in fabulous embroideries' to become the Wusun's de facto ruler. Later made regent for a young Wusun heir, she used the threat of Han intervention to impose peace, keep its occupants firmly in the Chinese sphere of influence and make sure the Wusun would never, ever have anything more to do with the Xiongnu.

## THE XIONGNU SPLIT

In Mongolia, the Xiongnu's long collapse continued. When the eleventh chanyu died, his wife was having an affair and conspired with her brother, a senior general, to have her lover seize the throne. The new chanyu, Yuan-Guidi (Huyandi in another spelling), in Sima Guang's words, 'turned out to be a hideously savage and implacable ruler'.

Driven into revolt by the chanyu's excesses, several tribes united to elect a chanyu of their own, Huhanye by name, son of the eleventh chanyu. He formed an army and started a civil war. Yuan-Guidi had neither the nerve nor the manpower to fight back and committed suicide. After two years of turmoil, five claimants to the throne whittled themselves down to two: Huhanye in the centre and his elder brother Zhizhi in the east. By the late 50s BCE, it was Zhizhi who was on top, about to chase his brother from the tent-city in the Orkhon valley that was the Xiongnu capital.

For Huhanye, there was only one source of help: China. That would mean surrender. He opened a debate with his officers. Most were appalled at the idea. Sima Guang summarises the tumult:

> Preposterous, intolerable! We Xiongnu revere the chivalrous and brave! Surrender is utterly despicable! Our kingdom was founded on horseback and warfare! Our motto is 'Wage relentless war!' To perish in battle is a divine honour! Han, mighty as it is, has never prevailed! Why be disloyal to our ancestors? If we surrender, our vassals will deride us!

One of Huhanye's top officers took the floor, and called for a reality check. There had been setbacks ever since the time of Huhanye's great-grandfather Chedihou. Now

> we do not have the resources to recover what we have lost. We have not seen peace for a long time. If we were to serve Han, we would be guaranteed peace, and our people would gain some respite. But we are destined to be annihilated if we choose to continue along the present path.

The tumult continued, then died. Zhizhi was on his way, with overwhelming force. What other course was open? Huhanye accepted the inevitable, and started to arrange the formalities for his surrender in the spring of 51 BCE.

In Chang'an, this news sent the court into a frenzy. How should he be treated? As guest or vassal? After much debate, the Emperor decreed that Huhanye was *voluntarily* making the Xiongnu, their enemies for centuries, a subject state. This – the unforced submission of a whole empire, never mind that it was an empire divided against itself – was unprecedented, overwhelming. 'I do not possess the virtue or moral aptitude for this grand and formal procedure,' said the Emperor, and he would therefore 'receive the chanyu with our national ceremonial etiquettes reserved for the most distinctive and esteemed guests'.

Coming to Chang'an in the spring of 51 BCE, Huhanye could hardly have believed his eyes. Built by the dynastic founder, Gaozu, 150 years previously, Chang'an, with walls twenty-five kilometres around and eight metres high, was home to some 250,000, equal to a quarter of the chanyu's own people. His whole tent-capital would easily have fitted inside the Emperor's main residence, the Everlasting Palace, a rectangle 8.6 kilometres around, with forty halls, standing on a platform fifteen metres high. And this was only one of seven palaces. Even at its height, Huhanye's empire had only a few scattered fortresses. Some are still visible today. You can stroll across one of these grassed-over squares in a few minutes.

The reception, outside the city, was 'incomparable', with 'dazzling and luxuriant gifts', listed by Sima Guang, among them: a royal carriage, a saddle (ornately decorated), a bridle (ditto), fifteen horses, twenty catties (equivalent to about twelve kilos) of gold, 200,000 coins, seventy-seven suits of clothes, eight thousand bales of brocade and fifteen tonnes of silk.

Then, joined by aristocrats and rulers of vassal states, Huhanye processed past tens of thousands of onlookers to the main bridge over the River Wei, where the Emperor greeted him, to roars of 'Long live the Emperor!', and led him in a formal entry into the city.

After a few days, it was time to return home, though what 'home' meant now was an open question. Huhanye asked if he and his people might settle just outside the Great Wall, north of the Yellow River, pretty much where Meng Tian had driven his ancestors from. And perhaps, in case of an emergency, he could find shelter inside the Wall? No problem. Off he went, with sixteen thousand Han troops, to his new base, where his hungry force – and presumably their families – received 34,000 *hu* of grain (which, if true, comes to 1,300 tonnes, which in turn is fair enough if Huhanye had ten thousand people in his care – that's 130 kilos each, enough to last until the next harvest).

So the Xiongnu were divided in half, the southerners under Huhanye in the borderlands, in the well-funded service of the Han Emperor, and the northerners under Zhizhi in control of the old heartland, nursing hopes of a revival. Obviously there was no point in Zhizhi taking on Han. Instead, revival for him meant reclaiming the west, initially Wusun.

Once there, Zhizhi, failing to make peace with Han, decided to lead his people even further west, out of harm's way, to Kangju, a kingdom on the Talas River in today's southern Kazakhstan – an unrecorded epic journey of 2,400 kilometres, taking several months. There followed an exchange of daughters as wives between the chanyu and the Kangju king, and finally a joint attack on the Wusun.

Back in the Xiongnu heartland, Zhizhi's migration had left the centre ground vacant. Since Huhanye's people had drained their new estates, he led his people north again, back to the more fertile pastures from which he had fled not long before. He was a vassal now, but safe, and with a guaranteed income from the Emperor.

Meanwhile, Zhizhi's military successes had made him 'insufferably insolent'. He argued with his royal Kangju ally, killed his wife (the king's daughter) in a fit of temper and then turned on the Kangju nobility, ordering hundreds to be killed, dismembered and tossed into a river. In full dictatorial control, he had his new subjects build a fortress, with a double palisade of logs, a moat and rammed-earth ramparts.

In 36 BCE, a Chinese commander of the frontier, intent on glory, led forty thousand men westwards. In the siege that followed – engineers undermining the walls, fires set against the wooden palisades – Zhizhi was wounded by an arrow in the face and fell down the battlement steps. Night fell, the fire spread and at dawn, to the boom of war-drums and the 'ear-splitting shrieks' of war-horns, troops piled earth against the ramparts, stormed up and over and the fortress fell. Zhizhi died of his wounds. We are told that 1,518 of Zhizhi's force died – a remarkably exact figure, so perhaps true – a thousand more surrendered, and 145 were captured. With Zhizhi's head sent off to Chang'an to be hoisted above the main street, victory was complete. The Han generals sent a message to the Emperor suggesting he issue an imperial edict 'disseminating a message to all our vassal states reading, "Kings! Whosoever dares to flout Han, no matter how near or far-flung, we shall have you executed!"'

## THE XIONGNU: RICH, BUT BROKEN

Back east, Huhanye was relieved at his brother's death, but apprehensive lest he share a similar fate. So once again, in 33 BCE, he went to Chang'an to pay homage to the Emperor, requesting the hand of a princess to re-establish the Peace and Kinship Treaty and turn himself into the Emperor's son-in-law. The Emperor agreed, and selected a woman from his harem who was of a noble family and who had not yet been invited into the Emperor's bed. Her name was Zhaojun, the now legendary Zhaojun. She is one of the Four Beauties, women whose looks caused fish to forget how to swim, the moon to hide her face, birds to fall from the sky and flowers to wilt. The few bare facts – she went north, she bore a son, Huhanye died, she married his stepson as tradition demanded, she bore two daughters, she vanished from history – were overtaken by multi-layered fictions that turned her first into a heroine, bringing civilisation to the northern barbarians, and then a goddess, one who could restore withered grasslands by playing her magical pipa (a Chinese lute). Her entirely spurious tomb on the edge of Hohhot is a major tourist attraction. She has inspired some 250 books, several plays, a TV series and a luxury hotel.

Huhanye was 'ecstatic'. 'I will be the border sentinel for Han,' he wrote. 'Not for this lifetime, but for ever.'

Two years later, in 31 BCE, upon his death, chaos loomed over the succession. Since the early days, the crown had gone from father to son. But, as we have seen, sons were sometimes too young, and so now the law decreed it should go from brother to brother, until there were no more, leaving disputatious cousins. One day, civil war would become inevitable. But for three decades there was peace, and royal visits, and a flow of more wealth than ever. From eight thousand bolts in 51 BCE, deliveries of raw silk rose to thirty thousand bolts in 1 BCE. Among the gifts was a lacquered wooden bowl made in the imperial workshop in Chang'an, and dated the fifth year of the Emperor Ai, which is 2 BCE. It was found in Noyon Uul, in Kozlov's tomb No. 6, which suggests that this tomb was that of the chanyu, Ujiuli.

Meanwhile, Han itself was in crisis. Emperor Ai, in his twenties, was besotted by a man named Dong Xian, a few years his junior, whom he had presented with ever higher offices, ever greater wealth and a royal mansion. Everyone knew about the affair. Once, so they said, when the two were asleep together, clothing entwined, Emperor Ai awoke and rather than disturb his lover he cut off the sleeve of his robe to ease himself out of bed. Ever after, homosexuality was referred to as 'the passion of the cut sleeve'. Courtiers were aghast. Astrologers said that the Emperor was under the malign influence of the planet Jupiter, which presaged a year of catastrophes.

A year? More like two decades. Ai died suddenly. In a flurry of accusations, suicides, banishments and executions, a usurper, Wang Mang, a minister-turned-Emperor, seized power to head a brief and bitter interregnum which lasted from 9 to 23 CE. Described by Sima Guang as 'restive, petulant and tetchy', Wang Mang announced the birth of a new dynasty, Xin – a surreal disaster of a dynasty, as we will see shortly.

## THE BURIED TREASURES OF THE XIONGNU

Ever since the discovery of Noyon Uul over a century ago, we have known that the Xiongnu élite had been extremely wealthy. But no one had any idea how widespread the wealth was until recently, or how much it reflected Chinese culture. The collapse of the Soviet Union and Mongolia's Communist government in 1992 opened the door to international research into Xiongnu graves – the ten thousand graves of local dignitaries and the several hundred 'élite' or 'royal' or 'terrace' graves, of which twenty have been excavated. All have a penumbra of subsidiary graves, hundreds of them. Dug many metres into soft earth, the larger tombs have sloping walls, in steps, so that they did not collapse as they were dug. Typically, the contents are similar to those in Noyon Uul – animal bones, iron horse trappings, Chinese carriages, bronze cauldrons, Chinese bronze mirrors, textiles and Chinese lacquered bowls and cups (apparently, the Xiongnu adopted eating habits from China). The burial chambers were of logs, containing the coffin, all covered with layers of pinecones and brush, which were set on fire before the pit was refilled.

The doyen of Mongolian archaeologists is Diimajav Erdenebaatar, a professor at Ulaanbaatar's National University. A burly man with a thatch of grey hair and a drooping moustache, he has a passion for his subject, and experience to match, having shared in the excavation of the vast cemetery known as Gol Mod 1 and masterminded work on its twin, Gol Mod 2 (Gol Mod means 'river wood', recalling their surroundings of mountainous fir forests and streams). His finds really need a specialised, large-scale, state-sponsored museum, which does not exist, so Erdenebaatar has made his own in the university.

His main focus is Gol Mod 2, which he talks about with pride, because he discovered it in 2001. He had started with Gol Mod 1, working with a team of French archaeologists. One day, wanting to get to another site, he decided to take a short cut, and asked a local to guide him. 'You know,' his guide said, 'we have another place, very like Gol Mod.' So on the way they checked it out, and he was astonished to see, in among the scattering of fir trees, a vast pile of rocks, with numerous smaller piles alongside.

'Obviously, it was a cemetery,' he said, the largest grave known so far, with over four hundred subsidiary graves, and richer than Gol Mod 1. 'It was like a gift from heaven.' He worked for three years on the main tomb to find the array of objects now in his museum. On the floor, for example, lay the iron rim of a chariot wheel, part of one of sixteen or seventeen carriages, all broken and all but one burned as part of the burial rituals (Erdenebaatar estimated the number of chariots based on the iron wheel-hubs). Chariots, covered in black lacquer and drawn by two or four horses, were an important part of the 'gifts' sent by the Han Emperors, and equally important as the official means of transport for Han envoys and Han princesses. Many chariots in other graves suggest they were status symbols for Xiongnu aristocrats, the equivalents of limousines for today's top diplomats. Most had parasols or roofs to keep off the rain and sun. Rock drawings and paintings of chariots show their horses prancing along, travelling (perhaps) across Ordos along Meng Tian's Straight Road. The top Xiongnu liked their own designs. Erdenebaatar's collection includes fourteen gold-coated plaques used to decorate horse-straps – gorgeous little cartouches and discs with bas reliefs of two mythological creatures. One is a sort of a unicorn with a deer's body, a horse's head and a single huge, curling horn; the other a *bers* (as it is known in Mongolia today), with the face of a snarling snow leopard, a single horn, a dragon's neck, wings and camel's feet (See the opening image of Chapter 1). Other objects reveal international connections with China and beyond. Small gold ornaments with turquoise inlays recall similar ones found in Afghanistan, which were quite possibly made there.[1]

The most intriguing of Erdenebaatar's discoveries, found in a large circular grave beside the main tomb, is a small blue glass bowl, only 7.5 centimetres high. It has white lines painted round the rim, and the delicate bulge of the body is strengthened with raised ribs. Glass was not a material used by the Chinese at this time. So where did this bowl come from and when? The surprising answer is: Rome in about

50 CE. That answer can be stated with confidence because there are six other similar pieces in Western museums.[2] 'I thought it had been traded all the way across Asia,' said Erdenebaatar. 'But when I was in Berlin a professor there said no, it was too rare and delicate for trade.' Could a Roman have travelled all the way across Asia, like a precursor of Marco Polo? Unlikely, said Erdenebaatar. 'It must have been a gift,' he suggested, carefully handed from leader to leader across the Asian heartland, until, perhaps, it arrived at the Emperor's court in Chang'an before being presented to one of the visiting chanyus.

A few days later, I set off for the two Gol Mod cemeteries. There were three others with me – Batmönkh, a guide with a passion for history, Tsend, one of Erdenebaatar's PhD students, and the driver, Mönkhöö, master of our Ukrainian 4x4 van. We headed west from Ulaanbaatar on tarmac, then north over the open steppe. They call this an ocean of grass, with good reason – distant horizons, a vast blue sky, no fences and a track network hundreds of metres wide, as if a giant had run a comb across the grass, made by drivers constantly choosing new tracks. After four hundred kilometres and a night in a friendly tent, we splashed through a stream, crunched through a snow-filled gully, wove between firs and arrived at Gol Mod 2.

Dominating a plateau surrounded by hills, what had once been a deep pit had been completely filled in. Stones outlined a shape like a giant paddle, the shaft marking what had once been a descending ramp and a square over the grave itself. Archaeologists commonly refer to tombs with entrance passageways, the paddle-shaped ones, as 'terrace tombs'. Larger ones are said to be those of the 'élite', while smaller ones are termed 'aristocratic', and the smallest, whether circular or rectangular, are 'satellite tombs'. The élite tomb we were looking at is the biggest yet discovered.

'It wasn't like this when I first saw it,' said Tsend. 'Those stones over there' – he pointed to piles of them a few metres away under fir trees – 'were all on top of the grave', which raised it to make a platform. It had taken a team of two hundred soldiers, released from duty, to clear the rocks and prepare the tomb for excavation. Twenty-one metres down, they found a coffin, broken by looters and then crushed under a protective carapace of rocks. The only human remains were a skull and a femur.

The main grave was part of a huge necropolis. There were 190 smaller terrace tombs nearby, along with 85 circular burials and 250 others. To one side of the main grave were twenty-seven circular tombs, forming a regular, gentle curve, for officials or relatives killed to attend their Emperor in death. Excavations showed that the coffins were laid out to follow the line of the arc, suggesting that this was a single ritual, all the killings and burials done together. Today, seeing the size of the main grave and the carefully placed subsidiary graves, you get an idea of the power of the chanyus to command in this world and the next, matching that of the Chinese Emperors they fought and emulated.

Concealment would have been impossible. The burial site covers a square kilometre, and it was created by a people confident that they could protect their tombs from looting or destruction by enemies. This was a fine place for aristocratic funerals – plenty of pasture, protected from winds by mountains, a nearby stream for drinking water and cooking, and lots of trees for fires, tomb-props and coffins. And beautiful, whether in high summer with the sandy earth unfrozen and soft for digging, or on a crisp autumn day, as this was, with the smell of the firs and a cold breeze sighing through the pine-needles.

Mongolians called this mysterious place Balgasin Tal, the City Steppe. I imagined myself as a time-traveller, leaving the present for the world two thousand years ago, watching sixty generations of Mongol herders flicker past, and then as the centuries slip by, seeing ghostly parades from earlier cultures – Jürchens, Khitans, Uighurs, Turks and half a dozen others – all pausing to wonder at this evidence of long-vanished predecessors.

I paced the outline of the main grave, not to record it – all the measurements are in the reports – but to feel its scale. Six paces across at the entrance, a forty-metre passageway, sometimes called 'the pathway to the other world', becoming wider as it approached the forty-metre-per-side grave, which – as the excavation showed – dropped the equivalent of a seven-storey building in a series of steps. Imagine a stepped pyramid with a sloping ramp leading almost to the top, and then in your mind turn it upside down. The stepped structure and the sloping walls were to prevent the soft soil collapsing. A back-of-the-envelope calculation suggests that the diggers – probably Chinese prisoners-of-war and criminals, not ordinary Xiongnu – had to shift 14,000 cubic metres of earth, which weighs about 21,000 tonnes. How did they do it? With wooden shovels, loading slings carried on a yoke by two men? From our time-and-motion study of Meng Tian's Straight Road, we know that a modern worker can dig five tonnes a day. The numbers of diggers and sling-carriers would have been constricted as they worked their way down, but round figures suggest four hundred men working for ten days, or two hundred working for about three weeks.

Nothing to match the First Emperor's tomb or the Straight Road, but still quite an operation, with no way to keep it secret. Digging was just the start. Expert workers fitted the tomb with timbers, dressed it with tapestries, then positioned the objects – the ones which are now in Erdenebaatar's museum. A procession of mourners, some perhaps destined to be sacrificed, carried the coffin down the entranceway and lowered it into its final resting place. The grave, once filled in, was made even more obvious by covering it with hundreds of stones and giving it a low masonry wall of roughly cut blocks. A layer of cinders near the surface showed that fire had played some part in the funeral rites.

Sunset and a biting wind drove us away. With the low sun turning car tracks into shadowy claw marks, we arrived at the nearest town, a scattering of plywood shacks either side of a stretch of steppe corrugated by car-track patterns. A two-storey flat-pack building proclaimed: 'Food Place. Hotel. Karaoke. People's Shop'. Someone came from the nearby village to cook mutton and rice. We were the building's only occupants. Next morning, we were off at dawn. Two hours later, splashing through the half-frozen Khünüi River, climbing a steep and forested ridge, descending through trees flaming an autumnal orange, we came to Gol Mod 1.

This was a place with a long history of archaeology. A Mongolian scientist, Dorjsuren (1923–97), started work here in 1956, listing over two hundred graves, half a dozen terrace tombs and several other satellite graves, opening twenty-six of the smaller circular ones. An attempt to excavate the massive main tomb ended when the sides of his eight-metre hole collapsed. Then in 2000 came the French, headed by Jean-Paul Desroches and the Mongolians under Erdenebaatar, who continued Dorjsuren's work, identifying 316 tombs (since then the count has risen to almost 400), of which 214 were 'aristocratic' or 'élite' ones, with entrance pathways. The entrances are aligned roughly north–south, so that as you descend into the grave you head north, in the direction of the seven stars that make the Great Bear, though whether this is significant is anyone's guess. Perhaps we should switch the point of view. Perhaps the dead were supposed to exit the tomb uphill and enter the afterlife by heading south, which – if traditional Mongolian practice is anything to go by – is the direction their tents would have faced.

The team cut the intruding firs, cleared wind-blown sand, then excavated two élite tombs and another seven 'satellite' burials. The most significant was the largest, labelled T1, carbon-dated between 20 and 50 CE. With the occasional help of a mechanical digger, eight hundred volunteers carefully scooped out several thousand tonnes of soil, revealing two layers; bronze and iron relics in the upper one, gold and semi-precious objects below. A rock floor was apparently designed to frustrate looters, but a deer horn, which had been used as a pickaxe, showed that looters had entered anyway, presumably by digging a long-gone tunnel. Seventeen metres down, the team found a double coffin of larch-wood planks, one inside the other – empty, looted, except for a few small pieces of jewellery.

In this case, the looters must have given up, because from the area round the coffin, the team gathered hundreds of items – fragments of vases, gold plaques, a bit of a bronze mirror, bones, silver ornaments, iron wheel-rims, chariot decorations, horse accoutrements, arrowheads, and several pieces of silk, wool and felt. A Chinese jade pendant drilled by a local artisan to make two holes for gold decorations. A bright bead made by fusing pieces of different-coloured glass – a complex operation, perhaps undertaken in Europe, involving the use of manganese, copper, iron and barium.

A lacquered tray offers rare support for written sources, like a torch spotlighting a find in a cave. The tray had a Chinese inscription recording its origins: made by, or under the supervision of, someone called Wu, working under seven other layers of supervision[3] – *seven!* This tray was the product of a vast and complex bureaucracy – in the Imperial Workshop, Chang'an in 16 BCE. As the authors of the article deciphering the inscription say, 'This is important as it is only the fifth absolutely dated object excavated from Xiongnu élite tombs.'

There was a mystery here, though. The two Gol Mod cemeteries, Noyon Uul and the other élite tombs were something new, radically different from the thousands of other Xiongnu tombs in Mongolia. Back in Ulaanbaatar, Tsagaan Törbat of the Mongolian Academy of Sciences gave me an explanation.

'All Mongolian élite graves date from the end of the second half of the first century BCE, soon after the Xiongnu submitted to Han, to the first century CE,' he said. We were in his office, cluttered with the books and papers related to his current research into the Xianbei, successors to the Xiongnu. 'So we're talking about a short period, only a few decades. In Mongolia, we have only eight places with these élite graves. They are in the shape of Chinese royal graves' – though without the Chinese-style mounds over the top – 'so we have to ask why we suddenly get these big Chinese-style graves full of Chinese – or Chinese-style – objects: chariots, buttons, jade discs, mirrors, ceramics?'

He paused, then answered his own question.

'I think something happened to Xiongnu ideology. It was to do with the balance of power. In 51 BCE, the Xiongnu under Huhanye accepted peace, acknowledging China as the superior culture. It must have been a severe shock, tolerable only because they received so much from China. I think that's why they adopted Chinese-style tombs and burial rites.'

It sounds right. Written evidence supports the suggestion of a radical change. Members of the aristocracy, who like most Xiongnu had names that were hard to transliterate into Chinese, started to give themselves simple Chinese names: Zhi, Dong, Zhu, Bi. As the American scholar Bryan Miller writes, 'They chose to appease the Chinese with whatever language became necessary, in exchange for a peaceful southern frontier and a steady increase in gifts.'[4]

One piece of evidence, or rather an absence, supports Törbat's thesis. Despite the Xiongnu's history of warfare, these are not the graves of men eager to proclaim themselves as warriors. As Ursula Brosseder says in her paper on terrace tombs, 'As far as we can tell, weaponry does not play a significant role among the grave goods, since bows and arrows or swords are mostly missing'[5] – and this suggests that the later chanyus and their top officials had decided to set aside symbols of their violent past.

It seems that the Xiongnu élite wished to overcome feelings of inadequacy and inferiority by collecting wealth and displaying it in 'ostentatious graves', in the words of the leading German prehistorian Georg Kossack (1923–2004). He relates this to other élites who adopted aspects of foreign cultures, such as the Roman aristocrats who collected Greek art. His theory suggests that the Xiongnu's new subservience seemed 'to stimulate the inner need to demonstrate that one is a member of an élite by borrowing foreign material goods and customs'. More recently, a comparable urge partly explains Europe's passion for Greek and Roman art, as initiated by the eighteenth-century German art historian and archaeologist Johann Winckelmann.

For the chanyus and their élitist retinues, the system worked. They were subservient, cowed by the Chinese conquest, but they were rich. They could not possibly have guessed how soon their comfortable world would end.

## A DYNASTY OF MADNESS, MERCIFULLY SHORT

For their profitable peace ended with a return to the old days of war, leading to a very unprofitable conclusion. War returned thanks to the disastrous rule of Wang Mang, the man who usurped the Han throne and set up the very short Xin dynasty, neatly punctuating two long periods of Han rule.

Wang Mang's dynasty started out badly and went downhill from there. His bright idea for restoring universal confidence was to bring in a currency reform – six different materials (gold, silver, tortoiseshell, seashell and two types of other metal) in twenty-eight different denominations. The people were so bewildered they refused to use the new system, which was promptly rescinded, leading to a boom in counterfeiting, which in turn entailed arbitrary arrests and banishments.

In a strange incident told by Sima Guang, Wang Mang tried to impose his will on the Xiongnu by deception. In 10 CE, a delegation of five generals, 'dressed in their most elaborate and luxuriant trappings', each in a carriage, each with his own military escort, brought the chanyu a new imperial seal, an incised stone beautifully wrapped in silk. The old seal was a formal acknowledgment that the Han Emperor and the chanyu (his name was Wuzhuliu in Chinese, Ujiuli in Mongolian) were equals, naming him as 'Emperor of the Xiongnu'. But the new seal bore the words 'Xin – Xiongnu chanyu seal', with no statement of equality. At a state banquet, the chanyu handed over the old seal, receiving the nicely wrapped new one and setting it aside for the next day. Later that night, one of the Chinese generals pointed out to his colleagues that, when the chanyu finally saw the new seal, he would be furious and demand the old one back. Better make that impossible. How? By smashing it. And next day, sure enough, the chanyu unwrapped the new seal, had it translated, objected bitterly that 'you have reduced the chanyu to a commoner!' and demanded the old seal back. The envoys showed the broken seal, and had the nerve to claim total innocence, saying 'it had destroyed itself spontaneously'. What could the chanyu do? Accuse them, and cause a diplomatic incident? Risk a pitched battle with the envoys' military escort? He swallowed his anger and accepted the new seal. But trust was gone, destroyed along with the old seal.

Word spread. Minor tribes in the Western Regions defected to the Xiongnu, who regained control of their traditional lands. In response, Wang Mang broke off diplomatic relations, arbitrarily changed the chanyu's title to a Chinese term meaning 'Surrendered Slaves', and prepared for a massive, five-pronged invasion with an army of 300,000. The aim was nothing less than the total destruction of the Xiongnu, which would all be funded by an economy still reeling from his currency reform.

A year later, in 11 CE, the troops still had not been fully gathered or deployed. In the border camps, as one general wrote, 'the morale of the soldiers has deteriorated and their weapons have become blunt'. They had turned the border regions into a wilderness while waiting for supplies that never came. The horses and oxen were dying, the men so weakened by carrying cooking utensils, logs and charcoal that they were prey to pestilence and unable to fight. Troops were becoming 'uncontrollably rowdy... and insufferably malicious'. No invasion was ordered and the demoralised troops stayed in their camps.

The dynasty plunged on towards its chaotic end. Wang Mang was obsessed with the idea that ancient rites would save the day, if only they could be understood correctly. Ministers ignored their duties to struggle with impenetrable texts. The court was plagued by executions, plots and suicides. Commoners prostrated themselves outside the palace, begging for relief from injustice. Civil servants went unpaid, and relied on bribes. Prices rose, and so did taxes. Ordinary people took to crime. 'Itinerant bands of marauders plundered, pillaged and robbed.' But to bring the Emperor bad news was to court execution; the way to promotion was to reassure him that all was well.

Wang Mang turned to ever more desperate measures. He offered rewards for anyone who could suggest new ways to invade and conquer the Xiongnu. One idea, described by Sima Guang, was a spy-in-the-sky over Xiongnu territory, which, if true, would have been the first attempt at manned flight (excluding the mythical Greek Icarus, whose beeswaxed wings melted when he flew too close to the sun).

> The inventor had fashioned two massive wings spun out of feathers and had his entire body covered with feathers from head to toe. Strings attached to rings were used to control the movement of the wings. The man then took off with his contraption. He left the ground for a few hundred steps and fell back to crash-land.

In fact, this is nonsense. This Chinese Icarus could not have left the ground. The laws of physics forbid it. No one would understand the principles of powered or gliding flight for another 1,800 years.* If the Birdman of Chang'an was real, he would have been good for a laugh, but not for a flight.

In 22 to 23 CE, Wang Mang made increasingly frantic attempts to shore up his waning power. He dyed his grey hair and beard black, selected 120 new concubines for his harem, freed all the criminals in his kingdom and offered the rebels a last chance to surrender or face total destruction at the hands of his million-strong army, reinforced with 'large numbers of tigers, leopards, rhinoceroses, elephants and other wild beasts'.

He was living a fantasy. Rebel groups, determined to reinstate the Han dynasty, united to form an army. Everywhere, ordinary people joined in the revolt. On the first day of September, rebels broke into Chang'an, then the palace, yelling for Wang Mang, who hid in a back room, delirious with panic, trying to decide with his astrologer what seat would be the most auspicious. Early next day, with his last loyal troops and family members being slaughtered by the mob, he fled to

---

* The first man-carrying glider was built by Sir George Cayley, of Brompton Hall, North Yorkshire, in 1804.

an island in the middle of a lake, where, finally, he was found, stabbed and beheaded. His head was set on a spike and displayed in public, until 'angry mobs viciously wrenched away the head, kicking it hither and thither'. So ended the shortest dynasty in Chinese history, leading to two years of chaos until the Eastern Han, lasting from 25 to 220 CE, brought stability once more.

## FALL, AND ANNIHILATION

All of which left the Xiongnu in excellent spirits. For a brief while, it looked as if the Xiongnu were about to restore Modu's empire.

But rivalry undermined them. An heir apparent named Bi* was pushed from the succession and took off with his followers to Ordos. His action split the Xiongnu into a northern, Mongolian branch and a southern Chinese-based one, which never left, becoming one of several 'barbarian' hordes living inside the Great Wall, until their capital Tong Wan Cheng was destroyed by the Northern Wei in circumstances we will get to later.

The northern branch – wealthy with Han gifts, their aristocrats burying each other in their lavish graves – lived on, in obscurity, because no one in China thought them worth recording. For forty years, chanyus came and went, occasionally raiding. Only in 87 CE did one emerge from the shadows. His name was Youliu, his name recorded because the up-and-coming tribe from Manchuria, the Xianbei, reached his capital, caught him, beheaded him and skinned him.

The real end was near. In Chang'an, a ten-year-old, He, had just become Emperor. It happened that an ambitious and arrogant general, Dou Xian, brother of the empress dowager and the boy-Emperor's uncle,

* Actually, Khailoshi-Jodi to the Xiongnu, renamed in Chinese sources, following the rule that Xiongnu leaders should have a single Chinese name.

was in prison after being implicated in an assassination. To regain his freedom and influence, he offered to crush the Xiongnu and end a 300-year menace for good and all. His sister agreed. In 89 CE, he headed north with a huge army of Han, Southern Xiongnu, Xianbei and several other 'barbarian' contingents.

What happened next is worth telling in detail, because the campaign was well recorded and because hard evidence for it recently emerged. Almost always, historical sources are marred by unsubstantiated claims. But here the source is backed by an inscription discovered in 2017. So, the story is actually two stories: the events and the discovery.

To record his coming victory, Dou Xian had with him Ban Gu, imperial librarian and the most eminent historian of his time. At fifty-seven, Ban Gu had been working on his monumental *Han Shu* (*Book of Han*), his history of the previous dynasty, for thirty years. History was a delicate business. He would eventually die in prison, accused by a jealous rival, but right now he was at the height of his prestige, acting as historian-at-large. He could not have been thrilled at the prospect. His advice was exactly the reverse of what was happening. The way to deal with the Xiongnu, he said, was to maintain 'hostile vigilance', because, in his words, 'Those who live beyond the Wall are greedy and desirous of gain; they have human faces but the hearts of wild beasts... the Sage Kings treated them like birds and beasts, neither concluding treaties with them, nor going forth and attacking them.' He kept quiet, and did what his Emperor wanted.

Things worked out well. Advancing in three columns across the Gobi in the summer of 89, Dou Xian first met the Xiongnu east of the Three Beauties range, where the Altai mountains dip into gravel, sand and gnarled saxaul bushes. The allies sent the Xiongnu, under a chanyu named Bei (note the Chinese-style name), in headlong retreat north-west. Dou Xian pursued them for 180 kilometres, out of the Gobi, across grasslands into the Khangai mountains. The Xiongnu regrouped on gently billowing plains near a hill named Yanran, and again suffered a defeat.

To mark his victory, Dou Xian ordered Ban Gu to write a memorial and have it engraved into a cliff face near the top of the nearby hill. When Ban Gu got home, he recorded what he had written: an account of the battle ending in a formal, traditional verse of five lines and seven characters per line.

This is what he wrote:[6]

> In the first year of Yung Yuan's reign [Emperor He as he became], in the autumn [actually July], the National Maternal Uncle, Dou Xian, was appointed the Commander-in-Chief to show the power of Han over the Xiongnu. Among his subordinate generals – as powerful as eagles and tigers – were troops from the Southern Xiongnu, Tenger Khan [the chanyu of the Southern Xiongnu*] and Shi, Rong and Di khans. The 30,000 horsemen and 3,000 chariots divided into four parts. When the troops were on the march, the dust covered the sky and the earth, flags flying, their armour outshining Heaven. They came to the Gobi, and killed many of the enemy, so that their bodies lay scattered here and there. Then passing mountains and rivers, they came to Yanran Mountain. They followed the footprints of the Xiongnu and set fire to their tents wherever they found them, expressing their anger against them. They comforted the souls of their ancestors, and fortified their rule so it could be passed down to their descendants, expressing the power of the whole land. This one victory assured peace for ever. Thus Our victory is inscribed on the rock of this mountain top, as an expression of Our royal power and virtue.

The verse, reproduced in the fourth-century *Hou Han Shu* (*Book of the Later Han*), runs:

> The fine Sovereign's armies campaigned into the desolate remote [regions],
> Destroyed the fierce and cruel, brought order to beyond the seas,

* This was his title, Heavenly Khan. He ruled from 88 to 93 CE, and his name was Xiulan Shisu-quuti (in pinyin), Syuulan Shiju-Khoudi (in Mongolian).

> Far-reached those distant [places], joined the territories and borders,
> Made *feng* [offerings]* at Spirit Mount, erected a glorious tablet,
> Recorded the splendour of the Emperor, renowned for ten thousand generations.[7]

The Yanran Inscription became famous as a memorial to the final, stamping-on-the-head-of-the-snake end of the Xiongnu menace. There was one problem: no one knew where the Yanran Mountain was, so no one could check the truth of the story, let alone if Ban Gu's record was a true copy of the inscription. There were several attempts to find it, with no success. In 1990, two herders avoiding a rainstorm sheltered beneath a cliff, noticed the inscription and reported their find. It was an inopportune time – Mongolia was embroiled in the collapse of Communism. But at least Mongolian scholars knew where Yanran Mountain was.

In 2014, scholars contacted Professor Chimeddorj, an archaeologist and vice president of the Inner Mongolia University in Hohhot. In July 2017, a joint Chinese and Mongolian expedition went to the spot, found the inscription and took rubbings. The following month, Chimeddorj and other team members from Chinggis Khan University in Ulaanbaatar announced that they could read 220 of the 260 characters (the rest having been eroded away), and confirmed that the one recorded by Ban Gu was the same as the inscription he had devised, almost to the day, 1,928 years previously.

Actually, it wasn't quite the end for the Northern Xiongnu. The so-called 'last of the chanyus' was killed in 93 CE. 'So-called' because sources do not agree on his name, and Mongolian sources list a further dozen pretenders to the title, on into the second century. But by then, the Xianbei ruled Mongolia, and if any Northern Xiongnu remained,

---

* The *feng* rituals were significant rites performed from the earliest times. Unfortunately, long gaps between enactments meant 'the details… have been completely lost.' The sacrifice performed was apparently considered good enough to count as *feng*.

they were nothing but bands of robbers. The rest had vanished into the hidden heart of Central Asia – until two hundred years later, on the far side of the continent, there appeared a tribe with a similar lifestyle and a strangely similar name, the Huns. That's another story (for which, see Appendix II).

*This was the womb from which the Xianbei said they sprang to build an empire in north China.*

## CHAPTER 4

# THE XIANBEI AND THEIR CAVE

## THE PUZZLING ROOTS OF A NOMAD EMPIRE

IN THE NATIONALITIES MUSEUM IN HAILAR, HULUNBUIR'S capital, there is a model of a cave mouth, as seen from inside, with a pretty view over distant forested hills. This, said the museum guide, was where the Xianbei (pronounced she-an-bay) came from. I was puzzled, because the only thing I knew about the Xianbei was that they had defeated the Xiongnu, in the second century CE, chased them out of Mongolia and then taken over the whole region, consigning the Xiongnu to extinction. How could a whole tribe and its army come out of a cave? And what possible connection could a cave have with the fact that they conquered much of the north and founded an empire?

For Chinese civilisation, these were difficult times. When the two rival empires of Xiongnu and Han fell apart, the whole of the north collapsed into a chaos of rival states, heralding an age of division which lasted from 220 to 581. Chinese historians call part of this period (304–439) the Sixteen Kingdoms of the Five Barbarians. Today this whole region, and more, is firmly within the Chinese sphere, as if China had swallowed these alien entities whole. But success was not all about conquest. Even when disunited, China was a magnet that drew the less civilised into its orbit. Barbarians sometimes *chose* to adopt Chinese culture, the Xianbei being a prime example.

To understand what happened, we must go back to the Xiongnu strongman, Modu. According to Sima Qian, having seized power from his father Tumen, Modu's first external challenge came from the Dong, a confederation of 'barbarians', one group of which were the Xianbei, herders who had immigrated from the Khingan mountains in what is now north-east Inner Mongolia. To summarise Sima Qian's story in Chapter 1, the Dong demand a stallion and one of Modu's wives in tribute, to which Modu agrees, but when the Dong king demands land, Modu strikes like lightning against them, destroys them and begins to build his empire.

For this chapter, the significance of the story is that one of the victims of this assault were the Xianbei. Rather than remain as Xiongnu subjects, they fled from Mongolia's grasslands, back to their original homeland, the forested hills of the Khingan mountains, and took refuge in a cave – the Ga Xian Cave, as it is called – the one of which there is a copy in the Nationalities Museum in Hailar.

I could not, of course, be happy with a copy. I had to see the real thing, because it posed problems. Are we supposed to believe this story, or is it simply a myth? Was the cave natural or did they dig it out? If natural, how does such a cave get made? Could a cave really be a home for an entire tribe? The museum guide said this was a protected site. Would I even be allowed in? Well, there was only one way to find out.

First, to pick up the story of the Xianbei after their flight back from Mongolia. Folklore puts them safe in their cave, where they stayed for 150 years. They had no writing, so we don't know anything of their lifestyle, but they were surely more than cave dwellers, hunting and gathering in the valleys, hills and forests of the Khingans, untouched by the constant wars between the Xiongnu and the Han Empire. If there was any truth in this, they would have preserved folk memories, kept alive by bards singing traditional songs and grandparents telling stories of the old days when they had co-ruled vast estates, raising herds and hunting, exchanging furs for silk with Han traders and then losing it all when the Xiongnu drove them out. And still, after such a disaster, would not their folklore preserve a burning hatred of their oppressors, the Xiongnu?

Can we be sure of this? Of course not.

But look at what happened when the Xiongnu fell under the sway of Han China. The Xianbei had been in their cave for 150 years when the Xiongnu started to collapse. A turning point came in 51 BCE, when the chanyu, Huhanye, went on his state visit to the capital Chang'an and submitted to the Han Emperor, receiving a treasury of gifts. That was the beginning of the end for the Xiongnu. Hooked on Chinese luxuries, fixated on Chinese culture, they forgot their old warrior tradition. The Xiongnu Empire divided in two, and those of them remaining in Mongolia collapsed into feuds, the start of a steady, inexorable decline that played out over the coming decades.

In the east, the Xianbei saw their chance, emerged from their cave and rebuilt their forces. In 87 CE, one group invaded the Xiongnu heartland, and seized their recently discovered capital, known as Long Cheng ('Dragon Wall') in Chinese sources. They caught the chanyu, Youliu, beheaded him, stripped off his skin and took it home in triumph, a brutal revenge for their humiliation almost three hundred years previously. Perhaps this disaster contributed to the Han victory over the Xiongnu at Yanran in 89. Some forty years later, the Xianbei took over the whole empire and what remained of the Xiongnu vanished into the heart of Asia.

In Mongolia, the Xianbei had little lasting impact, because their leader was no more than a robber baron, with no interest in government, preferring to raid rather than trade. But in China itself, a more effective group of Xianbei took over the region of the two lakes, Hulun and Buir, where they settled, thrived and spread, taking advantage of the chaotic disarray that marked the end of both the Xiongnu and the Han empires. Six of the Sixteen Kingdoms were run by Xianbei, one of which became the core of a dynasty, the Northern Wei (386–534 CE). This brought brief stability to these unstable regions, dominating north China for 150 years under their ruling clan, the Tabgach (Mongol) or

Tuoba (Chinese). The story of the cave comes into focus with their third ruler in the mid-fifth century.

In 443, Tuoba Taiwu (424–452) had reason to be proud of his clan's achievements and his own. He was a leader with many virtues, according to Sima Qian: strong, brave, always in the front line, frugal and free with good advice for his generals. Like all strong leaders, he was ruthless, perhaps rather too eager to execute people, and often living to regret his haste. There was no doubting his success, though. In the twenty years of his rule, tribes had been subdued, neighbours (like the marauding Rouran, who were now ravaging Mongolia) conquered, the Great Wall restored along the northern border, the ancient Chinese capital of Luoyang destroyed, Xianbei authority secured from Xinjiang to the Pacific, the north unified. Before Taiwu took over, his people had been in the process of adopting Buddhism. A former ruler had introduced Chinese script. Their subjects were Chinese. They had given their growing empire a Chinese name, Wei. But Emperor Taiwu despised the drift to all things Chinese, in particular the new fad for Buddhism, and he passed laws to wipe it out, with results we will return to later.

All this time, for over three hundred years, parents had told their children the story of their survival after they had been defeated by the Xiongnu. Scholars collected stories of their prowess, among them the one about Mulan, the woman who disguised herself as a man to join the Wei army and fight the Rouran (yes, the same Mulan as featured in the Disney film of 1998). Another story, also recorded in their sources. was about their cave, the symbol of their survival.

But where was it?

In 443, members of a small north-eastern tribe (probably Shiwei, about whom more later) came to Emperor Taiwu and told him that somewhere close to where they lived there was a cave where locals worshipped Xianbei ancestors. At this sensational news, Taiwu commanded two officials, Li Chang and his deputy Fu Qu, to mount an expedition, find the cave and there conduct ceremonies in honour of Heaven and Earth and his Xianbei ancestors. This was quite a challenge. It had been three hundred years since Taiwu's ancestors had left their forested base. The cave was 1,300 kilometres from the Xianbei capital, Pingcheng (part of today's Datong), across vast expanses of grassland where the wild Rouran lived.

Li Chang and his team, which would have been a wagon-train of tents and supplies, well protected by troops, set off for the Khingan mountains, travelling at a rate of twenty-one kilometres a day* across the grasslands and into the forested domains of bears, wolves and hunter-gatherers. Li Chang did not record their adventures, but after their two-month journey they found the cave, leaving an inscription to record their success, and returned with the good news.

## THE DWELLING-PLACE OF A LONG-DEAD IMMORTAL

A few days after my visit to the museum in Hailar, I was 350 kilometres to the east, just outside Oroqen town, named after the local minority. I was with my friend, Alatan. We pulled into a huge car park flanked by a new single-storey hotel catering to the tourists gathering on a wooden walkway. An electric tourist bus carried our little group a few hundred metres through saplings and bushes. A high ridge rose to the right, edging a broad wooded valley to the left. 'Welcome to the Ga Xian Cave,' the guide, Ms Ba, announced through her portable megaphone as we climbed out. Well, not quite. Ahead was an avenue ten metres wide paved with flagstones. It could have been a main road, but access to the cave was on foot. Was this to protect the site, or had someone known how to confer upon visitors a sense of significance? Make them walk, expend a little energy, feel they are approaching something worth visiting, something sacred.

* This was the average distance for royal expeditions, as shown almost a thousand years later by the distance between Kublai Khan's overnight stops as he processed from Beijing to his summer palace, Xanadu.

The one-kilometre approach led along a waist-high wall on which stood little pillars topped with what, to my eyes, were obviously frogs.

'Lions,' said Ms Ba. 'The totem of the Xianbei.'

Lions guard countless Chinese temples and palaces, but China had no lions of its own. They were imports by Emperors and kept in royal menageries. Sculptors seldom saw one. So they were iconic symbols of power, with a standardised appearance, which explains why they are frog-like. If you want to represent an alien or Jesus, say, you have to obey the rules. In China, if you wanted to carve a lion, it better look like a frog.

Ms Ba was talking. She said there were 108 pillars – a sacred number for Buddhists, recalling the 108 volumes of the Kanjur, the collection of basic Buddhist texts. The number suggested that the Ga Xian cave itself was sacred to Buddhism. Emperor Taiwu was a notorious anti-Buddhist, but this new religion played a big part in Northern Wei culture.

Had the Xianbei been the first occupants?

'The Oroqen people used to live here,' Ms Ba said, quoting folklore about the local people. 'But a ferocious nine-headed monster oppressed them and drove them out. They were saved by an immortal named Ga Xian, so they gave the cave his name. Then the ancestors of the Xianbei came.'

I wondered about the name, which was also the name of the tree-lined river we were walking along. Ms Ba offered several possibilities. Perhaps it meant 'bitter' in the Xianbei language, which was probably some Turkic or Mongolic relative. Or perhaps it meant 'hunting ancestor' in Oroqen. Or perhaps 'village', or 'valley', or 'home'. She shook her head at the uncertainty of it all.

We were near the end of the avenue of trees and pillars when I became aware that during our chat the ridge to our right had turned into a cliff, almost sheer, with parallel vertical scratch-marks that looked as if they had been made by the claws of a gigantic cat. A steep flight of steps led upwards through bushes.

And there, at the top, was the cave, a triangle of darkness about fifteen metres high. There was no barrier. Twenty or thirty visitors strolled in and out, listening to the loudspeaker commentary from their guide. I joined them, stepping out of the bright summer sun into the cool and gloom.

As my eyes adjusted to the darkness, I saw I was at the mouth of a huge chamber, some thirty metres wide, retreating back beyond a fence until it vanished into shadows. In the middle of the floor, in semi-darkness, lay an ominous pile of rocks which must have fallen from the roof long ago. But – I glanced upwards to check – the roof was safe enough now. Some immense force had scooped out the cave, grinding away at the floor and roof until it looked as if a gigantic tunnelling machine had been at work.

The guide was talking. The cave was 110 metres deep, she said. At the back it divided into two smaller tunnels, leading to four chambers, but we couldn't go back there for safety reasons.

'Do you know what made the cave?' I asked, with Alatan's help.

'It's natural,' she said briskly, as if dismissing the possibility of a tunnelling machine.

It took some additional research with geologists and cave experts back in London to come up with a scenario. Most caves are created by water washing away limestone, which is formed by the shells of uncountable billions of sea creatures. It is relatively soft, and usually drops of water seeping through it leave residues that build icicle-like stalactites and rock pillars (stalagmites). But the Ga Xian cave does not have any of these, because it is made of granite, formed of molten rock tens or hundreds of millions of years ago as this part of China continued its slow-motion collision with Siberia. Granite is uniform and impermeable to water, so granite caves are rare. They can form only in places where the granite is cracked, which allows water to enter and gradually, over millions of years, to wash away the rock and make a cave. That's what had happened here.

But that was only a start. As I stood there, looking at the arched roof and flat floor, it seemed to me that something else had been at work: ice.

Ten thousand years ago, this whole area was covered in ice, the latest in a series of ice ages. Imagine the ravine below as a vast river, flowing between the cliff and the opposite bank, two kilometres away. The climate changes, the water freezes solid. The ice is deep, maybe fifty metres. It covers the cave, for millennia. The climate improves, the ice breaks, grinding down the cliff face, leaving those cat-like scratches on the rocky surface. The frozen river turns back into flowing water. But the Ga Xian cave is like an ice-well, its contents kept frozen by the surrounding rock. Water flows in from above, which lubricates the melting ice. Both together scour the inside of the cave, creating a vast, drain-like tube. The upper section remains as a smooth, arched roof, while the bottom fills with sediment, making a flat floor. After the ice has gone and the river shrinks, the cave becomes a perfect base for humans as they set up home in the forests of Hulunbuir. Exit the Oroqen, if they were ever there, and enter, at last, the fugitive Xianbei.

What could the Xianbei have used it for? Well, probably not as a communal home for a horde of several thousand. The cave is about three thousand square metres in floor area, which, if you take an average house of seventy to eighty square metres, gives you living space for only about two hundred to three hundred people. Perhaps, in theory, you could double that by building more floors out of wood and using the smaller caves at the back, but that would create problems with food waste, toilet facilities and cooking. No, the cave has more in common with a cathedral or a temple than with a block of apartments. It is a magical space, not a domestic one.

In fact, the three thousand square metres of floor space is only half the size of St Paul's and one fifth that of St Peter's in Rome. It is space enough for two thousand people to gather while their shaman offers thanks to Heaven for their delivery from the Xiongnu. We cannot know what religious beliefs the Xianbei held, because by the time they adopted writing they had become thoroughly sinicised Buddhists, but nomadic tribes were nature worshippers and shamanists, who interpreted the will of Heaven in ceremonies of fire and animal sacrifice. Possibly, like others, they read the future by seeking meaning in the hairline cracks of a sheep's scorched shoulder bone. Perhaps those fallen rocks in the middle of the floor had been used as an altar.

This is not all down to my imagination. Archaeologists exploring the cave soon after its rediscovery in the 1980s found a medallion in the shape of an Ordos bronze, one of the little plaques which the inhabitants of Ordos used as belt buckles and as decorations for their horse equipment. So the Xianbei either made bronzes like this themselves, or got them by trade. However it arrived, it was an image of the Xianbei's *real* totem, not a lion as Ms Ba had said, but a flying horse, which, according to folklore, guided them when they started their migration south.* I think we can assume it was brought to the cave because the cave itself was a symbol of identity for the Xianbei.

If any further proof were needed that this is the right place, there, at the entrance, was the inscription left by the expedition headed by Li Chang in the summer of 443 CE. Its story links past and present. The cave and the story of the inscription had never been forgotten, because they are mentioned in the Wei history, but without maps or accurate references, no one knew where to look. Locals knew of the cave itself, but as Oroqen speakers, unfamiliar with Chinese, they had little interest in the inscription that identified the cave correctly Anyway, it is so faint it can hardly be read. Only in July 1980 did scholars arrive to research the cave. They noticed the patch of dusty rock just above eye-level, brushed it clean, found the inscription, and realised its significance.

Just inside the cave mouth, there is a copy and transcription of the 220 characters, which read from right to left in a style that was common until the early twentieth century. Alatan looked closer, and began to translate. 'In the fourth year of the True Lord of Peace, on July twenty-fifth...'

'You can read it!'

* Another version of this totem is on each of a pair of golden ornaments unearthed in 1960 near Manzhouli, and now in the Inner Mongolia Museum, Hohhot.

'Some signs are a little difficult, but yes.' It is one of China's most obvious cultural characteristics that its writing system has lasted so long. The age of the inscription, 1,600 years, is a good length of time, but Chinese writing had been in existence for many centuries by then. This, however, was a Xianbei tablet, not Han, and it had a few characters that would have baffled a Han scholar, because they record words in Xianbei, with its links both to Turkic and Mongol. 'It is signed in the name of the *Ke han*,' said Alatan. 'These two characters are the Mongolian word for "king" – *khagan* today ['khan', as it is in English]. And it is also signed in the name of the *ke dun*, the deceased queens. That is their version of the Mongolian *khatun*, queen, here used in the plural.'

It is rare for an ancient story to be so well served by archaeology. So here is the inscription, in full:

> In the fourth year of the True Lord of Peace, on the 25th day of the seventh month of the Gui Wei Year, Emperor Taiwu, Son of Heaven, sent ministers of the Six Departments and the assistant ministers of the Central Secretariat, Li Chang and Fu Qu, by offering stallions, oxen and furry animals, to declare to the whole country:
>
> God of Heaven, in the beginning, protected my imperial ancestors on that land for one hundred million years. The later southward migration was highly blessed. The unification of Middle China also benefited from my ancestors and grandfathers. They expanded and secured frontiers in four directions and blessed their descendants. Nowadays, I carry forward the spirit of Daoism. More holy halls are built, evil things are annihilated and imperial authority reaches the deserts in four directions. Despite the long distance, a hermit came to see me and kowtowed. Until then I didn't know the old site and where it was. Sighing with emotion, I longed to admire its remaining glory. The rise of the empire originated in my imperial ancestors. Like a cluster of melons on rattan, their descendants are well blessed. We return to express our gratitude to Heaven. May it bless our children and grandchildren for ever.
>
> In the name of:

God of Heaven,
God of Earth,
Ke Han, the imperial ancestors
Ke Dun, the deceased queens
Please enjoy the offerings.[1]

We made our way down to the little Ga Xian river below, running prettily over rocks and under trees. Stepping stones led across to an island, and beyond lay the broad valley that had once been a flood plain.

I turned and looked up at the cave, a black shadow in the sun-drenched cliff face. For a few seconds, I imagined a seventy-metre precipice of ice in a prehistoric world. A cuckoo called somewhere in the trees, the spell broke and we made our way slowly back to the electric bus.

## BECOMING CHINESE

Inspired perhaps by the knowledge of his people's origins, Taiwu went on a rampage of new conquests, striking northwards across the Gobi to crush the Rouran, the latest in the rulers of Mongolia, and westwards to annihilate the Southern Xiongnu and their capital, the only known Xiongnu city, Tong Wan Cheng ('Ruling Ten Thousand Cities'). The ruins – a six-kilometre square of guard-towers and walls – still stand after 1,600 years as a memorial to Taiwu's talent for destruction. Made of quartz sand, white clay and a cement of rice-flour, they look like whipped cream, which explains its modern Chinese name, the White City.

Taiwu's other great act of destruction was to attack Buddhism. His predecessors, familiar with it from their westward links along the Silk Road, had adopted it because they needed an ideology that set the ex-nomad rulers apart from their Chinese subjects. During the war against the Southern Xiongnu, some weapons were found in several

Buddhist temples. This convinced Taiwu that all Buddhists were in revolt against him. He banned the religion and ordered all Buddhist monks to be killed. Well, orders were one thing, carrying them out something else entirely. Buddhism endured.

These were cruel times. Every year brought war against neighbours or rebels, and inhumanity was routine. Describing a war with Song, Sima Guang listed some of the atrocities. Bear in mind that he was writing in the eleventh century, six hundred years after the events he describes, and he was himself from Song, so had an interest in portraying Song as the victim:

> When Wei forces encountered Song young men, the forces quickly beheaded them or cut them in half. The infants were pierced through with spears, and the spears were then shaken so that the infants would scream as they were spun, for entertainment. The commanderies and counties that Wei forces went through were burned and slaughtered, and not even grass was left. When sparrows returned in the spring, they could not find houses to build nests on, so they had to do so in forests.

Taiwu's reign ended in blood and chaos. His nemesis was a power-mad eunuch named Zong Ai, who, in 452, executed several minor princes, assassinated the Emperor, placed a young prince on the throne and then assassinated him as well. Zong Ai himself then became the victim of a plot in which he was subjected to the long-established Five Punishments, which were: face tattooed (usually with one's crime), nose cut off, toes or feet or testicles cut off, being lashed to death and finally decapitated prior to public exposure. As variants, executioners might choose to end the punishments with one of the old standbys – cutting the victim in half at the waist, which was a good way to test swords and swordsmen, or tying them to chariots which then drove off in different directions and tore the victims apart. Usually, criminals condemned to the Five Punishments had to endure just one. Zong Ai, for his sins, suffered all in turn, but kept his feet and testicles until the beating that killed him.

For the theme of this book – the northwards spread of Chinese rule – the most significant things about the Xianbei is that they were not conquered by China or any of its kingdoms: they *chose* to forget their culture and become Chinese. However, that was not their original idea. Recall that Taiwu's predecessors had adopted Buddhism as a state religion in order to preserve their non-Chinese traditions and keep apart from their Chinese subjects. 'We have complied with our appointed destiny and govern the Chinese as their prince,' said a Xianbei ruler in 335, even before the empire was formally established. 'Buddha being a barbarian god is the very one we should worship.' By Taiwu's time, however, it had become too successful for comfort. That was why Taiwu turned against it, viciously, but with no lasting impact. Twenty years after Taiwu's death, a successor, Xiaowen (471–499), was so committed to Buddhism that he abdicated to become a monk. By 477, Northern Wei had over six thousand temples and over seventy thousand monks and nuns.

This might also have been too much for later rulers, had not an unnamed Buddhist official declared that the Xianbei ruler should be considered a Buddha incarnate and that he should honour the fact by building a cliff shrine devoted to Buddhism. 'These were strokes of genius,' writes Ann Paludan. Rival religions were reconciled. Emperors and Buddhists could honour each other, and the ancestor-worshipping Confucians could use the shrines to honour their imperial ancestors. The unnamed official's declaration also refocused creativity. As Paludan puts it, 'The wealth, manpower and artistic resources which in earlier times had been devoted to imperial palaces and tombs were now channelled into lavish temple buildings and imperial cliff sites.'[2] So began a great era of Buddhist cliff-shrines, the first being the Yungang Grottoes near the Xianbei capital Pingcheng, now part of Datong. Work continued there almost until the dynasty fell in 535, creating fifty-three caves and 51,000 niches all filled with small Buddhas – a masterpiece of Buddhist art and, today, one of China's top tourist sites.

The Xianbei had become victims of what might be termed cultural drift. To assert their non-Chinese identity, the Xianbei had supported

Buddhism, becoming the first major state to do so; Buddhism had spread widely, becoming part of Chinese culture; and so the Northern Wei actually became a part of the culture they had intended to reject.

They employed Chinese officials in order to govern, they adopted Chinese institutions, they gave themselves Chinese names, they married their daughters to Chinese aristocrats, they emulated Chinese efforts to control their Chinese subjects. In 486, for instance, they gave every family at least twenty *mu* (about 1.3 hectares) of unused land, introducing the so-called 'equal field' system to control the population, ensure universal cultivation and prevent officials from building vast estates. A few years later, the Emperor solved the 'northern barbarians' problem not by building his own Great Wall* but by moving the capital to Luoyang, five hundred kilometres south, across the Yellow River, just after it turns east from the Great Bend. There he built a Chinese-style palace, prescribed Chinese dress at court and insisted on the use of the Chinese language.

In the long run, it did them no good. Border guards hated their effete masters, and in 535 they revolted, sacked Luoyang and killed two thousand officials. Decades of war and civil war ended in 581, when a new Emperor proclaimed the Sui dynasty, ensuring that this part of the barbarian north was now, and for ever, thoroughly part of the Chinese heartland.

* An official named Gao Lü recommended wall-building in a paper often cited by later dynasties as a solution to the 'northern barbarians' problem, but the Northern Wei chose to flee south rather than build.

## FAST FORWARD

*The Xianbei, within the orbit of China, overlapped another steppe empire centred on Mongolia, under a Xianbei subgroup, the Rouran. Between them and the Mongols, a thousand years later, lie several other empires (see Appendix I), one of whom (Jin), ruling from the city that would become Beijing, was the first major target for the Mongols under Chinggis Khan.*

An hour or two east of Mongolia's capital, Ulaanbaatar, Chinggis views his homeland. This, the world's biggest equestrian statue, exemplifies the power that China claims.

# PART II

# HIJACKING CHINGGIS

*Many in China see Mongolians as Chinese. Here's why. Chinggis Khan, born in Mongolia, founded a nation, and formed the world's biggest land empire. Under Chinggis's grandson, Kublai Khan, the empire expanded across much of Eurasia, including China. Relatives ruled elsewhere, but China was Kublai's. To rule it, Kublai declared himself a Chinese Emperor, founding a Chinese dynasty, the Yuasn. His estate included his original homeland, Mongolia. Under the Manchus (1644–1911), Mongolia became a Chinese colony. We'll get to the details later. Though Mongolia is now independent, all of this explains why there is a feeling in China that everything Mongolian – and everything to do with Chinggis – is really, truly, essentially part of China.*

*Mongolians at Holy Mountain (Bogd Uul), south of Lake Hulun.*

CHAPTER 5

# Chinggis in China

## The origin of the Mongols

CHINGGIS KHAN'S HOMELAND WAS NORTHERN MONGOLIA – the Khentii mountains, the sacred heights of Burkhan Khaldun, the Kherlen River curving away to the north-east, the grasslands giving way southwards to the Gobi – but northern Mongolia was not where the Mongols came from originally. Their foundation epic, the *Secret History of the Mongols*, says they came across the – or a – 'Tengis' (meaning sea or lake), which probably happened in the mid-ninth century.

What an academic storm that word has produced. What does 'Tengis' refer to? There are not many possibilities, because it designates a large body of water, such as the Mediterranean or the Caspian Sea. Some scholars argue that this Tengis must have been the biggest lake in east Asia, Lake Baikal in Siberia. But had the proto-Mongols really been living in the Siberian forests? It's doubtful. Other scholars say that 'Tengis' must be the only other large body of water in these parts – Lake Hulun, in north-east China, the larger of the two lakes – Hulun and Buir – which, remember, give their name to the Inner Mongolian region of Hulunbuir.

That's what Chinese sources suggest. The story starts with a forest people known as Shiwei. According to a few details in fifth-century records, they dominated the forests of the north-east, across Manchuria. They were not herders, having few horses, but lived in huts made of bent branches covered by the skins of the animals they hunted. Later accounts say they paid tributes in furs to the Turkic empire that ruled Mongolia in the sixth century and to the Tang in China from the seventh to the early tenth centuries. They were divided into anything up to twenty tribes, one of which lived in the western part of their range and was referred to as Meng-wu, or Mongol. They probably had links with the Xianbei: it was Shiwei, you will recall, who reported the existence of the Ga Xian cave to the Xianbei Emperor in 443, and 'Shiwei' and 'Xianbei' seem to be different transliterations of the same word. But the records are scanty, and no one knows if they spoke a form of Mongol, Turkic or Tungus. They emerge from their shadowy past only when the Meng-wu Shiwei moved on to the steppe and learned both herding and the crucial art of working iron.

According to folklore, they settled along the Erguna River (or Ergune or Argun in different spellings). The name of the river suggests that this is true: it probably derives either from the Mongolian for 'wide' (*örgön*), which it isn't very, or from *ergikh*, to wind or twist, which is something it does a good deal of as it wriggles northwards for one thousand kilometres, now forming the border with Russia. Then it joins the Amur, little known in the West, but we will hear a great deal about it in this and later chapters, because as the on-and-off border between Russia and China it flows with history and emotion. It is also the world's tenth longest river and a geographical oddity as the only major river in northern Asia that flows from west to east, rather than south to north.

Halfway to the Amur, there is a place that claims to have been the base for these soon-to-be Mongols. Some three hundred kilometres north of Hailar, the road runs past an impressive gateway – a broad arch flanked by four buildings, each topped by a dome in the style of a Mongolian tent. Flags fly from the roof. Beyond the entrance, forested hills rise in waves of green. A sign proclaims the site to be dedicated to the Shiwei.

The rolling forest beyond the arch covers almost four hundred square kilometres, the size of this protected area emphasising the significance of the subject to the local government. While driving me and two friends up a road that wound through an infinity of trees and hills, our guide told a story:

Once upon a time, there was a battle between the Mongols and the Turks (this being before Turkic tribes started their long migration westwards). The Mongols were reduced to two couples, who fled into a hidden valley in the Erguna Kun, a mountain or mountain range that has not been identified, but – since the Erguna River ran not far away – it must have been around here. On the other hand, this is a legend, so there may have been no Erguna Kun at all. Here, so the story goes, the Mongols lived for four or five centuries, growing in numbers.

There came a time when they wanted to get out. They killed seventy oxen and cows, and used the hides to make enormous bellows. With the bellows, they made a huge fire, so powerful that it melted part of the Erguna Kun, making a cleft through which they could escape. (Yes, there are some obvious problems with this story, like how did they get into the valley if there was no exit? We are dealing with folklore, so we should not ask too many questions.) Once free of the hidden valley, they crossed the Tengis – which, if it was Lake Hulun, was some two hundred kilometres to the south – and migrated six hundred kilometres north-west, across the grasslands of eastern Mongolia, to the mountains, rivers and grasslands of Khentii, which became their new homeland.

## YOUNG CHINGGIS

What happened over the next four hundred years is the main opening theme of *The Secret History*, with its mix of fact, folklore and anecdote. Scholars argue about which is which. This should be no surprise, given that the original Mongolian source, written in 1252, twenty-five years after Chinggis's death, was transcribed into Chinese characters as an aid for translators, was lost, rediscovered in the nineteenth century, reconstituted and only then translated into English and other languages. It was an immense, and ongoing, scholastic achievement.

A dozen legendary generations come and go, says *The Secret History*, with a medley of clan leaders, among them a widow named Alan the Fair, who has two sons, and then, after her husband's death and without remarriage, another three. She explains how this happened to the older two. 'Every night, a shining yellow man entered in with a brilliant light through the smoke-hole and lintel of the *ger* [tent] and stroked my belly; his brilliance dissolved into my womb. When he left, he would crawl out with the beams of the sun like a yellow dog.'[1]

Thus was conceived, by magic, the eleventh-generation ancestor of Chinggis Khan. His name was Bodonchar. Bodonchar the Simple, his brothers called him. Offended by the slur, he moved away and settled in northern Mongolia, where he and his heirs sired all the clans living in Mongolia when Temujin (the future Chinggis, named after a captive, whom his father had taken in battle) was born in 1162.

As so often among the Mongols, everything of significance over the past eight hundred years goes back to Chinggis. He is a living presence today, not only for Mongols. Greater-than-life-size statues of Chinggis and his family line the expressway leading into town from Hailar's airport. His spirit infuses the region.

A story in *The Secret History* tells us how, when Temujin was nine, his father Yisukei decides to find a wife for his son. The Mongols did not marry within their own clan. In a tradition that dated back a few decades, they chose their wives from a group known as Qonggirat (though spellings vary), who lived south and east of Lake Hulun. His own wife, Hoelun, was of this clan.

As it often does, *The Secret History* turns an event into a romantic tale with poetic additions. Yisukei is riding with Temujin across Qonggirat territory, aiming for his mother's original clan that lived further east, when he meets the Qonggirat chief, Deyi Secen (Deyi the Wise). *The Secret History* is clear where this occurred – near two mountains called Cekcer and Cigurqu, which are unidentified, but were supposedly somewhere west of the Orshun River, which flows between lakes Hulun and Buir. This is odd, because the area is a vast, flat slab of grassland, with just one prominent mountain, to which we will return later.

Offering hospitality to an old acquaintance, Deyi, who has a daughter of the right age, sees the political advantages of arranging a marriage. 'This boy of yours is a boy with flame in his eyes and fire in his face,' he says, and goes on to describe a dream he had had the previous night. 'A white falcon flew towards me clutching the sun and moon and alighted on my hand.' It is a good omen, because the falcon is both the king of hunting birds and the totem of Yisukei's clan, and white is the most auspicious colour. It means that Yisukei is destined for glory – if the two of them are linked through the marriage of their children. He reminds Yisukei of their traditional bond. The Qonggirat, he says, have always made alliances with their beautiful daughters.

> We Qonggirat folk, from days of old
> We raise our daughters fair of face,
> We sit them on our wagon's seat,
> Harnessing soot-hued bull camels;
> We send girls off to sit by your side
> On the high seat.
> Of old we Qonggirat folk
> Have lived by brides as our bucklers
> By pretty ones as our petitioners
> By the faces of our fair ones,
> By the graces of our girl children.

Let us go to my tent, says Deyi. Take a look at my daughter, Börte. And, of course, Yisukei sees that she is a beauty, with a strong character. In that stock phrase, 'He saw a girl with flame in her eyes and fire in her face, and he let her into his mind.'

Yisukei leaves Temujin with Deyi as a future son-in-law. On the way home he is poisoned by enemies, but before he dies, he sends for

Temujin. Ten years later, after many adventures, Temujin returns to claim his bride. She becomes his first love, and a powerful influence on him.

The Qonggirat remained a force in later Mongol history. Fourteen more Qonggirat women became queens of later Yuan Emperors, from Kublai Khan onwards. Marco Polo, whose *Travels** was the first to tell Europe about Kublai Khan's realm, worked for Kublai for seventeen years and described the process by which girls were chosen for the imperial bed. They were checked by 'certain elderly ladies, who make the girls sleep with them, in order to ascertain if they have sweet breath, and are sound in all their limbs'.

## A BATTLE CALLED COLD

As his star rose, Chinggis often campaigned on the Chinese side of the present-day border, intensifying feelings among the Chinese that Chinggis belongs to them. One of his most important battles is commemorated every year, in a festival that honours Chinggis himself and the Mongol deity, the Blue Sky. Before we get to the festival, this is what happened here eight hundred years ago:

In 1201–3, Chinggis was in the midst of operations to defeat his enemies, before declaring himself khan in 1206. His principal foe was his childhood friend and blood-brother, Jamukha, who had become his greatest rival and was head of an anti-Chinggis alliance. The two fought it out in a decisive battle at a place not far from where Yisukei met Deyi. *The Secret History* calls it Khuiten ('Cold').**

---

* Written about 1300. It has other titles, in scores of editions in dozens of languages: *Description of the World*, *Book of Marvels*, or simply the Book. It remains the best known and most influential travel book of all time.

** Khuiten is modern Mongolian. Atwood has 'Köiten'; de Rachewiltz 'Köyiten'.

Chinggis won a great victory, with divine assistance. The weather played a crucial role, thanks to some inept witchcraft by two generals named Buyruq and Qutuga:

> When they were pushing each other back and forth, up and down the slope, and re-forming their own ranks, at that very moment – Buyruq Khan and Qutuga knew how to use the weather-stone – they performed the weather-stone magic. But the weather-magic reversed and the magic fell on themselves. Unable to advance, it was they themselves who tumbled into the ditches, then, saying to each other, 'Heaven is not pleased with us,' they scattered.

During the battle, another chance event led to Chinggis gaining one of his greatest generals. As Chinggis put it afterwards, talking to a bunch of captives: 'When we were fighting at Khuiten and pushing each other back and forth and re-forming our ranks, an arrow came from high up on the ridge; it snapped the atlas bone in the neck of my white-mouthed straw-yellow armoured charger.' Who, he asked his captives, had fired the arrow? One of them spoke up. 'I fired it,' he said, then offered his services. If you kill me, he declared, I'll be no more than a bit of foul earth. But 'if I should be favoured, in front of the khan, I will charge for him, driving through the deep water, smashing through the smooth stone'. Chinggis was impressed, saying this is 'one fit to befriend'. In honour of the deed, he renamed the warrior Jebe ('Weapon'). He would become commander of Chinggis's heavy cavalry and one of the khan's 'four dogs', his closest companions.

Locals claim that the battle site is on the north bank of the Kherlen River as it flows from Mongolia towards Lake Hulun. Archaeologists have found many arrow-points here, though others point out that you can find arrow-points almost anywhere, and yet others think it was somewhere else entirely. One source backs up the *Secret History* by including a reference to men falling to their deaths from cliffs, of which there are none south of Lake Hulun. Christopher Atwood, the most recent translator of the *Secret History*, tentatively places it four hundred kilometres to the south-east, on another 'Cold Mountain', which has cliffs. As he wrote to me with gentle irony, 'The general principle of traditional Mongol nationhood was that "my *nutag*" [homeland, meaning anything from county to nation] contains within it at least a few, and preferably ALL the sites connected with the life of Chinggis Khan,' for if not 'it delegitimises their possession of the land.' About the only certainty is that the battle occurred in what is now China. Wherever it happened, this was one of the most significant battles in Mongol and Chinese history – imagine the difference if Chinggis had lost: no empire, no conquest of China, the world very different from the one we know.

## APPROACHING THE HOLY MOUNTAIN

China may have turned against their Mongols in recent years – more on that later – but some elements will be harder to displace than others. Take, for example, the festival that, for those who live in the Barga 'banners' (large counties)* of Hulunbuir, recalls the Battle of Khuiten. Of course, the festival takes place on Chinese territory, and in the light of new laws imposing Han norms and suppressing Mongolian and other minority cultures, it could be banned at a moment's notice. Perhaps I was privileged to be part of something that might never come again. But that's a thought that occurs in hindsight, as I read through my notes back home in London. No such cloud loomed over that bright June day.

When Bai Aijun, Deputy Chair of the People's Congress of Hulunbuir, briefed me on my research trip, he said I must certainly climb Holy Mountain – Bogd Uul, as the Mongols call it. When I asked why the

* The Barga (or Barag) Mongols were originally from the Lake Baikal area, a sub-division of the Buryats. After several migrations and deportations, they were settled by the Qing in Hulunbuir in three banners, Old and New, with New being divided into Left (east) and Right (west).

Holy Mountain was considered holy, the reply was, of course: 'Because of Chinggis Khan!' It was here that Chinggis fought his old friend and rival, Jamukha. When he was nearly defeated, he retreated up the mountain, and a storm gave him time to breathe, and he sent for reinforcements. That's why on 15 June every year thousands go up the mountain to give thanks and pray. I felt a rush of adrenaline. I had to be there, had to climb the mountain, had to honour the battle, Chinggis, the Blue Sky and the mountain itself.

At an official pre-festival supper in New Barga Right Banner, the local governor Bökh knew all about the Battle of Khuiten 'even though people argue about the actual site'. As if to underline the significance of the theme, on the wall was a picture of the Holy Mountain rising from the steppe, with a ribbon of worshippers ascending and descending.

The following afternoon, under a hot sun and blue sky, Alatan, 'Water' Xu and I drove south-east along a road as straight as an arrow over grassland that stretched to the horizon. Somewhere to our left, out of sight in the two-dimensional landscape, was the southern tip of Lake Hulun. Then ahead, a single hill broke the flat line of the horizon. It was only three hundred metres above the surrounding grassland, but it stood out like an island in a windless ocean.

The idea was to spend the night here, then make an early start, climb before the sun became too hot, then enjoy whatever else might be happening. Quite a lot, by the look of things. As we pulled into an enclosure of four tents and a shed, I heard a constant hum – cars in a steady stream heading for the mountain. More would be coming, all through the night. This was the heart of Mr Bökh's territory, Holy Mountain *sum* ('county'). It normally had a population of just two thousand. Up to twenty thousand were expected by morning. Most arrivals that evening would pitch tents or sleep under the stars, though we had it easy; we were glampers, sleeping in semi-permanent tents with concrete bases and proper beds.

I was still unclear about the arrangements. Over supper that started with many side-dishes, including skimmed milk cooked into various sorts of biscuit, I asked if we could take a car all the way to the summit.

'Most people walk,' said our guide, Li Ming.

'So there's a regular track?'

'There's a staircase. All the cars stop at the bottom.'

We were still five kilometres from the base, so the plan was to ride or take a car, then walk up. Fit young men could climb the three hundred metres in an hour or so. I feared it would take me a lot longer.

While we waited for more food, my hosts – the *sum* governor, the Party secretary, the director of archives and several more – emphasised the importance of the climb. People came from all around to meet each other, discuss local issues and introduce their children. The climb was a revered tradition, of course – hanging on the tent's trellis walls were two pictures of the mountain, honoured with fringes of blue silk – but there was more than tradition at work here. The officials had a political and social agenda that fitted the national policy – conservation and protection of the natural world. In this case, as Alatan explained after talking to the governor, the ambition was nothing less than the restoration of the original nomadic lifestyle. For this reason, climbing the Holy Mountain was both traditional and thoroughly modern at the same time.

Alatan's words hinted at a coming revolution, for until recently official policy had been to limit nomadism by fencing flocks in. Now, it seemed, herders would have to recombine pastures, removing fences, changing laws, recasting relations between herders. If I wanted to see the outcome, it would take many visits and years of research.

We were still waiting for the main meal. A sheep was on its way. 'It's very fresh,' said Li Ming. 'They killed it this morning.' To pass the time, I checked the shed next door, which served as the kitchen. Indeed, a cheerful chef was boiling bits of sheep in a huge vat.

Even here, no escape from domesticity. As I stood outside, listening to the passing cars and admiring the star-studded sky, my mobile phone rang. It was my wife in London. 'Darling,' she said. 'We have a problem. The vacuum cleaner is full and the cover is stuck. And I have a scene to finish.' She's a playwright. 'Do you know how to fix it?'

'Darling,' I replied. 'It is 10.30 at night here, I'm weak with hunger, I'm about to eat a boiled sheep and I have to get up at 4 a.m. to climb a mountain in honour of Chinggis Khan. I don't think I can remember the anatomy of our vacuum cleaner right now.'

'Fine. I'll just use it full.' She hung up.

When it finally arrived, the dissected sheep was a great relief from skimmed-milk biscuit, accompanied as it was by black blood-sausage, basically haggis, and the onset of toasts, luckily in tiny glasses. But there were lots of them, toasts to honour the climb, the officials, the meal, the one foreign guest, the grassland, the herds, the herders – I forget how many toasts, how many words of praise, how much respect was paid to how many officials, what honours were conferred on how many distinguished guests. From the blur, a memory: someone called Tana, with a tumble of black hair and a fiercely direct glance, who was in charge of tourism, and me asking her if she would be joining the climb the next morning.

'I'll stay at the bottom. Women are not allowed up the Holy Mountain.'

I wondered what she thought of a tradition that seemed to discriminate against women. Apparently neither she nor the other women saw it that way. They were content to follow tradition without feeling any sort of inferiority. Mongolian women don't do inferiority.

A meal as special as this would not be complete without song. There were many to choose from, songs about the grassland, about horses, about love. One of the officials stood and sang about night on the grasslands being beautiful. Tana, who was much less in focus than she had been, whispered a translation: 'I would like to write a letter to my love, but there is no postman here. The snow on the mountain is melting, and I am waiting for the spring wind to bring my girl to me to be my love.'

Suddenly, it was past midnight, and time for a few hours' sleep. Beneath the starry sky, Governor Bökh worried about the younger generation. 'They don't even know how to put up a tent, or how to herd. How will we protect our culture? How will we look after our future?'

## TO THE SUMMIT IN A THOUSAND STEPS

Dawn, and a perfect morning. The cars were still coming, making a backdrop of sound. A cloudless sky of soft blue, meeting the grass's soft grey-green at the horizon. The whole world glowed in the newly risen sun. Long shadows fell from tents, cars, horses and gathering people, most now in blue or green Mongolian dress, complete with silk belts. Half a dozen horses stood ready, two of which were for me and Alatan to ride the few kilometres to the base of the mountain. The saddle was Mongolian, with wooden bits jutting up front and back, which sounds uncomfortable but actually makes one feel secure. Carrying a whip – a chunk of wood with a leather handle – and with my knees bent to an acute angle by the short stirrups, I was in the hands of Erhelt, a weather-beaten Mongol who spoke no Chinese. On his horse alongside me, he led me as if I were made of porcelain to join the throng of cars at the base of the mountain.

We wove through the mass of cars and temporary shelters, into an enclosure of parked cars, dismounted, then walked towards a crowd standing near a giant circular shrine, an *ovoo*. It was made of stones and guarded by seven *suld*, war-standards topped by black horsehair, all joined by a spider's web of ropes and flags to an eighth *suld* jutting up from the middle. Ahead, in a line of officials, was Governor Bökh, dressed in a gorgeous red *deel* with a green waist-sash. Over a loud-speaker, a lama began to recite a long Mongolian prayer, calling for the blessings of Chinggis Khan and the Blue Sky, giving thanks for the good things filling every tent. The prayer was in eight-line stanzas, one line on a single note, falling a tone for the next line, rising again, falling, then ending with the three-fold affirmation from the crowd, *Khyrai! Khyrai! Khyrai!*, a call for good fortune which sounds like an English 'Hooray' and is shouted while circling both hands held out as if offering something. To a song playing over the loudspeaker, we all received little bags of rice, and corn for scattering on the waist-high *ovoo*, which we circled slowly three times clockwise, adding to the carpet of offerings that already covered the platform.

It was not yet 8 a.m., and time to start climbing. I set my floppy leather hat to guard against the sun. Water and I joined a mass of men and a few boys, making our way to the staircase. The wooden slats started to rise gently over the lower slope, in broad sections more like platforms than steps, three metres across. The sound of the loudspeakers died below us. A ten-year-old boy raced ahead, agile as a gazelle, while an old man with a three-pronged walking stick hauled himself up, step by laborious step. There was hardly a sound except the pad of feet on wood and the occasional greeting from people coming down, some on the grassy track beside the steps.

Halfway up, a platform invited us to pause with others to admire the view. What a view! The hundreds of cars below, reduced by the distance to the size of toys, stood in their enclosure as horses would have once stood. When we arrived, they had seemed to fill the whole area. But from above, they were no more than specks in the vastness of the surrounding grassland. People had complained how dry it had been this year. From up there, you could see it: the grass was grey with only a touch of green.

Now the stairs were steeper. Alongside the track was less grass, more rock, and herders were leading horses down. Perhaps I could have ridden to the top, and avoided this final climb. Then I was at the top anyway, immersed in crowds, from five-year-olds to teenagers in jeans, fathers with children on their shoulders, the middle-aged in their colourful *deels*. On a platform overlooking the cars and the steppe beyond, horses stood as if they too were admiring the view, saddled and ready to carry the weak or the lazy back down.

Water was with me, staring out over the horses on the platform, the columns of men climbing and descending, the cars in their enclosures, the grey-green grasslands, the distant horizon. Lake Hulun shimmered thirty kilometres away.

'Hulunbuir has eighty thousand square kilometres of grassland,' he said. He was a master of useful information. 'And this is the highest point.'

I turned through 360 degrees, and could see forty kilometres in every direction, with not a single hill, not another island in this sea of grass, which was – I did a little calculation on my phone – some five thousand square kilometres. This part of New Right Barga, which an hour ago had been my universe, was just one-sixteenth of all Hulunbuir's grassland. I felt like a child standing on the seashore for the first time, suddenly realising my insignificance.

Near the *ovoo* right on the top, a few advanced up the steps, hands touching in front of their faces in supplication, and prostrating themselves every few metres. At the top, a crowd two or three deep jostled to hang silk scarves on the stone wall of the *ovoo*, making a mosaic of reds, blues and greens, before joining in the slow-moving current of men circling the *ovoo* and tossing on to it their last handfuls of rice and corn. At a small *ovoo* to one side, a teenager in a blue *deel* splashed milk on the stones, a traditional way to honour the Blue Sky.

'Are you English?' A middle-aged Mongolian in a cotton jacket spoke in English. I nodded, suddenly aware that I was probably the only European on the mountain that day – perhaps, I thought, the first ever. He was from Mongolia, one of hundreds who had crossed the border for the occasion. But he had another reason for coming. 'I have a tour company. Here is my card.' He had seen an opportunity, in the interest that all Mongols have in coming here. It is a long and difficult journey cross-country from Ulaanbaatar, but next year, he said, he would arrange buses. He won't be short of passengers. Ethnic groups in all three nations – Russia, China, Mongolia – are bound together by social media forums, and are showing ever-increasing interest in their genealogies and cultural identities. As Caroline Humphrey writes, this 'is new knowledge for young people, many of whom barely knew about clans previously, or thought of them as just obscure preoccupations of aged relatives'.[2] This was an old festival, blossoming afresh every year.

As we went back down, passing the old man with his three-pronged stick still on his slow and steady climb, I wondered how and when all this had started, the folklore, the climb, the entertainments and sporting competitions, like those that were beginning as we arrived at the bottom. First, though, breakfast in a large *ger*. Over beef and lamb provided by the local community, the deputy Party secretary Ma Taiping offered a toast 'to show respect for the holy mountain and nature and humanity, and the harmonious relationship between them'. Mr Ma was a scholar as well as an official, so I asked him about the origins of the ceremony.

'It was a Mongol idea,' he said. 'They had always remembered the place since the Battle of Khuiten, when Chinggis defeated Ong Khan and his ally, Jamukha. But the Barga people arrived in the eighteenth century, so they built on the old memories. The mountain looks dark from a distance, so there's a local saying, "Khuiten dark, Khuiten peak, Khuiten holy".' Folklore often hides meanings in enigmatic sayings. This one seemed to reflect the belief that the battle had been fought either on, or at the foot of, Holy Mountain.

The festival had turned the mountain into a centre for entertainment – a stage with dancers in gorgeous colours – and for the 'three manly sports': archery, wrestling and horse racing, all with their own local variations. Archery, once done on horseback, had been turned into something utterly unwarlike under the Manchus. In Mongolia, they still use blunt arrows fired at little baskets. Here, at the foot of the Holy Mountain, archers use modern bows, with sights, to shoot at targets hanging from frames. The targets were of coloured rings, which fell out when hit by an arrow. The arrows are still blunt, but the bows demand strength and accuracy.

Near the targets was a man in a beautiful blue *deel*, Jeremtukh, director of the local archery association. 'New Barga is the only place that has this style of archery,' he said. I told him about my own bow – a simple Hungarian-made, Hun-style bow, far too powerful for me – and wondered if there was anything like it here. No, no one used old-fashioned bows here, because modern ones were much more accurate.

What about long-range archery? Did he know about Chinggis's nephew Yesunge, who hit a target at five hundred metres? The one recorded in stone by the Mongols in 1225? Of course he did. Everyone did. 'Do you do long-distance archery today?' I asked.

'Yes. The Hulunbuir record is 668 metres. It was done by a Canadian.' That was three times further than my pathetic personal best.

A short walk brought us to the wrestling, where a stand full of people and hundreds more outside crowded around the roped enclosure. In the centre, a dozen young men wearing tough, metal-studded leather jackets paired off, grabbed each other by the sleeves and tried to throw each other to the ground. Solid champions with slab-like shoulders – potential 'elephants' or 'lions' – waited with slim teenagers hoping to make their mark. Anyone could have a go, receiving a modest fifty RMB (the Chinese currency, about £5), which rose with every victory. Each new contestant was given an introduction over the loudspeaker, and every fall drew cheers from the crowd, most in *deels*, with hats or knotted handkerchiefs to guard against the sun.

It was not yet midday, but it was time to go. I would like to think I would be back one of these years. But I fear not. It's not just my age that is against me. China's new agenda looms. This festival is all about Mongol culture and Mongol history, and Beijing has ruled against both. At the stroke of a local pen in Hailar, a phone call from Beijing, a visit from some unnamed official, and all of this – the visiting thousands, the peacock displays of *deels*, the sideshows of wrestling and archery – would vanish, leaving Holy Mountain's staircase empty, the reasons for its existence lodged only in memory, until this generation died and the memory was lost. Who then would dare speak of Chinggis and Jamukha, or recall the significance of their battle?

## QASAR, THE 'WRITHING OGRE'

Or indeed other links between the thirteenth-century Mongols and today's Hulunbuir. Chinggis's half-brother Qasar plays a major role. They bonded in childhood, when Qasar helped young Temujin, as he

was then, kill his other, older half-brother Bekter for being a bully.*
When Chinggis was at his lowest ebb, defeated and down to a hard core of followers, he fled to an unidentified lake, probably no more than a muddy waterhole, known in Mongol and Chinese sources as Baljuna. Here Chinggis proved the strength of his leadership, as a Chinese source describes:

> Upon arrival at the Baljuna, the provisions were used up. It happened that from the north a wild horse ran up. Qasar brought it down. From its skin they made a kettle, with a stone they got fire, and from the river, water. They boiled the flesh of the horse and ate it. Chinggis Khan, raising his hand toward the sky, swore thus: 'If I finish the great work [by which he meant the creation of the empire] then I shall share with you men the sweet and the bitter. If I break my word, then let me be as this water.' Among the officers and men, there was not one who was not moved to tears.

This was a turning point. Allies – including the Qonggirat – came to him. Victory led to victory until one major enemy remained – the Naimans, now in alliance with Chinggis's childhood friend Jamukha. In 1204, the two clashed. *The Secret History* has a superb poetic description of the build-up, with Jamukha giving his ally, Tayang, fearsome portraits of Chinggis's generals. When it comes to Qasar, Jamukha paints a nightmarish image in verse, in which Qasar is a giant with superhuman powers. Mother Hoelun raised him on human flesh, he says,

> His body is three fathoms high,
> And he dines on three-year-old cattle.
> Wearing a three-layered armour,
> He is pulled along in his cart by three bulls.

---

* This cowardly act is well-described in *The Secret History*, as is Bekter's warning against violence and his mother's furious condemnation in imagery that was surely the work of an accomplished poet or bard, and quite possibly approved by Chinggis himself. Why would he do that? Possibly (I suggest) to show how *not* to behave if you want to ensure family – or tribal, or national – unity.

When he swallows a man complete with quiver,
It does not get stuck in his throat.
When he gulps down a whole man,
It does not fill his stomach.
When he is angry and draws his bow,
And releases a fork-tipped arrow,
He shoots and pierces ten or twenty men
Who are beyond a mountain…
Different from all other men,
He was born a writhing ogre.*

At his coronation in 1206, Chinggis gave Qasar the area between the Erguna and Hailar rivers. The result was that Qasar is still a presence in Hulunbuir, and beyond. As my guide, Miss Bo, in Hailar's Nationalities Museum put it: 'Qasar's later descendants, generation by generation, were scattered throughout Inner Mongolia.'

Alatan was listening, and added, 'He was known as *khat*, a title meaning "very strong"' – fair enough for someone who could swallow a man whole and shoot over mountains – 'Even today, people in Inner Mongolia say they are descendants of Qasar, especially here in the north-east. He was a Borjigin, of course, like Chinggis, but in Chinese the name is shortened to Bo. Her name' – he nodded to the guide – 'is Bo.'

## SCENES FROM THE PAST

Passing a dramatic contingent of horsemen galloping over a hillside – bronze statues, of course – we arrived at the head of the valley, a beautiful

* This is de Rachewiltz's version. It is looser, but simpler than Atwood's. The 'writhing ogre' is de Rachewiltz's rendition of '*gurvel mangas*', literally 'lizard ogre', but *mangas* is also a python, then known only from Buddhist literature, hence the metaphorical 'writhing'. Cf the fortress mentioned on p.68.

amphitheatre of grass and scattered trees looking like a picture postcard in the slanting afternoon light. Ahead, on the hillside, was a tent. A rough approach over tree trunks led up to the entrance. Inside were a dozen or more statues, all wonderfully lifelike: Chinggis holding court, displaying his international credentials with envoys of many nationalities – Chinggis himself on a carved wooden throne, full-bearded with a big fur hat, impressively good-looking, his beautiful queen Börte with a Mongolian headband, a shaman chanting a blessing, a Tungus from Siberia, a Persian merchant, a Chinese envoy.

Down from Chinggis's tent was a shaman's hut, guarded by a triangular passageway of tree trunks draped with black ropes, a division between this world and someone who has contact with the world of spirits. From loudspeakers came the ominous beat of a shaman's drum. Inside a shadowy tent, a chair and desk were covered with carpets decorated with swans (they seemed significant, but I have no idea what they represent). Above hung a facemask of black ropes beneath a cap covered with doll-like figures, like the little images (*ongod*), usually of felt, which are said to contain the spirits of the dead.

We walked on. Further down the valley was a muddy pond, labelled Lake Baljuna, as if this was the actual place where Chinggis drank the lake's 'muddy waters' with his few remaining companions.

On the other side of the path, on top of a steep little hill, loomed the statue of a man on horseback – Bodonchar, ancestor of Chinggis's family, the Borjigins. And even further down the valley, more statues portrayed the campsite of Chinggis's father Yisukei. It is a moment of high drama. Yisukei is returning from a campaign in which he has caught a Tatar chieftain. Actually, there are two of them, being led by a chain attached to Yisukei's saddle, but we are only interested in one, because his name is Temujin, which is the name Yisukei is about to give his new-born son. Servant girls dance a welcome. In front of the main *ger*, Börte holds little Temujin-to-be. The statues are of bronze, life-size, set out on grassland and surrounded by forest. In the low evening light, they made a striking pageant.

What are we to make of all this? Well, it is certainly not the exact place where the Mongols originated. Nor is it a museum. There is no archaeological evidence here. It is totally artificial, with no connection between this valley and the Mongols or their ancestors the Shiwei. And it does not present a narrative. Whichever order you choose to walk, the displays are mixed up – the 900s for Bodonchar, centuries for the shaman, 1162 for the campsite, 1203 for Baljuna.

But that's not the point. There is an authenticity and power in the scenes designed to create a belief that the whole of Mongol history belongs more to Hulunbuir and China than to Mongolia. Never mind that the Mongols migrated away from here to Mongolia, that Chinggis was raised there, and was buried there. This, here, on the banks of the Erguna and on the grasslands of Hulunbuir, is where his ancestral roots lie, this is where his mother and his first wife came from and therefore his story is part of Chinese history. Once upon a time this region was very un-Chinese, dominated by various steppe cultures, then it was disputed with Russia and Japan – more on that later – but now it is part of the new, revolutionary, resurgent China. By claiming the past, the site makes clear to visitors that the Mongols, Chinggis and his empire all belong to China.

The site itself is in the process of development. Captions to the displays are in Chinese, Mongol (both Uighur and Cyrillic scripts), Russian and English, in preparation for an influx of tourists. When it is all ready, and tourists come by the busload, who will doubt that this is indeed not only where the Mongols originated but where they and their story really belong?

*A reconstruction of Kublai Khan's 'cane palace' – or 'stately pleasure dome' as Coleridge called it – based on Marco Polo's description. A symbol of Mongol-Chinese union.*

# CHAPTER 6

# In Xanadu

## Fact, fame and fiction

AS EVERY ENGLISH-SPEAKING SCHOOLCHILD USED TO KNOW,

> In Xanadu did Kubla Khan
> A stately pleasure-dome decree.

The teacher may also have told the class that in 1797 Samuel Taylor Coleridge wrote the poem after a drug-induced dream, and so it has been widely believed that Xanadu is a fairy-tale place, of gardens, chasms, a sacred river, a woman wailing for her demon lover and caverns measureless to man. Its name, conferring a sense of exotic luxury, has been adopted by resorts, hotels and restaurants all over the world. It is also the title of a 1980 movie with Olivia Newton-John, initially reviled for its batty plot, which involved shape-shifting muses, Greek deities and a glitzy nightclub. It was the name of the fictional mansion built by Charles Foster Kane (with its hint of 'khan') in Orson Welles's film *Citizen Kane* (1941) and, more recently, the nickname applied by journalists to Bill Gates's vast mansion on Lake Washington, near Seattle.

So it's quite understandable to assume it's a fictional place. But it's real – a corruption of the Chinese Shang-du, the 'Upper Capital' of the Emperor Kublai Khan, grandson of Chinggis, heir to his empire. Coleridge had been reading about Marco Polo's description of the place just before he dreamed about it, and of its 'stately pleasure-dome'. That too was real. Five hours' drive north of Beijing, the ruined city is a superb archaeological site with a fine museum.

Its story starts in 1211, when Chinggis headed south to invade his main enemy, Jin, the empire ruling north-east China at the time. Before dropping from the Mongolian plateau through the mountains that guard Beijing – Zhongdu (Central Capital), as it was under Jin – he camped in a well-watered, well-protected grassland called Dragon Ridge (Long Gang). The years passed, Chinggis built an empire, then died, and his heir, Ogedei, took over as khan and built a new capital Karakorum in the centre of Mongolia. Other sons inherited their own sections of the empire. Kublai's father, Tolui, took over Chinggis's original homeland, Mongolia, backed by his wife, Sorkaktani. She was the most impressive woman of her times, as many acknowledged (and still do – she has a cult following among Mongols). As a Christian and a Kerait, not a Mongol, she was used to dealing with other cultures. Tolerant, assertive, intelligent and well-educated, she was shrewd enough never to remarry after Tolui's death in 1232, and remained in effect queen of Mongolia, working to guarantee futures for her four sons. She remained in the background during a nasty civil war, which saw a change in the line of succession from Ogedei's line to that of his brother, her husband, Tolui. Eventually, all her sons achieved power, Hulegu as Emperor of Persia, Ariq as a rival for the throne yet also a ruler in Central Asia, Mönkhe as Emperor in Mongolia and finally Kublai, who succeeded to the throne when Mönkhe died in 1259. He was well-prepared by his mother, who oversaw the recovery of her Chinese estate after it had been ruined during Chinggis's invasion. In his twenties, Kublai acquired and administered his own estate, hiring Chinese officials and building a solid tax-base.

So, even before his brother's death, Prince Kublai was straddling the two cultures, Mongol and Chinese. His top adviser, Liu Bingzhong, a

Chinese Buddhist, advised him to become more Chinese. That would mean building a seat of government, a capital. But he was not about to abandon his Mongolian roots by setting up in a Chinese city. His team of advisors, the Golden Lotus Group, agreed that Chinggis's campsite was the place: the last stop on the grasslands, but within reach of China's lowlands, a good compromise between steppe and farmland, tents and cities. It was a rich area for herders, and a blank slate, with no trees and no stone, all of which had to be carted in from far away, transforming open grassland into a new city.

The grasslands of Inner Mongolia are surprisingly close to Beijing on the map, a mere 250 kilometres as the crow flies, but they are in a separate world, even today. You head north-west, away from the city's dense traffic, along the expressway that carries most of the ten million who visit the Great Wall every year. Today's stone wall was not there yet, but the tree-covered ridges and precipitous ravines over which it undulates have not changed. The ancient route through them was once a track along a pass, the Juyong, so narrow that the southbound motorway has to take a separate route. You climb, then drop again for an easy hundred kilometres to Zhangjiakou, which once marked the frontier between lowland China and the plateau lands of Mongolia. Mongols (and foreign explorers) called it Kalgan, from the Mongolian word for 'gateway'.

Stephen Bushell, an English doctor attached to the British legation in Beijing, took this route in 1872, and left an account of the transition between China and Mongolia that had been true for the five centuries since Marco Polo's time. 'Reaching the precipitous edge of the Mongolian plateau, the eye ranges over a prairie with long wavy undulations, the first of the grass-covered Mongolian steppes… a "land of grass", the support of innumerable flocks and herds, where no tree is visible in a week's journey.' But it was all changing. 'Where the country is hilly and the valleys fertile… the Chinese agricultural settlers are numbered by the million, and… in nearby areas not a single Mongol remains, where two centuries ago the land belonged to them exclusively.'

The next foreign visitor was an American writer, Lawrence Impey, who was in Xanadu for a month in 1925 and whose article is still a prime source.[1] He too commented on China's implacable advance northwards. 'As if by magic, the frowning hills fall back on either side, yielding place to a land of undulating grassy plains, a natural ranching country, or so it appears at first sight. Here Chinese settlers have established their first farms, pushing on a few miles in every succeeding generation while the Mongols slowly retreat before them under the relentless pressure of economic superiority.'

At Zhenglan Qi, a dispiriting collection of Communist-era buildings, a new railway line brings in yet more Chinese settlers to plough and build in this once-Mongol frontier land. Just beyond, there are open spaces that would still delight Kublai's soul. In 1260, he had himself crowned khan in the nascent city then known as Kaiping, acclaimed by Mongol princes who overrode his ambitious brother, Ariq. Now he needed a dynastic name. A sage consulted the *I Ching* (*Yi Jing*), the 2,000-year-old *Book of Changes*, and, after casting the yarrow stalks and deriving hexagrams and puzzling over their transformations, came up with a final, auspicious oracle, with many positive attributes: Yuan, the sublime, the origin, the first, the great. Ariq came to seek reconciliation, and rather conveniently died, leaving a taint of fratricide and his brother Kublai as master of Mongolia, north China and Central Asia. By 1263, his new capital was ready, and Kaiping became Shang-du, and five hundred years later (to English speakers) Xanadu.

At the same time, Kublai saw that he could not, after all, rule his empire from Xanadu alone. He needed a proper Chinese capital, and so began to restore Beijing, still in ruins from his grandfather's siege in 1215. From 1267, he commuted between the two. Winters would be spent in the new Great Capital (Dadu), summers on the cool grasslands of Xanadu. His immense retinue – his two-wheeled carriage hauled by four elephants, his outriders, his staff and family all in their own carriages – wound into the mountains and on to the plains of the Mongolian plateau. The procession travelled some twenty-two kilometres every day, spending nights in twenty mini-Xanadus, towns set in walled squares and manned year-round by soldiers and officials awaiting their lord's arrival for just two days a year, on the journey out in June and back at the end of August. You can see the grassy mounds of the last of these overnight places just outside Zhenglan Qi.[2]

## REACHING XANADU

Xanadu itself may be seen by combining modern archaeology with a view through the eyes of Marco as he arrived with his father and uncle in 1275. Imagine a body of horsemen heading north over grassland. Out in front is a senior officer, wearing an armoured coat of overlapping leather scales, a formality given the accompanying guards, all with swords and pikes and bows. In the centre of the bunch are the three Polos, Marco's father Niccolò, his uncle Maffeo and Marco himself, aged just twenty. This is the second visit by Niccolò and Maffeo, who had spent several successful years under Kublai's protection. Wishing to rebalance his rival religions – Buddhism, Daoism, Confucianism – with an infusion of Christianity (his mother's faith), Kublai had asked the two Polos to bring a letter from the pope, some holy oil from Jerusalem and one hundred priests. Having picked up the teenaged Marco in Venice, they had acquired the letter and the holy oil, but only a few priests, who had changed their minds within days of starting out. Now they're back, seeking to redouble their wealth. Perhaps the Mongol officer turns and says in Mongol, for even Marco speaks it now: 'Shang-du! That's what *they* call it. To us it's Dzu Naiman Sum, One Hundred and Eight Temples.' Pale in the distance are waves of gently sloping hills. Directly ahead, on the open plain, stands a town: a wall, eight metres high, blocking everything beyond except roofs tiled in yellows, greens and blues, with one roof standing proud above the others. Across the grassland run many tracks, crowded with carts hauled by bullocks, camels and yaks, arriving full or departing empty. There may even be a glimpse, on a distant grassy slope, of a patch of white, not sheep as you might at first suppose, but the Emperor's own white horses, by the thousand. Beyond a little river, the tracks converge, to make what a Yuan poet, Yang Yunfu, called 'the broad imperial road' leading through a mass of round felt tents, horses, traders and food stalls. Beyond is a main entry, offset to the right of the wall's centre: an arch as high as the wall, fringed by bulwarks and topped by a guardhouse with banners waving in the breeze. A huge wooden door stands open. The Polos' guards hold back supply-carts, and barge a way through street-traders offering textiles, food and drink. The party clatters over paving stones through the entry. A road leads straight through a line of mud-brick houses for six hundred metres to a second wall, a second gate. That's the Inner City, where the Emperor, his family and his retainers live in wooden houses tiled in bright blues, greens and yellows, their eaves ending in circular tiles in the form of dragons, birds and animal heads. And there, stretched out on a 150-metre brick-faced platform, the ornate two-storey building with the roof they saw from afar: Kublai's palace.

It takes a bird's-eye view to understand the place as a whole. The city had a simple structure: three sections, all squares, nested inside each other in the style of other Chinese imperial cities. The outer wall made the biggest square of just over two kilometres a side, nine kilometres in all. This sector, the Outer City, was in the shape of a set-square, in the northern part of which was a park of gently undulating grass, where Kublai could play at hunting. In the south-east corner of the big square was a smaller one, the Imperial City, 5.6 kilometres in circumference, containing the mud-brick or wooden houses for workmen, craftsmen and officials and several temples, all laid out in a grid of streets. And inside this, a third square, the Inner City, which is just over two kilometres around, with royal residences and meeting halls with Chinese-style curled-up eaves and glazed tiles, all overshadowed by the palace itself. The three walled boxes, together with a halo of tents and herds around the outside, made a working city of about 120,000 people.

## DECAY AND OBLIVION

After the Mongol dynasty fell in 1368, Xanadu was trashed by the incoming Manchus, and then abandoned. For six hundred years, its palace, courtyards, buildings and walls decayed into an archipelago of ruins and grassy mounds. In 1872, Bushell found the site

> overgrown with rank weeds and grass, the abode of foxes and owls, which prey on the numerous prairie-rats [fieldmice] and partridges… The walls of the city, built of earth, faced with unhewn stone and brick, are still standing, but are more or less dilapidated… The south gate of the inner city is still intact, a perfect arch of 20 feet high, 12 feet wide… the ground in the interior of both enclosures is strewn with blocks of marble and other remains of large temples and palaces… while broken lions, dragons, and the remains of other carved monuments, lie about in every direction, half-hidden by the thick and tangled undergrowth.

Impey, in 1925, was more meticulous, tracing dozens of buildings, then adding: 'All over the surface are to be found bits of broken pottery and china in extraordinary profusion,' which he suggested had been thrown up by moles.

Twelve years later, a Japanese team arrived. These were interesting times, which are worth a little diversion. Six years before, in 1931, Japan had occupied Manchuria and the following year made it nominally independent as Manchukuo. The approach to Kublai's summer HQ actually straddled the frontier. Japan, with its eyes set on expansion into Mongolia and Siberia, had good reason to turn its gaze on Xanadu. If Japan could hijack the cults honouring the imperial founders, Chinggis and Kublai, then the Mongols could be brought on-side and expansion into their territory would become a whole lot easier. It was surely with a similar, though hidden, agenda that a team of nine scholars, under the leadership of Yoshito Harada of Tokyo Imperial University, arrived in Xanadu in July 1937.

Harada planned some proper archaeology, until he became aware of Mongol sensitivities about interference in this sacred place. He and his eight scholars contented themselves with a week-long survey, recording for the first time the Outer City, the Inner City, the palace mound and the forty or so buildings. Four years later, Harada announced the publication of his report 'in spite of the fact that our work was done when the situation was strained'. *Strained!* As they worked, Japan was about to be thrown out of Manchuria by a Russian and Mongolian army (see Chapter 11) and, at the time of publication, they were planning to attack Pearl Harbor. It was remarkable that the work was done at all, that it was done so well and that it was published. It is extremely rare – there is only one copy in the UK, as far as I have been able to discover.[3]

From then onwards until quite recently absolutely nothing was done. War and civil war saw to that. Under its Communist regime, China showed no interest, for the Mongol/Yuan dynasty – established by barbarians from beyond the Gobi – was a chapter they would rather forget.

## CHINA MOVES IN

When I first went to Xanadu in 1996, I thought I knew roughly what to expect. The plans of the site made it look very neat, but up close it was not neat at all. There were no signs on the approach roads. With my guide, William, we drove straight in. There was no fence, no gate, no charge, no custodians to block the way along the track that cut through the Outer City wall. The sky was pure Mongolian blue, the breeze gentle and the only sound a cuckoo. A glorious wilderness of waving grasses and pretty meadow flowers rose and fell gently over the billows made by eroded, overgrown walls. I couldn't make much sense of it.

But others obviously could. Half a dozen men were at work with tape measures, posts and bits of string. They were archaeologists marking out the start of an excavation. Their leader was a professor with the attributes of a TV presenter – slim, good-looking, a voice as mellow as an operatic baritone. He pointed out walls, the remains of buildings, the base of the palace, the setting once known as the Golden Lotus Flower Plain. We were both short of time, and I forgot to ask for his name-card.

I walked on my own through the waving grass towards the palace mound, and came across a crude little out-of-place statue – Turkish, pre-Mongol – standing as if on guard, brought here perhaps by Kublai's people, or found here and simply left alone. Nothing had changed in a hundred years. The ground was still strewn with rubble, the base of the palace was still there, a heap of earth about fifty metres long standing some six metres high above the grass. The palace mound was flanked by two others – the remains of three great buildings creating what I took to be a three-sided courtyard. Paths made through the grass by wandering tourists wound to the top at either end. The front was an almost sheer earth face, punctuated by a line of holes, evidence, I thought, of long-vanished roof-beams that held up a canopy. I imagined dignitaries dismounting in its shade, before climbing steps to be received by the Emperor himself on his dais.

There was nothing solid up there now. A platform of earth had survived seven hundred years, despite the fierce summer downpours and rock-cracking frosts of winter, yet of the buildings themselves there was no trace. Had they all been reduced to the rubble at my feet? I picked up some, all shapeless bits and pieces, nothing even to suggest what they had once been. A bit of glazed pottery. A drab grey roof tile. Stones that looked like nothing more than stones. But what rubble, what stones: the dust of Xanadu! The bits and pieces are still in a plastic bag in a desk drawer. How on earth can I do them justice? Reader, if you have an answer, please tell me.

I was back in 2004. Change was on the way, reflecting change everywhere in China. A fine new highway ran east from Zhenglan Qi, a sign in both Chinese and English marked our entry to 'Yuan Shang-du', and a road led due north across pasture to a tourist camp of round, white Mongolian tents. Two right-angle bends took us to a fence, a gate and a little museum, with two attendants and an entrance charge. After that, though, I was on my own, as before, and equally baffled by the indeterminate ruins. Foreign tourists got no help, for the authorities had not yet appreciated the significance of the place, especially for English speakers. I was still free to stroll the hummocks and the palace mound and the grass-covered rubble.

Not for much longer, it seemed. Archaeologists had been at work. Along one side of the courtyard stood a line of marble statues, all headless, all found at nearby sites, all damaged by the incoming Manchus when the Mongols were thrown out in 1368. In the centre of the yard was a glass cabinet containing an immense block of white marble, two metres high. It was part of a pillar, a base perhaps. I tried the door. To my astonishment, it opened. Feeling as privileged as a prince and guilty as a schoolboy, I ran my fingers over marble that might have been touched by Marco Polo and Kublai himself – brilliantly carved bas reliefs of intertwining dragons and peonies, symbols of both war and peace. Once, it had been one artefact among many, proof of long-ago magnificence, the skill of Kublai's Chinese artists, and the labour involved, for the closest source of marble is seven hundred kilometres away.

It was also evidence to resolve a rumbling academic dispute about whether Marco Polo was ever actually in China. Well, he was. He uses Mongolian terms and Mongolian names. How else would be know the name of the Qonggirat, the group from which Mongol Emperors chose their queens? Crucially, he begins his description of Xanadu: 'There is at this place a very fine *marble* palace.' And finally, there is the Pleasure Dome itself, which we will discuss shortly.

The greatest change was not at the site itself, but the approach to it. The first glimpse of Xanadu was the tourist camp, some forty small Mongolian *gers* and three huge concrete ones, with double domes. The camp was the creation of a local businessman, 'Benjamin' Ren; Chinese who deal with Westerners often give themselves a Western name. Benjamin was remarkable in several ways: handsome, outgoing, generous, ambitious. His *gers* were cunningly adapted with double beds, lighting, running water and loos; and double-domed restaurants, which employed locals to cook Mongolian banquets and entertain with Mongolian music. He arranged sleeper-buses, so that his tourists would snuggle down in Beijing and awake seven hours later in Xanadu. He dreamed of tourists by the thousand, by the ten thousand. I feared that no one would ever again see the place as I first saw it, a virgin wilderness.

Where had it all gone, the remnants seen by Bushell, Impey and the Japanese? Benjamin had an answer. In the nearby town of Duolun – Dolonnur ('Seven Lakes') in Mongol – many of the domestic buildings have rather fine brickwork and tiles. Xanadu, he said, had been mined brick by brick, tile by tile, by local householders.

By 2008, Xanadu had changed again, and not in the way Benjamin had hoped. This time I was determined to understand what I was looking at, with the help of China's greatest Xanadu expert, Professor Wei Jian of Renmin University in Beijing. We met a couple of days before departure to plan our trip, with the help of an English-speaking graduate named Helen. Originally a prehistorian working on Bronze Age and Stone Age sites in Inner Mongolia, the professor had become intrigued by Xanadu in the early 1990s because no one had done any work there for sixty years. He had the intensity and charm of a Chinese David Attenborough. I told him of my previous visits, of my meeting with an inspirational archaeologist…

'When did you say you were there? 1996? You know…' He paused. 'I think… I seem to remember meeting a foreigner…'

We stared at each other, then, in bilingual unison, light dawned. 'It was you!' Of course it was: twelve years rolled away, and I recognised the athletic frame, the direct gaze, the verve, the operatic voice.

We approached Xanadu in driving rain. It was utterly miserable. Oh, well, I said. We can stay at Benjamin Ren's *ger* camp, and have a banquet.

But no: at the camp gates, it became clear that something had gone terribly wrong with Mr Ren's plans. The camp was abandoned, with grass rank between circles of damp concrete where *gers* had once stood. One sodden *ger* remained. I knocked on the door. A decrepit old woman

Xanadu as it is today.

appeared, carrying a cat. She told us that Mr Ren had gone off to live in Hohhot. There had been no tourists this year or last. The rain came on harder. Never mind, said Wei as we headed for our hotel in Dolonnur, we will return tomorrow.

Next morning, after a breakfast of milky tea with curds and the remains of a well-muscled sheep, we drove back to Xanadu, under a heaven that was mercifully blue. We pulled up at what used to be a wire fence, and before that nothing at all. Now there was a grand four-metre portico, with two copies of the marble pillar for supports and a lintel like something from Stonehenge. It was flanked by a huge stone bas relief of armies and courtiers crowding around a massive Kublai, sitting knees splayed on his throne. An incised plaque provided a brief biography, in Mongol, Chinese and – in anticipation of mass tourism – English. As so often in China, no one had bothered to check the English with someone who actually speaks it. 'Mongolian dubbed him saint, virtue, marvellous, merit, doing well on both civil and military.'

In the courtyard, the headless statues were gone, and so was the marble pillar. To one side were four electric buggies for tourists, but we were the only takers. We drove down a track for a kilometre, over the little river, to a mound that had once been the south gate before it fell in. Its centre had been cleared of fallen bricks, and the sides revealed the lower parts of an arch. When Bushell saw it in 1872 it had been intact. But in a 1908 photograph, its crest was only two delicate layers of brick. Sometime in the following thirty years, it fell, for Harada found no trace of it in 1937. Now it was partially revealed again by Wei. 'This was the main gate in Kublai's time,' he said. 'You can tell from all the bricks that it had a building on top of it. But that was destroyed when the rebels came at the end of the Yuan dynasty. And there was a wooden gate as well. We found some of the framework.' So this explains what Marco saw: a massive wooden gateway blocking the 5.8-metre entrance, topped by a guardhouse, with bulwarks either side making an entrance tunnel of twenty-four metres. (I paced it.)

From the top, one sees the low remains of walls, mostly stripped of their brick facades, running away for several hundred metres, before turning north at right angles to form the square of the Inner City. Wei took me to a section of wall that he had restored: brickwork about six metres high sloping back at a fifteen-degree angle, so that you could run up it, if you were an athlete in a good pair of track-shoes. The top would have been flat, paved, easy to patrol. Every four hundred metres a U-shaped bastion stuck out, but there were no guard-towers; the wall was built to assert status, not to withstand an assault.

A track led across long grass to the platform on which the palace had once stood. We stopped at a nondescript bump with a hole dug in it.

'It was here that I found the marble pillar!' Wei said. 'So I knew this was an important place.'

That discovery made him wonder about the name of the palace. Several sources refer to a magnificent, *marbled* building called the Pavilion of Great Tranquillity. Scholars always assumed the pavilion and the palace were one and the same. Here, though, was proof that marble was used in another building, whereas no marble has ever been found at the palace. 'The marble pillar I found has a dragon design, the imperial symbol. For this reason, I think this, not the palace, was the Pavilion of Great Tranquillity, where important administrative functions were held.'

Where did that leave the palace? We walked over to the fifty-metre earth platform on which it used to stand. I asked about the holes, which I thought had been left by long-vanished roof-beams. No, said Wei, the earth platform had needed strengthening, and had had a skeleton of timbers, which had rotted away to leave the tell-tale holes.

The palace mound, with two wings on either side, embraced a courtyard, with access from below by wooden staircases. Yes, wood, because no stone – certainly no marble – was found nearby, which means the whole palace was made of wood, like a temple, except for its tiled roof. 'We think it had over 220 rooms. If I'm right about the Pavilion of Great Tranquillity, then this palace was actually the Pavilion of Harmonious Brightness,[4] a place of celebration. At the full moon there were parties here, because the moon is round, perfect, harmonious, bright like the palace and Kublai's dynasty.'

## THE PLEASURE DOME

We drove on, through what had been the north gate of the Inner City, out into the hunting ground, once home to deer, rabbits and birds, past a series of faint ridges – the North Yard, said Wei, where Kublai kept a zoo of rare animals, among them his elephants and a snow leopard trained for hunting. Then, in what looked like a blank slab of grassland, nibbled by herds and scattered with dried dung, Wei got out of the buggy. He stood arms akimbo, as if conjuring up a show on an empty stage.

'It was here, John, that Kublai built his Cane Palace, the one described by Marco Polo. It was a hundred and eighty metres all around!'

If he was right, this was the base of the creation that has come down to English speakers through the first few lines of Coleridge's famous poem:

> In Xanadu did Kubla Khan
> A stately pleasure-dome decree
> Where Alph the sacred river ran
> Through caverns measureless to man
> Down to a sunless sea.

These opium-induced images have absolutely nothing to do with Xanadu, which has no caverns and is several days' hard ride from a sea that is no less sunny than any other. But there was a step-by-step link between dream and reality. Coleridge's source, which he had been reading before he fell asleep, was Samuel Purchas, who in 1625 published a re-edited and extended version of the massive three-volume book of travels by his friend Richard Hakluyt. *Hakluytus Post-humus, or Purchas His Pilgrimes* summarised in archaic language Marco's eyewitness account, which had been available in English for two hundred years:

> In Xamdu did Cublai Can build a stately Palace, excompassing sixteene miles of plaine ground with a wall, wherein are fertile Meddowes, pleasant Springs, delightfull Streames, and all sorts of beasts of chase and game, and in the middest thereof a sumptuous house of pleasure, which may be removed from place to place.

But here's a question: what made Coleridge dream of a *dome*? He mentions the image several times: 'stately pleasure-dome… shadow of the dome of pleasure… sunny pleasure-dome with caves of ice… that sunny dome!' Yet Purchas makes no mention of the shape of his 'house of pleasure', nor does Marco. But the idea is there, implied by his account, which runs as follows,[5] a little reduced:

> He has another Palace built of cane, of which I must give you a description. It is gilt all over, and most elaborately finished inside. It is stayed on gilt and lackered [lacquered] columns, on each of which is a dragon all gilt, the tail of which is attached to the column whilst the head supports the architrave, and the claws likewise are stretched out right and left to support the architrave. The roof, like the rest, is formed of canes, covered with a varnish so strong and excellent that no amount of rain will rot them. These canes are a good 3 palms in girth, and from 10 to 15 paces in length. They are cut across at each knot, and then the pieces are split so as to form from each two hollow tiles, and with these the house is roofed; only every such tile of cane has to be nailed down to prevent the wind from lifting it. In short, the whole Palace is built of these canes… The construction of the Palace is so devised that it can be taken down and put up again with great celerity; and it can all be taken to pieces and removed whithersoever the Emperor may command. When erected, it is braced against mishaps from the wind by more than 200 cords of silk. The Lord abides at this Park of his… for three months of the year, to wit, June, July, and August… When the 28th

> day of [the Moon of] August arrives he takes his departure, and the Cane Palace is taken to pieces.

All the pillars, roof-beams and tiles were of 'cane', by which Marco meant bamboo, a word that did not yet exist in any European language. In Kublai's realm, a bamboo structure had only recently become a possibility, because bamboo grows in the tropics, which in China means the south. Kublai did not complete the conquest of the south until 1279; but he did control one southern province – Yunnan, which is rich in bamboo. Kublai himself had led the conquest in 1253. Perhaps, probably – no, almost certainly – the idea of using bamboo occurred to Kublai, or his advisers, only because the Mongols ruled Yunnan.

Now to its shape. Marco says only that the bamboo was split into half-tubes 10 to 15 metres long and about 0.3 metres across ('about three palms'). To seal a roof with these half-tubes, they would have to be placed in overlapping rows, like semicircular roof tiles, with one set of rows facing up, the other facing down. But can you make a *round* roof out of *straight* bamboo?

Yes, you can. You must. You have no choice, as a bamboo dealer pointed out to me. Not only is bamboo a superb material – lightweight, many times stronger than oak, easy to cut, long lasting – it is not in fact straight: it tapers. Well, of course it does. That's what most trees do as they get higher. Bamboo, when cut into fifteen-metre lengths, has one end thicker than the other. Placed on the ground next to each other, the stems fall *naturally* into a circle. The same is true when they are cut in half to make long, overlapping tiles, 628 of them to be precise. Once in position, fixed to an encircling lintel, the bamboo poles would make a fine protection against rain and sun, and allow a refreshing flow of air. Everything will fit together to make a building big enough to hold a crowd of a several hundred.

The Palace was collapsible, standing for three summer months until Kublai's departure, then taken apart and stored. There were no foundations: the structure was secured against gales by two hundred silk ropes. The roof weighed in at about twenty-five tonnes, but it acted like an aerofoil. A high wind might lift the whole building. Hence the need for the two hundred ropes. There are many other considerations – designers would want pillars to stop the roof-timbers from buckling, a way to attach the tiles to the lintels, lacquer to seal the tiles against rain – but, in brief, Marco's specifications are good enough to re-create the 'pleasure-dome'.

In 2019, I found two Xanadus. One was the real site; the other, a few kilometres away, was the creation of a Chinese businessman and lover of all things Mongolian named Ge Jian. His many concerns include hotels, a wine company, clothing and a passion for both Chinggis and Kublai, and a production company. He has made a 20-part TV series on Chinggis and was just completing an 86-part series on Kublai (yes, really, 86 parts, though the last I heard it was stuck in the censor's office). For the series, his people had created a life-size wooden city – his own version of Xanadu. It was much more than a studio lot. Once the show was on TV, it would have shops and hotels for the tourists who would flood in – an alternate Xanadu that would be a representation of a historical reality, with a reality of its own.

Nearby, the real Xanadu, Yuan Shang-du, has become almost what it should be. A good museum, set into the nearby hill, displays Wei's marble pillar, the little Turkish statue I had seen years before by the palace-mound and a mass of other finds. On the site itself, fenced and ticketed, wooden walkways and platforms allow visitors to wander from ruin to ruin, enlightened by multilingual captions.

Perhaps one day out on Kublai's hunting ground, those who manage the site will raise a cane palace that would be familiar to Kublai and Marco. If so, they will learn something about the relationship between China and Mongolia, then and now. Kublai's house of pleasure, the 'pleasure-dome', the Cane Palace, was one of the most astonishing – perhaps the most original – creations of its time, an unprecedented and never-equalled combination of a Mongolian shape and Chinese materials, all symbolising Kublai's vision of a united

Mongol-Chinese empire. But it would also symbolise the rising tide of Chinese culture right now, for the designers, the cash, the materials and the site itself, chosen by a Mongol khan for a Mongol empire, would all be Chinese.

*The Chinggis Khan Mausoleum in Ordos, the Lord's Enclosure as the Mongols call it. A Chinese design incorporates Mongolian tent motifs, where members of an authentic ancient cult guard inauthentic relics.*

## CHAPTER 7

# RIVALS FOR HIS SPIRIT

### A BURIAL THAT WASN'T

TAKE THE MOTORWAY SOUTH FROM ORDOS CITY, PAST THE apartment blocks of newly built Kangbashi, leaving the international airport somewhere away to your left. You drop into a valley, filled with a mass of tents – a tourist camp, where a pole carries a standard of two loose black horsehairs, like vast ponytails, and a notice that proclaims this to be 'Holy Land'. Beyond, over the next hill, you turn into a large car park next to an immense paved terrace with a discreet line of shops along one side. It's all very grand and imposing. You feel a sense of awe, and you should because – as the sign back there said – this is holy soil for Mongolians. You have arrived at the Mausoleum of Chinggis Khan, where the founder of the world's greatest land empire has undergone a profound change, from ruthless conqueror to a demigod of peace.

Ahead is a five-arched marble entrance leading to an auspicious flight of ninety-nine steps – ninety-nine being the number of minor spirits subordinate to Blue Heaven, the deity of the Mongols. On a platform a little way up is a bronze statue of Chinggis on horseback, his left hand on his leg, his right hand bunched into a fist, symbols of his abilities as both administrator and warrior. Beyond you can see the reason for all this, the temple itself, a central dome flanked by two wings ending in two smaller domes. Like a Christian cathedral, the Mausoleum is both a focus for rituals and a tourist attraction, one of China's finest. When I first came here, it was a bit off the beaten track, with an annual tally of 200,000 visitors. Now it has over a million, with space enough for more.

All three domes, with their blue and gold patterns, are inspired by Mongolian tents, but they are also clearly Chinese, with curled-up eaves. The story of how it came into existence, however, reveals less of a Mongol-Chinese combination than another hijack – an ancient, wholly Mongol cult in the service of modern China.

Its background involves two mutually exclusive traditions, folklore versus truth. In the first version, the Lord comes to a beautiful pasture, so beautiful that he says, 'This is where I wish to be buried when I die.' So it comes to pass after his death in 1227, some five hundred kilometres to the south-west. Those who buried him there wish his remains to be undisturbed. But they also want to remember the spot. How is this to be done? Female camels have excellent memories, so they find a camel with a baby to which she is giving milk. They kill the baby camel and bury it next to the Lord's grave. Then, each spring, they release the mother camel, and she returns to the spot where the baby camel was buried. Every year this happens, and every year people are able to honour their khan, until the camel grows old and dies, and all knowledge is lost of the exact place where the Lord lies.

In fact, though, he is not buried here, but in his homeland, in the Khentii mountains of northern Mongolia, on or near a mountain on which he had many dramatic escapes from his enemies. That mountain, known as Burkhan Khaldun, is probably today's Khentii Khan, though no one is certain, because Burkhan Khaldun may have been a range not a mountain. Nor does anyone know the burial spot, because it was kept secret. Horses were driven over the grave so that only a select few knew its position. The grave – in fact a cemetery for several other Mongol-dynasty Emperors – had to be honoured. Chinggis's heir Ogedei decreed a solution: in the words of the seventeenth-century historian Sagang

Sechen, 'eight white tents were raised for the purpose of veneration'. A clan, the Darkhat, was appointed to care for the Lord's possessions and supervise the rituals by which he was venerated, ensuring that Chinggis would watch over his people for ever.

At first, the focal point for the White Tents was the gravesite. Seventy years later, the Mongols ruled all China as the Yuan dynasty. After the death of Chinggis's grandson, Kublai, in 1294, one of his grandsons, Kamala, was put in command of Chinggis's *ordos*, his tent-palaces. As the Persian historian Rashid al-Din says, the estates included 'the Great Khorig [Forbidden Precinct] of Chinggis Khan, which they call Burkhan Khaldun, and where the great *ordos* of Chinggis Khan are still situated. These latter are guarded by Kamala. There are four great *ordos* and five others there, nine in all' – yes, the sources disagree about the number – 'and no one is admitted to them. They have made portraits of them [the family] there and constantly burn perfumes and incense.'

At some point during the Yuan dynasty, the main shrine became not the *place*, but the *tents*, which moved between several sites, forming the heart of the cult for the worship of Chinggis's spirit. After the collapse of the Yuan dynasty in 1368 the tents followed the Mongols back to the grasslands.

A secret grave, a forbidden area, a shrine of movable tents: the evidence for what happened to Chinggis's body was ephemeral from the start. Many clans and places wanted a share of him. With the Eight White Tents as the shifting focus of worship, stories arose that Chinggis was not on Burkhan Khaldun at all, had never been taken there in the first place. Hence the rise of the local legend that he was actually buried in Ordos.

## A PLACE OF WORSHIP

As the years passed, the Eight White Tents wandered back and forth across the Gobi, to the Altai mountains of the west, to the eastern grasslands, to the semi-desert of Ordos, now together, now apart, their number and contents varying, until, in the early seventeenth century, they settled on a well-watered spot on the eastern edge of Ordos. This place became the Ikh Juu, the Great Monastery, otherwise known as the *ordos* of Chinggis Khan, which later gave the name to the whole region. The descendants of those set to guard the palace-tents improvised tales until, with the passing of the generations, it became accepted locally that this must have been the place where Chinggis had wished to be buried, and therefore *was* buried, though no one knew the exact spot. Soon, under the influence of Buddhism, the beliefs and rituals associated with this setting became encrusted with Tibetan lore.

By then, there were three tents for Chinggis's three wives – Börte (his first love), Yisui (his second wife, and valued adviser) and the fictional Gürbeljin, a Tangut queen who, in one legend, dealt Chinggis a fatal cut and threw herself into the Yellow River, though in another version they loved each other, and she drowned herself in grief.* The other five were for sacred objects, including a little pot with jewels and grains to symbolise wealth, a mirror for perception, coloured ribbons for the regions and peoples of the empire, the accoutrements of his divine white horse, and a mare's-milk bucket made of red sandalwood, used by Chinggis to gather the milk of ninety-nine heavenly mares before setting out on campaign.

The temple and its rituals were, and still are, controlled by the Darkhats, an élite, exempted from taxes and military duty. So things remained for some seven hundred years, with the Darkhats developing ever more specialised tasks, as happens with many other priesthoods. They were all men, and all the tasks were inherited from father to senior son. There are two main divisions, which spring from two of Chinggis's generals, Bo'orchu and Mukhali. Bo'orchu had become

* The legend explains why, in Mongolian, the Yellow River is the Queen's River (Khatun Gol).

Chinggis's *anda* – his blood-brother – after he helped young Chinggis regain some stolen horses, later becoming one of his greatest generals. His descendants were responsible for the Mausoleum's arcane ceremonies, and always looked back to their Chinggisid origin. Rihu Su, in a PhD thesis on the cult, quotes one Darkhat, Surihu:

> When Chinggis Khan was about to pass away, our ancestor, Bo'orchu, was at his bedside. He was very sad and crying as he said: 'What will happen after the Great Khan passes away? What will happen to my descendants?' Finally, Chinggis said, 'After my death, your descendants will live with me, generation after generation.' So this task was assigned to Bo'orchu. After Chinggis Khan died, we, the descendants of Bo'orchu, have been engaged in making offerings and guarding the mausoleum. And the duties have never been stopped. I am the 39th generation of Bo'orchu's family.

The second group, descendants of Mukhali, viceroy of north China, cared for the war standards – spears with yak tails below the point – and the ceremonies that honoured them.

Both groups spawned subgroups and sub-subgroups, with individuals responsible for the minutest points of ritual, such as caring for the horse-headed clappers, etiquette, chanting, reading decrees, arranging offerings, supervising liquor ceremonies, boiling sheep, carrying lanterns, butchering horses and monitoring lookouts.

As the original shamanistic rituals gave way to Buddhist ones, Chinggis became a reincarnation of the bodhisattva (or 'Buddha-to-be') Vajrapani, the Thunderbolt-Bearer, who in Tibetan mythology fights demons to protect Buddhism. Rites settled into a series of four great seasonal observances, of which the greatest occurs in the spring, each with its songs, prayers and incantations, many beginning with words which, if the names were changed, could just as well be used by a priest invoking Christ:

> Heaven-born Chinggis Khan,
> Born by the will of sublime Heaven,
> Your body provided with heavenly rank and name,
> You who took overlordship of the world's peoples…

The prayers invoke virtually anything connected to him – possessions, actions, looks, wives, children, horses, pastures – to ensure the Lord's help in overcoming demons, illnesses and other evils.

The ceremonies are great public events. One, for example, takes place on 21 March in front of the main *ovoo*, a sacred pile of rocks that stands on a rise overlooking the whole site. It commemorates the Golden Pole to which Chinggis tethered his pure white horse. A legend claims that a thief took the horse and as a punishment was made to represent the Golden Pole, standing all night holding the horse with his feet buried in the ground. Today, a pole represents the criminal, and people run from the *ovoo* to scatter milk on the pole in a ritual purification.

Originally, the Mausoleum and its rituals were only for Mongols, an exclusiveness for which its guardians were prepared to die. In a story told at the Mausoleum, when the Manchu Emperor Shunzhi died in 1661, the Mongols refused an official decree to mourn. Summoned to Beijing to explain themselves, a group of Darkhats said they had been ordered to remain in mourning for one Emperor only, Chinggis Khan, all their lives: 'We would rather die obeying our late Emperor's order than live violating [it].' The Manchu officials granted the Mongols freedom to follow their own ways, pretty much unmolested, for almost three hundred years.

Owen Lattimore, the great American Mongolist, historian and traveller, was one of the very few outsiders to observe the ceremonies. He came to Edsen Khoroo, the Lord's Enclosure, in April 1935, in time for the spring festival. Arriving for this 'Audience with Chinggis Khan', as he called his vivid account, he found five tents (not eight) flanked by two dozen *gers*, ox carts, tethered horses and lines of poorer tents belonging to traders and servants.

The ceremony started with a humble approach to Chinggis's tent. Inside was a low silver-plated table, which was the altar, and a silver-plated wooden chest, the 'coffin'. This was supposed to contain the bones or ashes of Chinggis himself – impossible, of course, if Chinggis had been buried secretly in northern Mongolia. Lattimore noticed a Manchu inscription in the silver, which suggested it was no more than three hundred years old. There followed ceremonial observances, including the offering of silk scarves, a nine-fold prostration, the drinking of milk-wine from silver cups, the offering of a sacrificial sheep, and many prayers. Lattimore noted how traditionally Mongolian the ceremony was, with Buddhist lamas performing only a small role, their main task being to blow immense curved Tibetan trumpets, producing a sound like 'the splitting of gigantic trousers'. At the end of the ceremonies the following day, all five tents were lifted on to carts drawn by two sacred white camels, then taken back to a walled enclosure.

## THE WORLD AT WAR, THE TEMPLE MOVES

War, which Lattimore just managed to avoid, changed everything. The rivalry between shamanism and Buddhism gave way to three-way political rivalry. Japan, expanding into Inner Asia from Manchukuo, its colony in Manchuria, faced two Chinese challengers, the Nationalist Guomindang under Chiang Kai-shek and Mao's Communists. From Manchukuo, Japan planned the conquest of Mongolia, China and Siberia. The first step was to take eastern and central Inner Mongolia, which acquired its own puppet regime, the Mongolian Autonomous Government. By now, the Japanese had decided that Chinggis was the key to empire in Asia, complete with a revolutionary calendar which had as its founding date the year of Chinggis's birth. In 1937, they advanced to the Yellow River. Shortly afterwards, a representative of the Royal Japanese Army appeared at the Mausoleum to demand that the Mongolian leaders commit themselves to the Japanese, and move the Eight White Tents and their contents into Japanese custody. The provincial bosses pointed out that if the tents and their relics were moved there would be riots, which would not benefit the Japanese cause. The invaders saw the point, and retreated.

But now the Mongols were forewarned. The Japanese had in effect driven the Mongolians into the arms of the Chinese, with lasting consequences. From now on, for the Chinese of any political persuasion, Chinggis became a Chinese hero, a Chinese symbol of resistance.

When the Mongols asked the nearby Nationalists for help in moving the relics to a place of safety, they agreed, planning to move everything by truck and camel to the mountains south of Lanzhou on the Yellow River, six hundred kilometres to the south-west.

On 17 May 1939, two hundred Nationalist soldiers arrived unannounced at the Mausoleum, explaining to the astonished locals that they had come to protect it against the 'East Ocean devils'. They promised that all expenses would be paid, that some of the Darkhats could go along and that all ceremonies would continue. Hundreds, then thousands, came, spending the night in lantern-lit tears and prayers as the tents were loaded on to carts. At dawn, the carts headed south at walking pace towards Yan'an, Shaanxi province, almost four hundred kilometres away. Yan'an was the 'holy land of the Revolution', where Mao Zedong set up the HQ of the Communist Party's Central Committee at the end of the Long March. Because Chinggis, the progenitor of Kublai Khan's Yuan dynasty, was seen as a Chinese Emperor, both sides united to praise him as a symbol of resistance, and the Communists allowed the convoy with its Nationalist guardians to enter their territory.

Then the Communists took over and changed gear. Camel carts gave way to eight trucks, one vehicle for each tent, the leading one bearing the coffin. Near Yan'an, watched by a crowd of twenty thousand, the convoy drew up at a room designated as a funeral hall. A huge scroll proclaiming Chinggis 'The Giant of the World' was flanked by a couplet:

> The Mongolian and Chinese nations are more closely united,
> Continuing in the spirit of Chinggis Khan to fight to the end.

An arch hung with a sign – 'Welcome to Chinggis Khan's coffin!' – led to a shrine laid with wreaths, one from Mao himself. A dozen senior Party and army officials paid tribute in a four-hour ceremony, with an oration praising Chinggis as 'the world's hero'.

Three days later, the convoy again passed into Nationalist hands. In Xi'an, 200,000 people packed the streets, eager to honour Chinggis as the founder of a Chinese dynasty, as a great ancestor (even if not theirs) and as a Chinese leader in the mould of the First Emperor, China's unifier. How strange it seems, given that Chinggis had further dismembered this part of an already dismembered China. It was his grandson Kublai who had brought it all together.

On 1 July, another five hundred kilometres to the west, in the Xinglong mountains south of Lanzhou, the convoy arrived at Dongshan Dafo Dian, a Buddhist temple that was to be the Mausoleum's home for the next ten years. This glorious place, once hidden in towering forests, is now opened by a winding road. A little river tumbles through a huddle of houses. Pagodas crown forested peaks. Day-trippers climb winding stairways to the temple. Inside, a golden statue of Chinggis as a Buddhist deity is flanked by war standards and a square tent. It is all quite new. The original temple and its contents were destroyed by fire in 1968, and restored in 1987. Nothing would be authentic anyway, because in 1949, as Communist troops approached to wrap up the civil war, the Nationalists shepherded the Mausoleum away again, two hundred kilometres further west to the great sixteenth-century Tibetan monastery of Ta'er Si, where monks welcomed it with chants and prayers.

## THE COMMUNISTS TAKE OVER

For the next five years, with the Nationalists and Japanese defeated, the Communist Party had its hands full with post-revolutionary matters. Inner Mongolia was in the hands of Ulanhu, who brought a slow return to normality. At last, local and national officials turned to the Mausoleum. For Mongols and Chinese alike, Chinggis deserved something better than a few tents – a temple. In spring 1954, by truck and train, the hero's bier and his 'relics' returned to the Lord's Enclosure, in time for the laying of the foundation stone on 20 April. The new temple, with its three *ger*-like domes, opened two years later.

The year 1962 marked the eight hundredth anniversary of Chinggis's birth. Mongolia itself had to pretend not to care, because it was subservient to the Soviets, who despised Chinggis for sending the Mongols to seize Crimea and much of the Russian south. But China, still smarting from its split from its former ally, knew very well how to use the cult of Chinggis. In the Lord's Enclosure, thirty thousand people, mostly Mongols, participated in an excess of adoration, which suited the official line perfectly. Inner Mongolia would be firmly pro-Party, pro-China and anti-Soviet.

But when Mao unleashed the Cultural Revolution in 1967, Chinggis suddenly fell from grace in a wave of xenophobia. In Mongolian lands, the Mongols, once brothers-in-arms and proud defenders of China, became victims. The prime political target was the so-called Inner Mongolian People's Revolutionary Party, accused of wanting total independence for Inner Mongolia, with the long-term aim of reuniting with Mongolia itself and establishing, presumably, a new Mongol empire. The Party urged everyone to unite against the threat of 'pan-Mongolism'.

In Cultural Revolutionary eyes, the Mausoleum was the seething heart of treason. In 1968 the Red Guards tore the place apart, destroying almost every 'relic' – the sacred bow, the coffin, the war standards, the tents. Almost certainly, none of these objects was authentic, but all had a certain symbolic eminence, some perhaps being several centuries old, but now there is no way to check.

So don't expect authenticity. Facing you as you enter is a shadowy marble statue of our hero as a Buddha figure four metres high, finished in 1989, as attested by the signature of the artist, Jiang Hun. The 'relics', dating from the 1970s, are as fake as Splinters of the True Cross: the Sacred Bow and Quiver, the Chamber of the Miraculous Milk Bucket, and the Holy Saddle. What of the contents of the silver coffin, which Lattimore had been told held the Lord's body, or ashes? The one destroyed by the Red Guards? On my first visit in 2002, with the help of my Chinese-Mongolian friend Jorigt, I asked Nachug, the head of the Mausoleum's Institute of Chinggis Khan Studies. All he knew was that it supposedly held 'the last breath of the Lord'.

'You mean – just air?'

'No, no. Inside the box was a clump of hair from a white camel. And it was this hair that held the last breath of Chinggis Khan. You see, the hair had a little blood on it.' Somehow the legend about the body had slipped away, leaving a mere trace, the stain of a bloody cough caught on a twist of camel hair used as cottonwool to clean the royal lip. 'And there was also the umbilical cord. That was what was in the coffin that we worshipped here.'

'Were they really in there?'

'Well, the box was never opened. Only worshipped.'

We were back to hearsay, legend, rumour, almost certainly myth, but all well illustrated by murals. They displayed the glories of Chinggis's rule in figures that reminded me of 1930s fashion plates, with their suave elegance and fabrics falling in neat folds. Nothing marred the perfection of the costumes, the good looks of the men and women. Here Chinggis presided over his united empire, there Kublai conferred the title of dynastic founder upon his grandfather, who hovered, dragon-flanked, in Blue Heaven. Musicians serenaded, maidens presented silk scarves, foreigners offered tributes from afar, for Chinggis bridged east and west, stimulated a transfer of art, scholarship and trade, and assured the wellbeing of all. Of dead bodies there was no trace.

But there is authenticity of a sort in the beliefs, the prayers, the songs, the ceremonies, enough anyway to win the respect of a foreign sceptic, especially when in the company of a Mongolian. Jorigt made sure we had something to offer the spirit of Chinggis. From one of the gift shops that lined the entrance courtyard we bought a length of blue silk – a *khatag* – a bottle of vodka and a brick of tea. Inside, Darkhats in suits and brown trilbies stood watch, dour as guard dogs. To assert their authority, a sign warned against photography.

A young Darkhat, Bulag, guided us past the looming marble presence, set against a huge map showing the extent of the Mongol empire. Humbly we trooped into a back room, where three tents stood beneath an array of banners. This was the Mourning Hall, the three tents being for Chinggis himself, for his senior wife Börte and for Gürbeljin, the Tangut princess, reviled elsewhere as a murderess but here adored for her loyalty. We laid our *khatags* and our bottle down. We knelt. We lit incense. Bulag muttered a prayer, in Mongol: 'Holy Chinggis Khan, John and Jorigt have come here today to pray at your tomb. We beg you to grant them good luck in their work.'

## THE BIRTH OF A NEW RELIGION

Does the spirit of Chinggis still have power? Well, this is not a place of miracles, where people are cured of diseases. But many Mongols, and also Chinese, because he is after all an ancestor, believe that Chinggis-in-spirit mediates between earth and heaven, and will, on occasion, intervene if asked in the right way.

We sought out Sainjirgal, once the chief researcher at the temple. Now retired, Sainjirgal was living in a nearby town, in a neat little house set round a tiny courtyard down a side street. He was in his seventies, but his twinkling eyes and ready smile made him seem twenty years younger. He had been a teacher, but had become intrigued by the worship of Chinggis Khan – 'I am not a Darkhat, but I am a Mongolian. He was my ancestor' – and had found his life's work collecting the rites, prayers, songs and beliefs of the Mausoleum. His work was well under way when the Red Guards came, destroying whatever they could. 'I was in prison for over a year, then sent to do manual labour, and that was sometimes worse than prison. They tied me with arms outstretched, and beat me with canes. They made me stand close to fires and burned me.'

'But why?'

'Because I worshipped Chinggis Khan, and this had become a crime! They also said I was a spy for Mongolian independence fighters, and for the Russians.'

When he was finally freed in 1974, after six years, the Mausoleum had been turned into a store for salt. 'Yes, a salt-preserving place! For the next ten years! It was to prepare for war.' I had not known how intense and widespread had been the fear of war with the Soviet Union (a story told in more detail in Chapter 13). He resumed life not broken, but inspired. 'I knew I had to fight for our culture. I had to publish the history of my ancestor.' His book, *The Worship of the Golden Chamber*, had just been published in a new edition, six hundred pages, beautifully printed in the Mongolian script.

Later, Nachug revealed an even deeper level of Chinggisid theology. Strolling round the immense courtyard in front of the temple, we came to a platform of rocks and grass on which fluttered yak-tail war standards, the symbol of Mongol military prowess. Nachug told the story of how Chinggis came by them:

> Once, when Holy Chinggis was fighting to unite the Mongol tribes, he despaired, and addressed Heaven. 'People call me the Son of God, but yet I fail! I beg Khökh Tenger, the Blue Sky, to give me the power to win!' At once,

> the heavens thundered, and something fell among some trees. He was unable to reach the object. So he commanded his generals to cut the trees and get it. It turned out to be a yak-tail standard. In thanks, Chinggis sacrificed 81 sheep, leaving the remains for the 'sky dogs' [wolves]. So the standard – the *suld* – became like a flag, a sign from the Blue Heaven uniting the Mongols, going before them in battle. That is why we worship the *suld* today.

Then he added a conclusion that put the whole Mausoleum and its ceremonies in a new light: 'This is a form of worship even higher than that of Chinggis Khan. If Chinggis Khan himself worshipped the standard, then it must be higher than him. It is a symbol of Heaven itself.' As such, it has a power of its own. I had thought until this moment that Chinggis was a god. Now I saw that in the pantheon he inhabited he was not at the pinnacle, only near it, a demigod. Perhaps with a hint of something even more mystical, a sort of Mongolian Trinity, with God the Father, Son and Holy Spirit mirrored by Blue Heaven, Chinggis and Standard.

It was a surprise to discover that the Mausoleum is the heart of a religion in the making, with genuine spiritual aspirations, formulated by its own theologian, Sharaldai. In his book, *The Power of Eternal Heaven*, he explains the nature of Chinggis's semi-divinity. I caught up with Sharaldai in Ulaanbaatar, where he had come for a conference on Chinggis Khan studies. Over our hotel tea, with the help of another friend, Erdene, he instructed me on the subject of Chinggis's divinity. 'The worship of Chinggis Khan is a way of connecting us to the Eternal Heaven.' He used the term that, in Chinggis's time, became superior to the more ancient concept of Blue Heaven. 'There are three levels,' he went on. 'The basic tenet of Eternal Heaven philosophy is that we on Earth are part of Eternal Heaven, our system of nine planets. People say we human beings are the highest level of a hierarchy of life. That may be so in terms of biology. But in terms of philosophy, we are a part of Eternal Heaven. To think of ourselves as the top of a hierarchy is to separate ourselves from Eternal Heaven. Our task is to reintegrate ourselves with creation. That's what people don't appreciate today.'

'So when one worships Chinggis Khan, does one worship Eternal Heaven *through* Chinggis?'

'It is so. Also, you can worship Eternal Heaven directly. You see, there are three components: Eternal Heaven, the power of Eternal Heaven and *being subject to* the power of Eternal Heaven.'

He'd lost me. This was as arcane as medieval arguments about the nature of the Trinity, on which Catholic and Orthodox churches still disagree, after a thousand years of dispute. 'Christians say that God is three in one: Father, Spirit, Son.'

'There are similarities. But Eternal Heaven has real power. Chinggis knew that all living things owe their power to Eternal Heaven, and he was able to use it to lead. You can see how we Mongols did this by looking at our three national sports, wrestling, horse racing and archery. A strong body, good horsemanship, accurate shooting. By these means, we conquered half the world. But...' He raised a finger. 'To use power in such a way was not Eternal Heaven's true purpose. In conquering, we saw that this was not the way to live, bringing suffering to others. What we learned was that the time had come to stop fighting, and live by talking.'

'What does this mean for today?'

'We are in the process of discovering. In the world today, there is no philosophy of life! There is science, but science only looks at the surface of things. All the world's leaders have forgotten about the existence of the power of Eternal Heaven.'

This was the real purpose of the Mausoleum, Nachug said – to awaken not just Mongols but everyone to their place in the universe. 'It doesn't matter whether the objects are genuine or not. The real significance lies in the connection with Eternal Heaven. So, in this sense, as I say in my book' – he pointed to the page for emphasis – 'Chinggis Khan is a spirit for all of us. We are created by Eternal Heaven. If we follow the way, then we shall all be eternal.'

It was an unlikely, extraordinary vision. If Sharaldai's message spreads, there will be those who will teach that Chinggis's life was the first faltering line on a graph, which strengthens and soars over eight centuries to these astonishing conclusions: that violence, whatever its initial success, must ultimately fail; and that all conflict should be resolved in peaceful discussion.

This is surely the oddest of Chinggis's transformations: in life, from a nobody to world-conqueror; after death, to a demigod; and now to a spirit of universal harmony.

## A BRIGHT PRESENT, A DARK FUTURE

In 2017, I returned to the mausoleum with Alatan and 'Water' Xu, to find that over the past fifteen years it had become bigger and better and easier to reach. You can avoid the ninety-nine steps by riding in an electric cart. Chinggis's black war standards have a fine new platform. The place where they perform the spring ceremony – the main *ovoo* and a dozen small ones – are all made permanent with cement and stone, linked by a cobbled path. The ceremony itself has been declared a National Intangible Cultural Heritage by UNESCO. And the space in front of the Mausoleum has acquired a lawn that would not disgrace an English country house.

Inside, nine offering tables of Vietnamese mahogany were donated by Xi Jinping, then vice president, in 2009. He came to honour Chinggis as a symbol of national unity – after all, Chinggis's grandson Kublai had been responsible for fixing China's modern borders, including Tibet and Xinjiang. Huge new frescoes illustrate incidents from Chinggis's life – the capture of the scribe Tatatonga who devised the script that is still in use today; the Great Western Campaign against the world of Islam, which 'connected east and west' (still with no hint that this terrible event killed millions and destroyed a dozen cities). The most impressive mural, to my eyes, is one depicting the Battle of Khuiten (detailed in Chapter 5), when Chinggis defeated his blood-brother Jamukha thanks to a sudden 'Heaven-sent' storm that tumbled Jamukha's troops into ravines.

Sharaldai had been dead for five years, but the traditions of the Mausoleum are as strong as ever, as our guide, Altan Erdene ('Golden Treasure'), explained. He was living proof of the enduring traditions, being the fortieth-generation descendant of Bo'orchu, son of Bulag, who had prayed to Chinggis's spirit for me all those years ago. One of the hundred or so guides, Altan Erdene was proud of his role and his ancestry. He pointed out a glass box that contained five hundred silver ingots, each fifty-gram ingot representing one of the Darkhat families chosen by the Qing Emperor in the seventeenth century to look after this place in perpetuity.

Perhaps if my grandson comes here in twenty years' time, he will find Altan Erdene's son carrying on his grandfather's and father's role as guide and protector – the forty-first generation from Bo'orchu.

Or perhaps not, for in 2022, China began the outright suppression of Mongol culture, in particular the language. Today, the Mausoleum lives with a paradox. This very Mongol institution, which might have been seized by the Japanese, was saved by the intervention of both Nationalists and Communists, then resurrected in its present form thanks to post-revolutionary China. Now, though, the Party is in full control. Beijing no longer needs Mongolian support, and the rulers can afford to adopt an agenda of repression in their pursuit of national unity. Better to suppress the old spirit, with its hints of 'pan-Mongolism' and Mongolian national identity.

Where will this leave Chinggis and his Mausoleum? Well, certainly under firm Chinese control. It is a prime tourist site, much praised as such on Chinese websites. It may be allowed to go its own way, with its traditions tolerated as the charming, harmless, entertaining rituals of a subject people. Perhaps the Party will shrug off the idea of a threat. What harm could there be in colourful costumes, a few prayers and libations of milk?

But what if these rituals, with their Mongol-language prayers, acquire a political tinge? What if they were to act as rallying points for Mongol cultural identity? What if the Lord's Enclosure threatens to become a symbol of something that might tear at China's precious unity? What if Chinggisid theology acquires a political agenda, with Chinggis not simply as a help in ages past, but a hope for freedom from Beijing in years to come? Then, I think, Beijing would unleash the full force of its anti-Mongol legislation, and the Mongol-speaking Darkhats would be silenced, the tourists banished and the Lord's Enclosure reduced to rubble.

The Great Wall snakes over ridges north of Beijing.
It was no sooner built than redundant.

# PART III

# THE EVER-SHIFTING FRONTIER

*China's northward advance was never straightforward. The frontier shifted constantly, depending on China's policies and the ambitions of feuding nomads. In 1368, with the Mongols expelled, the incoming Ming had more to worry about than the Mongols. For almost fifty years, both sides kept clear of each other. But Mongol rulers, still dreaming of past glories, yearned for revenge and booty. Their raids were a menace. Only in the mid-fifteenth century, after one of the worst military disasters in history, did the Ming address the problem. For two hundred years, they worked on defence, obsessively, locking themselves behind the Great Wall. Further expansion northwards came only in the seventeenth century with a new dynasty, the Manchus – an expansion that went into sudden reverse two centuries later.*

*In an ink painting by Ch. Rashdanzan, a horse archer shows what the Chinese army was up against in 1449.*

# CHAPTER 8

# DISASTER AT TUMU

## A MEMORIAL TO A CATASTROPHE

A FEW KILOMETRES BEYOND THE GREAT WALL AT BADALING, past the tourist buses and the T-shirt salesmen, my guide Cheng Yinong told the driver to turn off the motorway on to the old road, where trailer-trucks pulled in for tea and dumplings. Cheng was a post-grad writing a thesis on medieval towns and their defences. There was something he wanted to see. Guarding eyes against a gritty autumn wind, we crossed the road to a line of single-storey brick houses. A lane led past stacks of dead sunflowers and cornhusks to an incongruous rammed-earth wall, frowning over the shacks below.

'Tumu Fortress,' said Cheng.

Through a gap-toothed hole in the wall crowded more low houses, among trees that had sprouted in unkempt corners. But grey earth walls looming over distant roofs showed this was indeed a fortress, the inside of which had long since clogged with houses, lanes and courtyards.

'This is an important place,' said Cheng. 'Near here in 1449 Mongolians beat a great Ming army. Very important, especially for me, because before, not many towns had walls' – they had no need of walls, of course, because before the Ming threw them out, the Mongols ruled all China – 'and after Tumu they built walls.'

We wandered round a corner to, of all things, a little open-air theatre, which faced the town's administrative offices, and a small temple. 'This temple was built in memory of the officers who fell here,' said Cheng. 'Oh, locked. Sorry.' But we had been seen. A woman appeared, along with four shy colleagues, one of whom had a key. While they whispered and giggled about the foreigner, the dust and shadows of the one-room temple whispered of disaster. On the wall was a roll-call of sixty-eight officers and officials who had died near here in the summer of 1449. The plaque spoke of a foolish Emperor in the power of a malign eunuch; of the loss of 500,000 soldiers; of the building of this, the Ancestral Temple of Loyalty. *Half a million* troops killed? Was that possible? This was a story worth further research.

Having thrown out the Mongols in 1368, their successors, the Ming, were faced with a question: what was their China to be? Theoretically, since they had replaced the Mongols, they might lay claim to the whole empire as established by Kublai Khan. But even in his lifetime, much of it – Central Asia, Persia, southern Russia – fell away into independence. For the Ming to secure even Kublai's heartland – China, including Mongolia – would be unrealistic, because the defeated Mongols had reclaimed their own homeland. So the Ming made do with Kublai's Chinese estates, minus Mongolia.

That forced the Ming to wrestle with an ancient problem: how best to deal with the northern barbarians? They could not rely on the Wall, because for a century and a half under the Mongols it had all been inside the Mongol Empire and, being made of earth, it was an eroded and unmanned wreck. But no matter. The new dynasty's military was strong, the northern borders were in the hands of pro-Ming clans, and the Mongols back on their grasslands were too divided to be a threat.

Success in consolidating the new regime was largely down to the founder's youngest son, usually known by his reign title Yongle (1403–25). As a prince, in 1382, he masterminded the reconquest of Yunnan. As Emperor, he shifted the capital back to Beijing, and began turning Kublai

Khan's palace into the Forbidden City as it is today. He planned to make China into a world empire, and very nearly did so thanks in part to his reconquest of Yunnan, where he had adults killed and the male children castrated by the hundred. Among the castrati was a Muslim boy, Ma He, who was taken into the royal household. Later given the honorific name Zheng, he grew up to be an imposing and brilliant commander, becoming Yongle's top imperial aide in a series of massive new projects that would proclaim China as the world's greatest power. These included a fleet that would explore the world and solicit 'tributes' from lesser powers. The Emperor commissioned several hundred new ships, among them sixty-two gigantic four-masted 'treasure ships', which were 145 metres long and 54 metres across (though scholars dispute all details of numbers and sizes). In seven expeditions between 1405 and 1433, Zheng He would lead the fleet to explore the southern coasts of Eurasia to the east coast of Africa.*

Meanwhile, on the other side of the Great Wall, the Mongols clung to the idea that they were still the 'real' rulers of China, calling themselves the Northern Yuan. But the Mongols were their own worst enemies. Westerners (Oirats) rivalled easterners (Khalkhas), squabbling and feuding as their ancestors had done before the rise of Chinggis. For China, peace depended on these inter-tribal rivalries, and on three docile buffer-zone tribes on the Manchurian border known as the Three Guards. But it was not enough. A leader named Arugtai refused to pay the usual tribute and won over the Three Guards. In an attempt to assert his authority, Yongle unleashed five campaigns between 1410 and 1424, each one involving some 250,000 men, and none to any great effect.

All Emperors claimed the Mandate of Heaven, but in Yongle's case Heaven seemed a little reluctant. In 1421, lightning set fire to the new Forbidden City and burned down much of it. The distraught Emperor

---

* Academics reject the idea, popularised by Gavin Menzies in *1421: The Year China Discovered the World*, that Zheng He's ships reached the Americas, or even Australia.

put out a public request for help in understanding what he had done wrong. A flood of opinions blamed him for wasting the nation's wealth on foreign adventures and vast schemes, including those of Zheng He and his fleet. As if in support of the criticisms, disasters multiplied. The Emperor suffered strokes, impotence, sex scandals at court and rebellions. In 1424 he embarked on one last campaign to crush the Mongols, the biggest of all, only to discover that his opponent had vanished over the steppe. It was too much. Yongle, broken by failure, died on campaign.

His son and heir having died after a brief reign, his grandson (Xuande, 1426–35) reversed all Yongle's large-scale projects. After a final voyage in 1430, on which Zheng He died, the great ships returned to the junkyard, and Zheng He's records to the bonfire. China, which might have seized the world as European nations were soon to seize it, turned inwards again, back to its traditional business: defence against the barbarians beyond the Great Wall; it was concerned not with forward campaigns, but with the regarrisoned Wall itself.

## THE ROOTS OF A NIGHTMARE

So, after the great reset, the northern frontier in 1440 seemed safe enough, secured by vassal Mongol tribes. Chinese colonists began to settle in Mongol territory. The expensive and exposed outer defence points beyond the Wall had been pulled back, and the Wall itself largely rebuilt. Beijing was supposedly safe behind two lines of the Great Wall, one running across the mountains either side of the Juyong Pass, the other through today's Zhangjiakou, backed by armies based in two walled cities, Datong and Xuanhua. The Emperor, Yingzong,* was a boy

* This was his temple name. Usually, Emperors are referred to by their reign name. Unfortunately, this one reigned twice, with different reign names, Zhengtong and Tianshun. It is simpler to use his temple name.

of twelve, but he was well supervised by his wise and strong-minded grandmother, the Grand Dowager Empress Zhang. A major concern of hers was to limit the influence of the eunuchs, particularly their boss, Wang Zhen, whose self-serving, malign, overweening ambitions were the very opposite of Zheng He's.

Two years later, all this began to unravel. The key event was the death of the Grand Dowager Empress, which gave Wang Zhen, one of China's most notorious villains, the freedom he wanted. He controlled the eunuch bureaucracy, the secret service and soon the mind of Yingzong, now a foolish fifteen-year-old. It was Wang Zhen who would build the road on which the Emperor would march to disaster.

The young Emperor had been raised to admire soldiers, and in 1449, aged twenty-one, he decided it was time to prove himself in action. There was only one region from which invasion threatened: the Great Wall frontier, beyond which lay what could become a unified power, the Mongols.

It so happened that a force for Mongol unity had recently emerged. His name was Esen,* and he had inherited control of the western Mongol groups, the Oirat. In the 1440s, he took over what are today Uzbekistan and the other Central Asian -stans, then the Chinese–Mongol borderland groups along the Gobi to Manchuria. His base was what was known as Zungaria, which Esen made into the heart of the last empire of the steppe nomads. His success suggested he might become another Chinggis and lead the Mongols to reclaim China.

One way Esen increased his popularity at home was to exploit the 'tribute system' by which China dealt with the 'barbarians'. The system, designed to buttress China's superiority complex, served several unstated functions, best understood by the liberal use of inverted commas. The idea was that, since 'barbarians' were 'inferior', Chinese Emperors could deal with them only in so far as they showed evidence of being good

* Esen, pronounced Yisun, means 'nine', a number of 'special symbolic significance for the Turco-Mongolian peoples' (de Rachewiltz, *Secret History*).

subjects. Trade with inferiors was beneath Chinese dignity. So, if barbarian leaders brought 'tribute', such as horses and furs, Chinese Emperors would shower them with 'gifts', like silk, iron goods and (later) tea. The reality behind the euphemistic exchange of barbarian 'tribute' and imperial 'gifts' was both trade and bribery to keep the peace, always with the (unstated) threat of blackmail – that if the Emperor's gifts were not good enough, the barbarian leaders might go on the warpath. Esen exploited the system by sending ever bigger 'tribute missions', which would arrive in Beijing expecting to be housed, entertained and rewarded with 'gifts' for their 'submission'. In 1448, two thousand of them arrived. This was nothing but extortion.

Wang Zhen, the eunuch who had the Emperor's ear, was no diplomat. He took a cut of every deal, had his own secret service, rewarded toadies and punished critics. Finally, with Esen's power and demands alike increasing, he decided to force a crisis and then capitalise on the Emperor's passion for military glory. When the latest oversized mission arrived in 1448, Wang Zhen cut the expected 'gifts' by eighty percent and curtly rejected Esen's request for a Chinese princess.

Such treatment demanded a response, for without 'gifts' Esen could not keep his commanders happy. Within months, reports came from the Great Wall of raids and skirmishes and scouting parties, suggesting that Esen was planning a major attack. This was the chance Wang Zhen was looking for. Let us, he said, campaign across the Wall, with the Emperor in command and himself as generalissimo. He, Wang Zhen, would lead an army of 500,000 in a march beyond the Wall that would destroy the nomad armies once and for all; then, in triumph, he would command a victory parade for the Emperor.

Wang Zhen was no generalissimo, and this was lunacy. Officials banded together to say so. The defences are adequate, they said in a memo to the Emperor. This is the height of summer, they wrote, the heat is intolerable, there is little water and fodder; the Emperor's absence would paralyse government. 'Armies are instruments of violence; warfare is a dangerous business,' the officials protested. '[Yet] the Son of Heaven, though the most exalted of men, would now go personally into those dangers. We officials, though the most stupid of men, say that this must not occur.' Yingzong, parroting Wang Zhen's words, refused to listen: 'The bandits offend against Heaven... We have no choice but to lead a great army in person to exterminate them.'

What he did not know was that Esen, intent on wringing better trading concessions from China, had sent four columns, two to attack the garrison towns of Datong and Xuanhua, and two more to divert attention elsewhere. None of them had any problem crossing the Great Wall, as Frederick Mote says in his brilliant account of the battle.

Events now pick up in pace and immediacy, as if in an epic movie. On 4 August 1449, the Emperor departs, swaying northwards in the imperial palanquin, his army of 500,000 trailing behind. Wang Zhen alone has about a thousand carts for himself and his entourage. A secretary tries to talk sense into the Emperor, throwing himself in front of the entourage: 'Your Majesty may make light of your imperial person, but what of the dynasty, what of the state?' Wang Zhen curses the man, who is ignored. Moving at twenty kilometres a day, the immense procession heads north-west, through the mountain pass that runs through today's Badaling. It's hot, but also raining. The sodden troops are near mutiny. No one can speak to the Emperor except Wang Zhen, whom officials must always approach on their knees. The head of the Directorate of Astronomy says the signs are bad. 'If it is to be so, then fate has ordained it so,' says Wang Zhen. At Xuanhua, six days and 130 kilometres from Beijing, two distinguished old officials plead for the campaign to be called off; Wang Zhen makes them kneel for a whole day in punishment. Still it rains. No one can remember such rain in August. The Mongols watch and wait for their chance.

The thirteenth of August is a bad day, and not just because of the continuous rain. At Yanggao, thirty kilometres north-east of Datong, Esen thrashes an army sent from the city against him the previous week. Three days later, the Chinese see the sodden battlefield, still strewn with thousands of unburied corpses, and 'the chill of terror grips all hearts'. The commander who escaped death by hiding in long grass, tells Wang Zhen, 'Give it up! If you go on, you will simply fall into Esen's trap.'

And now, at last, Wang Zhen begins to have second thoughts. He decides to declare the mission accomplished and return to the capital. As the expedition sets camp the following evening, a black cloud descends precisely over it and hangs so low it seems to press down on people's heads, though beyond the camp on all sides clear sky can be seen. Rain falls through the night, accompanied by lightning, inducing fear and disorder.

After another nine days of this, the Emperor, his eunuch and their entourages are back where they were some three weeks previously, thirty kilometres from the inner wall at Badaling, camping near the little town of Tumu. Behind them straggle half a million men, spreading westwards up the valley of the Yang River. Further west still is the rearguard, two days' march and fifty kilometres away.

Early on 30 August, messengers gallop into the imperial camp with the news that the rearguard has been attacked. With what result? Wang Zhen decides that the imperial party should wait for news. That evening, the son of one of the two rearguard commanders gallops in and reports that the rearguard was ambushed in a narrow defile and 'The government troops have virtually all been killed or wounded.' The two generals lie dead on the field of battle.

At once, a large force of cavalry – maybe thirty thousand, maybe fifty thousand, sources being as usual vague – is sent back to fight the Mongols and rescue survivors. It is commanded by a venerable old general, Chu Yung, who owes his position to his father, a high official under the early Ming a good sixty years before – a typically inept choice by the campaign's self-appointed civilian leaders. Chu Yung was 'full of respect towards scholars and officials' and 'appeared to be quite heroic, but both his courage and his tactical sense were deficient' – as any military man would know, because he had been blamed for bungling a campaign against the Mongols only five years before. To pile idiocy on idiocy, the man who should have been in charge – Xueshou, a Mongol who had served the Chinese with distinction – is made second-in-command. Chu Yung leads his force straight into an ambush, and is killed along with his men. Xueshou is also killed, but dies heroically, his arrows spent, his bowstring broken, wielding his bow like a club until he falls to Mongol swords. His attackers then find out who he is.

'He is one of us,' they say. 'No wonder he was so strong and brave.'

## THE EMPEROR CAPTURED

The next day, as the Emperor reaches Tumu, officials urge him to keep moving through the inner wall and the Juyong Pass, deploying a rear-guard against Esen's approaching army. But now the imperial wagons are ahead of the thousand carts full of Wang Zhen's possessions. He wants to wait for them. When the war minister remonstrates, Wang Zhen curses him: 'You fool of a bookworm! What do you know about military affairs? Say another word and you will be beheaded on the spot!' The minister, dragged away by guards, is left weeping in his tent.

Now the rain has stopped, the heat builds and the imperial party is short of water. There's a river nearby, but the Mongols have caught up, and a flanking party blocks access to the river. By late afternoon, the Chinese and their horses are not only parched; they are surrounded. That night, guards report that 'numbers of the enemy on all sides swell beyond all expectations'.

Next morning, 1 September, the sun rises in a clear sky. The Mongols hold back, and send a letter offering peace talks. The Emperor sends a reply, stating his terms, but at the same time Wang Zhen orders an advance. The imperial palanquin struggles forward in the midst of jostling guards. The Mongols attack, cutting off the imperial party from the army. 'Throw down your arms and armour, and be spared!' comes the cry from the Mongols. The Chinese soldiers panic, strip off and run, only to be cut down. In the Emperor's group, the Emperor, in his armour, climbs from his palanquin and sits on the ground, while his guards fall under the hail of arrows. A Mongol soldier breaks through and, unaware of the Emperor's identity, is on the point of killing him to seize his armour when a Mongol officer stops him.

'Are you prince Esen?' asks the Emperor, without revealing his identity. 'No,' replies the officer. His brother? Any of his other brothers? The Emperor names them in turn, at which point the officer suspects that this is someone important, and leads him away. His identity is revealed. He is kept for two days nearby, and is allowed to send a messenger to Beijing to announce his capture and order gifts. Meanwhile, all the Emperor's senior staff have been killed, including Wang Zhen, perhaps murdered by his own enraged officers. A quarter of a million men lie dead; the rest have scattered – and it is these who make up the half-million mentioned in the Tumu memorial.

Esen is astounded to discover that the Emperor is his prisoner and has him sent back to his camp at Xuanhua, where a debate ensues about what to do with him. 'He is the enemy of our Mongol khans,' says one old officer. 'Kill him.' One of Esen's brothers slaps the old man. 'The Emperor of China is no ordinary mortal. Look how he sat there unharmed through the thick of battle,' he says. 'We have all been the recipients of China's beneficence. If we keep the Emperor unharmed and return him, we will earn undying gratitude and fame.' Esen agrees.

What now? The Emperor is well treated, being given a few survivors as servants. The Mongols feast, entertain him, offer him a Mongol wife (who is politely declined) and discuss what use they can best make of him. Jewels arrive, sent in panic from the Forbidden City. Obviously, as Mote says, Esen has not engaged in this major military enterprise 'just for a few mule-loads of baubles' – he wants to be acknowledged by his own side as the new Great Khan; but from the Chinese, he wants no more than a steady flow of trade and gifts.

Instead, fate has presented him with an astonishing prize. The way to the capital lies open. As an enthusiastic captive eunuch tells him, he could use the Emperor as a bargaining chip to force all border garrisons to open their gates, and seize the capital itself. All north China could be at his feet. The half-rebuilt Wall would become irrelevant even before it is finished. But Esen's sudden good fortune leaves him totally nonplussed. He is not set up for conquest, let alone regime change and administration. He dithers, withdraws to make new plans and advances on Beijing only after six weeks' delay.

That allows the Ming time to pull themselves together. Out go the incompetent eunuchs, in come new brooms, including a minister of war, Yu Qian, who backs a new candidate for Emperor. The old one is now to be designated the 'Grand Senior Emperor', and is suddenly redundant. Yu Qian castigates as cowards those who advise surrender, reorganises the defences, restocks the granaries, restores confidence. By the time Esen arrives in mid-October, he is too late. When he offers his captive, he is told it is the dynasty and the nation that matters; 'the ruler is unimportant'. In brief: no deal. Esen knows he could not take Beijing. After five days he turns back, resumes tribute payments and quietly sends the ex-Emperor back to Beijing with no demands attached.

Thereafter, he focuses on extending his power at home. In 1453 he declares himself Great Khan of the Great Yuan, claiming the mantle of Kublai and Chinggis. But he lacks followers. And those he does have are not loyal. One of them assassinates him the next year, and the Mongols go back to raiding and futile feuding.

## THE FRONTIER TURNED TO STONE

Tumu brought the problem of the northern frontier into sharp focus, and fossilised both attitudes and policies. From now on, there would be no forward bases the other side of the Wall, and no campaigns into Mongolia. The Great Wall would be the frontier. It would have to be rebuilt more strongly, well maintained and well garrisoned. But without defences beyond the Wall, occasional breakthrough raids by Mongols had to be expected. That meant that the communities on the Chinese side would become armed camps. The whole strip of land within the Great Wall became a very Long City – the alternative translation of 'Great Wall' – living with the ever-present threat of invasion.

Or *perceived* threat; because, in fact, after Tumu the Mongols kept to themselves. Meanwhile, the Ming began to devote immense ingenuity, cash and manpower to building the stone wall as it stands today, running for one thousand kilometres around Beijing and onwards to the Pacific. 'If there is one weak point,' wrote its chief architect Qi Jiguang, 'the whole is weak.'

It is, as ever, a wonder: an eight-metre-high cliff of bricks – something over fifty million of them* – three thousand towers, and forts for troops and stores, and crenellated roadways, and walkways, which all run from the Yellow River to the Pacific and vary with the different terrains. Some sections can accommodate five horses side by side, a rollercoaster of stone trodden by millions every year, which in some places turns into staircases that ascend almost vertically. Some sections, shaken apart by earthquakes, are 'wild', closed off by barbed wire. Simatai is a breaking wave of rock, with a foaming crest of stone that narrows to a curtain between an abyss and a precipice. It's the width of a shoe, as I discovered by squeezing past the health-and-safety warning. Beyond, the crest peters out in loose stones, and beyond that soars the Tower for Viewing the Capital, where a rock-climber can, at dusk, see the lights of Beijing, if he or she cares to risk life, limb and a hefty fine.

* Perhaps, possibly. No one knows the true figure, but the stone sections, with numerous doublings and triplings, link the Yellow River to Shanhaiguan on the Pacific. Estimates of hundreds of millions, even billions, of bricks rely on the false assumption that all the rest, 7,000-kilometres of rammed earth, are also made of brick.

Tumu defined China's attitudes and the government's agenda for almost two centuries. Work on the Wall became a national obsession, prejudice against Mongols an item of faith. The Wall was prejudice in stone, literally petrified, so massively over-engineered that no Mongol would have dreamed of assaulting it head on.

Instead, when a challenger arose, forces came from the far west, around the end of the Ming's Great Wall. This was Altan Khan, remarkable not only for his raids on China but also for converting to Buddhism, being instructed by a Tibetan priest, for whom he invented the title Dalai Lama. The result of his raids was that the Ming granted him a grand title and opened several centres for trade fairs, which was enough for both sides to agree a peace treaty in 1571.

So, in the late sixteenth century, it was not the Mongols who were the main menace, but the rising power to the east, the Jürchen, soon to be renamed Manchus by their ambitious leader Nurhachi, which gives us the name of the region – Manchuria. In the 1640s, rebellion against the Ming was brewing within China. The Ming sank into corruption, mismanagement and panic. A rebel leader broke into the Forbidden City, driving the Emperor to hang himself on Coal Hill, in his own gardens. Meanwhile, at the eastern end of the Great Wall, a local Chinese general had the bright idea of soliciting help from the Manchus. Naturally, they accepted. Far from barring the way to enemies, the Wall did the opposite. The Manchus poured through the open gate at Shanhaiguan, chased the rebels out of Beijing and in 1644 took over.

China's Emperor was a foreigner once again, one who ruled on both sides of the Wall. In the blink of a historical eye, the Wall became irrelevant, and a new era opened on the northern frontier.

*Emperor Kanxi: he backed the 1689 treaty with Russia and the 1691 takeover of Mongolia. Both events still permeate Chinese attitudes.*

## CHAPTER 9

# TWO PRIESTS AND THE NEW FRONTIER

### 'A RATHER EXTRAORDINARY STORY'

IN CHINA'S FAR NORTH, RUSSIA IS EVER PRESENT, ACROSS the Erguna River, or, if you go way north, across the Amur. You see tourist information and museum captions in Russian, eat in Russian restaurants with waitresses dressed up as Russians. In Manzhouli, on the border, much of the city is devoted to Russian tourism, with a hotel in the shape of a *matryoshka*, a Russian nesting doll which looks as if it should have other hotels hidden inside. Russian-style clubs employ long-legged Russian pole-dancers. But Russian influence spread across the whole area long before tourism. The railway to Harbin was built by the Russians. A century ago, after the Revolution, the city's hundred thousand Russian refugees – or at least those who had got their cash out – could shop at Churin's department store, visit the opera and hear the Harbin Symphony Orchestra playing Glinka and Tchaikovsky. Russia wraps around north-east China like a fur hat, and runs through it like meltwater.

Yet in the late seventeenth century, China's border was several hundred kilometres further north and east. What had happened to make the Chinese gain a large chunk of Siberia and Manchuria from the

Russians? The simple answer involves Russia's advance across Siberia in the seventeenth century, an advance that brought Russian traders, explorers and some extremely unpleasant bandits up against the outer reaches of the Qing dynasty under the Manchus. The two empires needed to agree a border.

The practical issues were formidable. Horses, riverboats and rough tracks linked an archipelago of scattered outposts. Vast distances and weeks of travel separated this borderland from the two capitals; Moscow was over 4,000 kilometres away, and Beijing 1,500 kilometres. Both sides were rivals for the same territory, both sides distrusted the other, neither knew anything about the other, no officials spoke both Chinese (let alone Manchu) and Russian and neither side had much experience in international relations. The unmapped borderland between Russia and China was a tinderbox of colonists, traders, outlaws and rival tribes.

Yet these two hostile contestants managed to make peace instead of war.

There is a little-known story here. It involves two priests, who belonged to a group of Jesuit missionaries, respected in China not so much for their religion as for their scholarship. One, Jean-François Gerbillon, was French. The other, Thomas Pereira, was from Portugal. As well as being fluent in their own languages, they spoke Manchu, Chinese and – crucially – Latin, the language used by most Christians, including well-educated Orthodox Russians. To negotiate with the Russians, the Emperor Kangxi* asked them to act as interpreters and as advisers to his Manchu- and Chinese-speaking officials. Both priests kept diaries. Gerbillon's, in French, was published in 1736, but at thirty-five years old he was the junior. The diary of Pereira, ten years older, was discovered only in the mid-twentieth century and published in 1961. Meticulous and vivid, Pereira's diary – the main source for this chapter[1] – reveals the characters, emotions and prejudices of those involved, particularly

* Kangxi is the reign name of Xuanye, the second Emperor of the Qing dynasty. Scholars often call him 'the Kangxi Emperor'. I call him Kangxi to keep things simple.

those of his own team. As the diary's translator, Joseph Seres, puts it: 'It is rather extraordinary that a small group of Europeans, foreigners to both Russia and China, missionaries of a religion hardy tolerated, if not persecuted in both countries, should have played the role of intermediaries in highly important diplomatic matters between these two great Empires.' Rather extraordinary indeed. At crucial moments of high drama, the two priests saved the negotiations from collapse. Pereira's reactions – patience, exasperation, flashes of humour – give his account the pacy immediacy of a film script.

Before I tell their story, let me explain how Russia and China first came face to face across the wilderness of Inner Asia.

## TWO EMPIRES MEET

Russia had been pushing east for two centuries. First came adventurers, so-called Cossacks, who were little more than robbers, eager for furs, principally sable, which they took by force from local tribes. In 1581, one of them asked the Tsar for help, backing his request with 2,400 sable furs. Sable – 'Siberian gold' that fetched high prices in Europe – inspired a myth that Siberia was a place of fabulous wealth. The Tsar, Ivan IV, sent troops, and from then on expansion eastwards became a state exercise in empire-building. Russians seized river valleys, crushed tribes and built forts, which became towns. This was not easy. Tribes fought back; of which the Buryat Mongols were the toughest. There were retreats, punitive raids, diplomatic approaches, alliances to set tribe against tribe, 'tributes' of furs demanded and received.

Quite rapidly, Russians planted colonies, leaping from river to river, making tracks through the forest. Unlike the Spanish in South America, they could not enslave communities nor were they driven by missionary zeal. This was a commercial enterprise, based on a tenuous network of forts, tracks and river traffic. By 1601, there was a postal service, with horses and post-stations and several hundred couriers. Churches and monasteries encouraged the spread of Orthodox Christianity. In 1618, a twelve-man expedition under Ivan Petlin followed the Great Wall to Beijing, where Petlin, used to wooden houses, was awed by all the stonework and the markets crammed with velvets, damasks, silks, dozens of different vegetables and 'a fragrance of cooking that seemed to have come from Heaven'. The Ming had a vague memory of Russians, because some had been caught up in the Mongol Empire and settled in Beijing, but the Yuan records had been forgotten and the Ming had no interest in trade. Petlin's visit led nowhere.

Far to the north, a local base, Yakutsk, arose on the Lena River in 1632, and seven years later Russians reached the Pacific coast, in the bay known as the Sea of Okhotsk. Here they heard intriguing reports: that further south there was a great river – the upper Amur to locals, the Heilongjiang to the Chinese (not that the Russians learned the river's name in either language) – where tribes of farmers traded grain for sable.

In June 1643, a southward expedition, consisting of 132 men under a vicious leader, Vasily Poyarkov, set out from Yakutsk, keen to find better supplies for their grim Arctic settlement. Travelling by river, he reached the Stanovoy mountains, which divide northward-flowing rivers from those that flow south – to the Amur, as he would discover, and on to the Pacific. Beyond, lay scattered communities of Ewenki reindeer-herders and Daur farmers, a subgroup of Mongols, all ripe for the taking. Leaving a small contingent to guard the middle Amur, Poyarkov and the rest sailed downriver for six hundred kilometres south-east and followed the Great Bend in the Amur for another seven hundred kilometres north-east to reach the river's mouth. Rather than fight the current back upriver, they travelled north along the coast for six hundred kilometres, and inland for another six hundred kilometres back to Yakutsk. In their three-year trip, they lost fifty men to famine, several to floggings – Poyarkov beat some to death himself – and twenty-five who were killed by the warlike Daur. Frankly, it was remarkable that any at all survived, given that their brutality alienated the locals and guaranteed near starvation, which they escaped by eating their own captives. Poyarkov was recalled to face charges, and vanished from history. Still, the adventure opened up the Far East for Russia. Poyarkov's report was the first the Russians knew of the Amur, the only river that links Siberia to the Pacific – the *lowe*r Amur, that is. They still had no idea about the upper part, or what lay to the south.

So they didn't know that the new Manchu rulers of China considered this to be in their sphere of interest. They soon found out. In 1650, a small force of two hundred Russians under the rich, piratical Yerofei Khabarov returned to the Amur, and came across an impressive fortification manned by fifty Manchu horsemen who had been sent to collect tribute. The Russians attacked, took the fort and told nearby chiefs that they should declare their submission to the Tsar. Continuing on down the Amur, Khabarov discovered another fort, named Boli, where he proposed to spend the winter of 1651–2, backing his decision with demands for tribute and hundreds of murders and rapes. 'With God's help,' he recorded,[2] 'we cut them all down... big and little we killed 661.' Appalled, the tribes decided to claim protection from the Manchus. Horsemen galloped off to Beijing 1,500 kilometres away.

The Emperor, Shunzhi, authorised force. In March 1652, even before spring had unfrozen the Amur, two thousand Manchu and local horsemen attacked, but were defeated. Guessing he was about to have more trouble, Khabarov abandoned Boli, headed back upstream and sent for reinforcements.

By chance, Moscow, which had heard of Khabarov's brutalities, had already decided to recall him and take over. The Tsar favoured trade, not war. Russians wanted Chinese products, like cotton cloth for clothing, along with rhubarb, an ancient medicine for diseases of the liver, spleen and kidney. In 1654, Fyodor Baikov, heading a trade mission to Tobolsk, was dispatched to Beijing with a letter from the Tsar, arriving in March 1656, only to be stymied by protocol. The Manchu wanted Baikov to bow at the door of a temple, but Baikov had been ordered to bow only to the Emperor; the Manchu officials wanted Baikov to hand over his letter, Baikov said it was for the Emperor in person. After six months of stand-off, the Manchus expelled Baikov, saying he 'had not the slightest inkling how to show respect to a sovereign'. He returned to Moscow with good information and a good profit, but no diplomatic progress.

Meanwhile, another expedition had been mounted from Yeneseisk, two thousand kilometres to the west. The commander, Dmitri Pashkov, proposed to Moscow the founding of a town on the Shilka, which joins the Erguna at the northern tip of Hulunbuir to form the Amur. Moscow approved, and made Pashkov commander of all local forces. With 560 men, his march through the Siberian wilderness took two years. In 1656, having reached the Shilka, Pashkov turned up the Nercha River. Three kilometres upstream, he ordered his men to build a fort, the core of the new town of Nerchinsk, which will shortly become the focus of our attention. Without enough men to maintain an effective force, Pashkov retreated, leaving a small garrison in Nerchinsk.

In 1665, a new era opened. A Russian on the run after killing a local commander fled, with eighty-four other outlaws, to a village on the Amur belonging to Daurs. Known as Yaksa, it was run by a man named Albaza. Perhaps because the Russians were too brutal to resist, he allowed them to stay. The little colony thrived, and became known to Russians as Albazin (Albaza plus a Mongolian genitive to mean 'Albaza's Place'), though locals and their Manchu masters continued to call it Yaksa. Once established, the colony of outlaws begged Moscow for a pardon, which was granted. In 1671, Albazin was given a commanding officer.

The result: Albazin became the focus for the struggle for the whole Amur River and the lands on either side. Russia started a brutal colonisation – a 'wild east' equivalent of America's advance into its 'wild west'. This region was a no-man's-land of tribes, soldiers, deserters, runaway serfs and bandits. Local tribes were forced to pay tribute. The Russians, mainly young traders used to violence, seized local women for sex and slavery. Again, several tribes appealed to the Manchus for protection. But the Manchus, still busy imposing their rule on rebellious areas, could only advise the tribesmen to use 'scorched earth' tactics, burning and abandoning their fields, thereby depriving the Russians of supplies.

Traditionally, China had despised the 'Northern Barbarians', attempting to control them by excluding them with the Great Wall, by occasional invasions and by making allies of this or that tribe, 'using barbarians to control barbarians', to use a stock phrase. But the Manchus were 'barbarians' themselves. They had a natural connection with the other barbarian peoples, mainly the Mongols but also other tribes who lived close to the Manchu homeland. They were not about to abandon Yaksa/Albazin, let alone the rest of the Amur.

Once secure in the south, the Qing – the Manchus' dynastic name – could focus on the north with a new policy: occupy and protect. For a while, this was more theory than practice, because in 1661 the first Manchu Emperor, Shunzhi, died of smallpox and his successor, Kangxi, chosen because he had survived smallpox and would therefore be immune, was a boy of seven under the control of regents. Six years later, at the age of thirteen, he seized power for himself, and began one of the most illustrious eras in Chinese history.

A major problem was the north, where western Mongols were at war with eastern Mongols, some of whom considered asking the Russians for help, some the Manchus. The whole of what was then the Mongol borderland – Mongolia itself, Buryat Mongolia by Lake Baikal, Inner Mongolia and the far west (Zungaria) – was in the balance. The Emperor needed a secure border within which to assert his authority. For that he needed a peace treaty with Russia.

He did not have much to build on. The Russians had twice tried to establish relations, and had been rejected both times, because their envoys refused to comply with Chinese protocol. A third envoy managed to get a polite letter through to Kangxi, who sent a positive reply. Weeks later, his letter reached Moscow. Tsar Alexei set up an official mission, which reached Beijing in May 1676. Again, protocol was the stumbling-block. The mission head, Nicholas Spathar, made a number of sensible requests, asking about what languages to use, and suggesting exchanges of ambassadors, merchants, goods and maps. But then it all went wrong. An exchange of gifts was cancelled when Spathar refused to receive his gifts kneeling. Kangxi refused to answer the Tsar's letter because of Spathar's 'disobedience'. Manchu officials insisted Russia would have to admit inferiority, along with other unacceptable conditions. After three months, Spathar left, empty-handed.

Kangxi lost faith in the idea of peace, and sent an army of ten thousand troops to Aigun, a newly fortified river port thirty-five kilometres down the Amur from its confluence with the Zeya. With this as their base, the Chinese raided Russian outposts. By 1683, the lower Amur was cleared of Russian bases, and the Chinese could turn on the toughest outpost, Albazin, four hundred kilometres north of Aigun – upstream, against the current – and with a garrison of 450. In 1685–6, in what the Chinese still call the Battle of Yaksa, Albazin was besieged by the Chinese, abandoned by the Russians, destroyed by the Chinese and finally reoccupied by the Russians, with eight hundred men and twelve cannon.

Their work is still visible. The travel writer Colin Thubron was there in the 1990s, and used the present to evoke the past: 'They crowned the bulwarks where I walked with a long palisade, buttressed by corner towers, and skirted with a deep ditch concealing sharpened stakes. A raised gun turret turned their cannon in any direction, and the breastworks were lined with baskets of resin to illuminate night attacks.'[3] The Manchus responded with a siege, barring the river with boats and raining cannon fire from three lines of earthworks. Of the 826 invading troops, says the Chinese website Baidu, only sixty-six remained alive. But the siege continued.

Moscow got the message. Fighting for the Amur was not going to work. They sent envoys to prepare peace-talks. Arriving in September 1686, they asked Kangxi to raise the siege of Albazin. He did so, partially, promising a further reduction when the exotically titled Russian High Ambassador Plenipotentiary Fyodor Golovin arrived in Yakutsk in two years' time.

Talks about talks continued, with slow-motion exchanges of letters across Eurasia. The empires would meet in Nerchinsk, on a tributary of a tributary of the Amur, in the borderlands claimed by both powers. In Beijing, delegates were named, headed by one of the Emperor's uncles, Songgotu (minister for bodyguards), and a Han official, Tong Guogang (Beijing's governor). For the first time in history, China was about to negotiate with a foreign power as an equal. Kangxi, one of the most brilliant of Emperors, had the talent needed. In this many-sided war game, with his empire as the prize, he understood what he was playing with – soldiers, weapons, tribes, missionaries, merchants, rivers, cities, trade goods. He had a feel for tactics, too. He saw that if you want to win *this*, then you better be prepared to lose *that*.

His delegates felt themselves to be in a strong position, having held back the Russians and aware that Kangxi was favoured by the Mongols (mainly because, as Buddhists, they saw Kangxi as pro- and the Russians as anti-Buddhist). The officials wrote a confident note to the Emperor stating their intentions. 'The territories occupied by the Russians are not theirs, nor is it a neutral zone... The Amur has strategic importance which must not be overlooked.' In other words, they aimed to keep or take over land far beyond the Amur. 'If we do not recover the entire region, our frontier people will never have peace.'

Unfortunately for them, the Mongols of Zungaria, the last steppe empire and a growing power in the far west under their leader Galdan, chose this moment to invade Khalkha, present-day Mongolia. Galdan, ambitious to build an empire to rival the Manchus, saw that he could not do this with a nomadic culture. He encouraged his people to settle down and start farming. A Russian envoy reported that the Zungars grew wheat, barley, millet, rice and fruits, and that they traded with India, Tibet and China. Possibly, Galdan would seek help from the Russians, which, in the diplomatic game the Chinese were about to play, would be unacceptable. Kangxi had to move fast and carefully.

He urged his ambassadors to be flexible. If you insist on keeping Nerchinsk, he wrote, you will leave the Russians with no place to shelter. What then? They will feel threatened, and could turn nasty. 'You should try to retain Nerchinsk. But if they beg for it, you may draw the boundary along the Erguna.' But there was a deeper problem. Yes (to continue the gaming metaphor), the Chinese had the advantage of playing on home ground, because the local population favoured China, but his true agenda – peace and a border that both sides would respect – needed understanding on both sides. How was that to be achieved, given that neither spoke the other's language?

Kangxi had an answer. He often consulted the two Jesuit priests, the long-established Pereira and the new arrival, Gerbillon. Pereira was the key, having been invited to court in 1672, seventeen years earlier, because of his musical talent. Like Mozart, he could hear a tune once and write it down. He became the Emperor's music teacher, and the two played duets on the dulcimer, an instrument with strings struck with hammers. But he quickly revealed other talents. His Christian colleagues told Rome about 'his extreme dexterity in the handling of affairs... his moral virtues and prudence... his humility and love of poverty'. So he wrote in his diary. He was not backward in putting himself forward.

Kangxi knew that both men spoke Latin, and so surely did Christians on the other side, as well-educated members of the Russian élite. The priests would have told him about how to conduct international negotiations, which in Europe were based on the so-called Law of Nations ('Jus Gentium'), a body of customary practices dating from Roman times. This constituted a first draft of what is now called international law. Behaviour at high-level conferences was supposed to reflect innate and universal social values: treating people as equals, allowing them the right of reply, setting aside past hostilities, recording proceedings, keeping promises. Anger, browbeating, threats, denigration, insults – all these had to be avoided, a difficult task for mandarins who considered themselves the pinnacle of civilisation. Kangxi had the wisdom to see that he could assure peace with Russia only if old attitudes changed. The two priests would be just the people to bridge the cultures, oversee fair negotiation and produce a Latin version of the treaty acceptable to both sides. This could best be achieved on China's edge, away from its traditional culture and prejudices. His deeply conservative officials would not approve, but so what? This was the Emperor's decision. Discreetly, avoiding all publicity, he gave the two priests clothing and gold-embroidered saddles, and urged his uncle, Songgotu, to look after them just as he would the Emperor himself.

## INTO THE HEART OF ASIA

When it left in mid-June, the expedition was more like a migration than an embassy trip. Nine top officials, the two priests and 1,400 others – troops, servants, cooks, grooms and more, with their horses (which with spare mounts numbered about four thousand), sheep, oxen and camels loaded with tents, two boats, nets for fishing and provisions for five months and a journey of 1,500 kilometres, one way.

Two weeks and 325 kilometres later, they were in Mongol territory, in midsummer, at Dalai Nur ('Great Lake'), a lake much larger, deeper and lusher than it is today. Pereira noted that 'it contains such an incredible quantity of fish that it looks like a school of sardines', or 'like ants on an anthill'. When some of them went fishing, using the nets and boats, they caught so many fish that they could not pull the nets into the boats and had to wrestle their catch to the shore.

Northwards, on the edge of the Gobi, it got tougher. 'These regions are wastelands,' Pereira wrote. 'Almost completely covered in sand and without inhabitants. For thirty or more leagues at a time, we saw only a few tents of shepherds tending their sheep, horses and cows, from whose milk they draw their poor subsistence.' Not entirely a wasteland, though, because they saw white-tailed gazelle by the thousand.* They organised a hunt, circling in to trap and shoot as many as possible with bows and arrows, but could get only a few of these athletic animals. Moving on at twenty-three kilometres a day,** in mid-July they crossed the Kherlen River, flowing 'quietly and smoothly' between its treeless banks south-west of Lake Hulun.

At this moment, Pereira makes his first mention of the Erguna, which will play an important role in the coming negotiations with the Russians. But he makes a mistake. He says, 'After leaving the lake, the Kherlen River continues its course under the name of Argun [Erguna].' No, it doesn't. The Erguna flows from the east, makes a sharp bend just fifteen kilometres north of Hulun, and then heads away north-east. Well, in fairness, he didn't have GPS. It is hard to do geography on horseback, relying on reports of places you cannot see.

As they approached the edge of the grasslands, the going got worse. It rained. In a flooded river, horses trying to cross on a mat of willows got stuck in the mud and drowned. While the priests crossed in the boats, some of the entourage swam across naked. Others, preserving modesty, tried riding in their clothes, only to have them soaked or swept away. Provisions were lost, and horses panicked, throwing their riders to their deaths in the tumbling water. The mosquitoes were a plague. They drew blood from the animals, and 'tormented us to such a degree that those who were able were forced to make thin silk gowns with visors or hoods, which covered the heads like a net... I would say that this region could very well be called the kingdom of mosquitoes.'

A week from their destination, messengers began to travel back and forth between the Russians and the Chinese. Teams of several hundred went ahead to cut back bushes and lay branches to make a decent surface

---

* There are still many in eastern Mongolia, but none in northeast China.

** This was average for a royal procession. Kublai Khan's overnight stations between Beijing and Shang Du (Xanadu) were about this distance apart. See Chapter 6, p. 141 and note 2 p.352.

over the mud. Now they were in the forested hills of southern Siberia. Pereira was impressed by the otters and the elks.*

Then, as they reached the fast-flowing, clay-coloured waters of the Shilka,** ninety boats appeared. These vessels, manned by a thousand Chinese soldiers and another two thousand servants, and with cannon mounted on their prows, all assembled on the Amur as part of Kangxi's military build-up, were now hauled upriver against the current to bring his embassy new supplies. Numbering almost four thousand, with several thousand horses and camels, this immense throng camped on flat land opposite the mouth of the crystal-clear Nercha – Nipchu, as the Chinese called both town and river. They had been travelling for forty-nine days. The Russian fort almost overlooking the confluence of the two rivers had troops, but they were vastly outnumbered by the Chinese, a fact that underlay the Russians' nervousness over the next few weeks. That evening, the ambassadors and their senior officials dined on birds caught earlier. Musicians in the boats celebrated a full moon, answered by Russian trumpeters in the fort – an idyllic start, apparently, to negotiations.

Next day, 1 August, fifteen sheep and ten cows arrived as gifts from the Russian governor. No word yet from the ambassador himself, Fyodor Golovin, who had not yet arrived. On the second, a mini-embassy came headed by a 23-year-old. After being given a polite welcome, the young man asked icily if his hosts had come to make war, given the size of their force. He then suggested that both sides should be represented by the same number of officials and troops.

Until this point, despite the tough journey, there had been a sense of optimism. Neither side wanted to continue violence, both sides wanted

---

* He chose to use the Mongolian name, which he spells 'Kam dar gan', which is his version of the modern Mongol *khandgai.* Why did he bother? It has no significance in his narrative. The answer, I think, is that he loved such details. He was a natural ethnographer.

** Pereira calls it the Black River, assuming it is the upper Heilongjiang ('Black Dragon River') or Amur. Today, it is the Shilka, which joins the Erguna some four hundred kilometres north-east to form the Amur/Heilongjiang.

a treaty and, whatever the differences, both sides were positive. But in what follows a theme emerges – the loss and regrowth of trust, a crucial element in international relations.

That bureaucratic request for equality of numbers planted a seed of suspicion. The Chinese were puzzled. Why not just get on with it? We have ten days, they said, then we have to go. Winter is coming. Well, let's make it the seventeenth, said the Russians. Ambassador Golovin was due any time now. Agreed, but Chinese anxiety grew. It had already been two weeks, and that was just to the first meeting. Were the 'Moscovites' (as Pereira calls them) to be trusted, uncouth barbarians that they were?

More gifts came from the governor – milk, cows, vegetables. In the Chinese camp, suspicion grew. Perhaps the gifts were poisoned. Pereira sighed, picked up a radish, sprinkled a little salt on it, and ate it. The rest watched and waited. The act, in Pereira's words, seemed 'foolishly daring'. When he did not fall down dead, one of officials said, 'There is no deception,' and he too took a radish. The others copied him. As everyone ate, Pereira explained the need for trust in negotiations: 'One must have faith in the natural goodness of men.'

Days passed. Worries returned. The 'Moscovite' ambassador was too slow. The Manchu leader, Songgotu, wrote a letter, probably in the common language, Mongolian, wondering what the problem was. A reply came…

Let me interrupt for a moment. These events had already involved several letters and visits across the river. There would be many more. This was not an easy trip. To get from Nerchinsk, the messenger, probably with an escort, had to ride or walk the three kilometres to the Nercha's junction with the Shilka, which was some 250 metres wide with a strong current. They then had to either arrange a ferry or tackle the river on horseback, which meant at least a wetting, more likely a total soaking while hanging on to the horse. It was risky. Frequent downpours raised the water level. Already the Chinese had lost several men and horses, and there would be many more losses. Each crossing must have taken an hour or two, depending on conditions.

This particular letter was rather sharp in tone. The governor expressed surprise at the size of the Chinese delegation, and suggested they were a bit too close for comfort. Would they please move further away? To which Songgotu replied impatiently, directly to the messenger, that they had no choice – they needed pasture for their animals, and they were surrounded by rivers, swamps and mountains. Perhaps if the governor could suggest a better campsite, they could move. In a further exchange, the governor took the point. They could stay where they were, but trust retreated further.

Ambassador Golovin, a fat 39-year-old aristocrat, arrived, as the Chinese knew from the sound of trumpets and flutes, but he did not cross the river. Days passed. Then came not a visit or a start to talks, but a request to move some of the boats. The cannons on their prows looked threatening. Pereira thought the delay and this petty request were ploys to assert authority. The Chinese and Manchus were wary. Why did Golovin not send his Latin interpreter? What was going on? Clearly, trust was draining away ever faster.

On the twenty-first, progress: an agreement that both sides should have three hundred soldiers, with two stipulations by the Russians: only five hundred soldiers in the boats, only three hundred to disembark, and the boats themselves to be the same distance from the meeting place as the town. Songgotu agreed, but, next day, when the moment came, all of the eight hundred soldiers disembarked on the Russian shore – an obvious sign of suspicion, an obvious threat. Pereira wondered who gave the order. His question embarrassed Songgotu – who had a change of heart and asked Pereira for additional help as a negotiator. He and Gerbillon went to see Golovin. But trust had gone. Golovin said he had no confidence in any agreement.

Back on their side of the river, Songgotu and the other ambassadors said the Russian demand for fewer Chinese troops meant he was about to launch an attack. Pereira was appalled. 'Making myself surgeon to this disease, I said they should have confidence in the Moscovites and that the dispute about the number of soldiers was a question of honour not a plot.' To no avail: 'Everything, even my yelling at them, was unsuccessful.'

They refused point-blank to continue talks. Pereira was at a loss. They had come to make peace, and here they were on the brink of war.

He tried again, with fine words:

> Sirs, you must realise that the Moscovites are human beings endowed with reason and are not wild beasts. They are not so perfidious as under the pretext of peace to wish us harm. It would be an insult to the whole world and make us the laughing-stock of the world, if, after all the expenses, pledges and hardships, we returned not having opened the door on which we have knocked and not having met the Moscovites face to face after being in their home.

What would the Emperor say? 'It would not I think please him in the slightest' – an understatement designed to summon images of heads on poles and bodies torn apart by horses galloping off in opposite directions. Sensing victory, Pereira sealed it with melodrama:

> I offered to have the barrel of a Moscovite gun stuck into my ribs for the duration of the conference as a security against all risk, since if they have some evil design, undoubtedly, I, being the most exposed, will be the first to die.

Stunned silence, broken by Songgotu. He praised Pereira for his loyalty, experience and wisdom, and finished: 'I alone shall cross the river with him.'

That did it. Everyone followed, ferried over to make preparations. Tents were raised by both parties. The Russians put out a grand table and silk-covered chairs. The Chinese, having assumed they would sit on the floor in the Chinese style, decided they had to sit in the European fashion and set carpenters to work all night to make benches.

## TALKS START, AND STOP AGAIN

The next day, 22 August 1689, dressed in their finest robes, the whole delegation – two ambassadors, the priests, a hundred back-up staff, a body of soldiers – were ferried across the river, meeting up with their horses, which swam. The Russians paraded with equal pomp – troops marching to a band of flutes and trumpets, the bulky Golovin in furs and silks with his aides on horseback. At the main tent, all dismounted together and made their way inside. Top people sat, the Russians on their silk-covered chairs, the Chinese on their rough, impromptu benches, the two priests between them. Interpreters stood by, translating Chinese (possibly a bit shakily, since the main speakers were Manchu) and Russian into Latin, and vice versa. The Russian–Latin translator, Golovin's aide, was a brilliant Pole named Andrei Bielobitski, who had studied philosophy and theology in Kraków and then become Golovin's Latin teacher. As the go-between with Pereira, he would play an important role in what followed.

It was not an auspicious start. The Chinese were irritated by the Russian finery – their nice chairs and two fine silver cups – when they themselves had only lacquered wooden bowls for their tea. Barbarians were not supposed to have such things.

Lacking a chairman to manage proceedings, both sides began 'long useless disputations', reviewing past letters, expectations, insults and outbreaks of violence. This was not going as planned. Pereira, ignoring his lack of a formal position, interrupted and told his officials that they were wasting time, that the violence had been mutual, that they should move on, negotiate the division of land and secure peace.

Songgotu resumed by suggesting that the border should be right there on the River Nercha. Golovin said, in effect: no way, this area was Russian and the border should be the Amur.

Deadlock. End of proceedings.

The next day was exactly the same – the river crossing, the parade, the formalities, the proposal, the deadlock. To Pereira, these were opening gambits, maximum demands on which to negotiate. But back in their camp, the haughty Chinese officials, totally unused to opposition, said it was all over. Obviously, they muttered, the Russians didn't want peace. Better treat them as enemies, and go back to Beijing. For the second time, as Pereira said, 'war was practically declared'.

But, he insisted, neither the Emperor nor the Tsar wanted this! Golovin was only trying to fight his corner with normal negotiating tactics! This was all down to the inexperience of 'our ambassadors... Neither the Tartars [Manchus] nor the Chinese had negotiated in this manner before.' Don't make mountains out of molehills, he said. Don't confuse high-class people like these with ruffians. Some Chinese are thieves and drunkards, but that didn't mean that they all were. It was the same with the Moscovites. Don't despair! We can get this done! Again, the Emperor's uncle spoke up in support, persuading the others to let the priests do the negotiating.

Towards Pereira and Gerbillon, who were almost always together, Golovin was friendly and open to suggestions. Eager for clarity, he worked through his Latin translator, Bielobitski, to avoid misunderstandings. One matter Golovin wanted clear: they were discussing Mongol territory and the Mongols had resisted the Russian advance, so no Mongols were to be involved in these talks. Pereira agreed. As usual when great powers negotiate, lesser powers are excluded. The Mongols were to be crushed, or absorbed, or ignored.

Pereira, with Gerbillon, went back to the Chinese envoys, and reported his progress. Now, at last, they got down to the core issues. China wanted Russia to abandon claims south of the Amur. Russia wanted China to abandon claims to the west and north of the river. All this was proposed in exchanges of messages carried by the long-suffering Bielobitski back and forth across the river. All seemed set fair for another, perhaps final conference.

And then, in the conference tent on the twenty-seventh, it all went horribly wrong. The problem was Albazin. China wanted Russia to give it up; Russia refused. The fort was a red line for both, and amazingly no one had talked about it, each locked into their own assumptions. China had twice taken it and, having in their view kindly allowed the Russians back, saw it as rightfully theirs, so assumed that Russia would give it up. Russia saw it as their property temporarily 'loaned' to China. The ambassadors were eyeball to eyeball, and neither blinked. 'We concede nothing,' said Golovin, coldly. 'You ask too much.' The conference broke up. Pereira left with tears in his eyes, exhausted.

Back in camp, some Chinese were incensed at the failure. They made plans to cross with the whole army and blockade Nerchinsk, forcing compliance by threatening violence. Making peace by making war? It was crazy. But Pereira, like a good poker player, kept his cool. 'I still hoped the Moscovites would send people to look for us as they did not want to return empty-handed.'

He guessed right. He had just fallen asleep in his tent when he heard a yell from the Emperor's uncle: 'The Moscovites are coming!' Golovin had blinked. It was the Latin interpreter, Bielobitski, with startling news. The ambassador wanted a third conference. As Pereira learned later, he had been pressurised by the governor to 'deny everything' as a negotiating tactic, and realised he had made a dreadful mistake. Emotion had trumped reason. Now he had a proposition, which he would make in the morning.

Pereira, a great negotiator, at once seized on the change of attitude. Perhaps Golovin had decided to agree that the Russians would hand over Albazin. He had declared it to be a red line, and it really wasn't. But perhaps by the morning he would have regained his nerve. Deals are made when both sides are so exhausted that they will do anything to get the deal over the line. Pereira made one more push. The morning, he said, would be too late. The time for propositions was right now, in the middle of the night.

Bielobitski agreed to deliver the message, but added, 'Most Revered Father, assist us.' He was addressing Pereira as Christian to Christian, saying in effect, 'Let's work together.' He left, and Pereira was 'overcome with joy'.

Now what? His bosses had been determined on a river-crossing with their troops. They planned to meet up with some Mongol rebels and seize a dominant position in case of war. Now they hesitated. The ambassadors asked Pereira what they should do. That placed him in a quandary. He said he was just a priest; he was not authorised to make such decisions.

'I said that the Emperor had sent me only to negotiate peace, which had nothing to do with crossing the river.' Your Excellencies, he said, you have your instructions, so follow them. But how? What was for the best? They had no idea, and begged for his guidance. For almost an hour they argued, in an agony of indecision and wasted time.

Finally, Pereira saw the problem: they were scared of failure – a botched advance, a lost battle, a failed treaty. They knew that he, a man noted for his honesty, would tell all to the Emperor if asked, and the Emperor would blame them, and they would end up with their heads on posts. Their only escape was to make sure he would be to blame – in the event of failure. They could do this by refusing to make the decision, thus forcing him to make it. What a dilemma. To offer any advice would be to exceed his authority. And if he spoke, whatever he said might lead to disaster – deaths in the river, a battle, perhaps war, and goodbye to the treaty. And if he survived, would he get back to Beijing? If so, to what sort of a reception from his religious bosses and the Emperor? Then he Pereira glimpsed a way out. 'God,' he wrote, 'who is always at hand to help, came to my rescue.' Whatever happened, he assured them, *he would not tell the Emperor*. And 'with this, they were content'.

## DISASTER AVOIDED

The Chinese then did what they had decided. Leaving the priests behind in the darkness in case Bielobitski returned, a contingent of troops took boats, sneaked a few kilometres downriver, keeping close to the bank, crossed and set themselves up on a mountain overlooking the town. Back in camp, the dawn brought no sign of Bielobitski, so the priests followed the troops, escorted by a few horsemen. It had been raining heavily: we know this from Gerbillon, who recorded the weather every day. Crossing the swollen Shilka with horses, 'some persons and beasts perished, which is the usual loss in similar transactions'.

Meanwhile poor Bielobitski had arrived at the Chinese camp, found everyone gone, discovered their foolish plan, and followed them. Pereira, having caught up with the army, saw him striding along a mountain track and, guessing why he had come, ran to him in delight, 'asked him everything all at once', grabbed his hand and led him to Songgotu and the other envoys. Three things were instantly clear: 1. Bielobitski would have to report all this to his superiors; 2. If the truth came out – that the Chinese had mobilised their army to get their way – all would be lost; and 3. Bielobitski was eager to help.

If this were in a film, it would make a charming scene. I have slightly modified Pereira's words:

EXT. HILLTOP. DAY
Two hundred fully armoured soldiers part to allow BIELOBITSKI and PEREIRA through to join SONGGOTU.

BIELOBITSKI
(*to* Songgotu)
Why are you here?

PEREIRA
(*aside to* Songgotu)
Reply prudently. If you don't you put everything at risk.

SONGGOTU
(*to* Bielobitski)
We ran out of pasture. We are here to look for fodder.

BIELOBITSKI
In that case, why are you in armour?

SONGGGOTU

It is our custom. And... it's a mark of personal dignity...

(*emphatically*)

... indicating *no hostile intention.*

BIELOBITSKI

In that case, why occupy a high place in the mountains with all your squadrons?

SONGGOTU

The place is infested with Mongols. We don't know the country. To feel safe, we sent our troops on ahead to make a campsite.

It was not quite so dramatic, because Bielobitski was talking to Pereira in Latin and Pereira was translating into Manchu. Still, Bielobitski accepted these outrageous excuses with a straight face, and invited Pereira and Gerbillon back to his HQ to sort out details and resume the conference.

The Chinese, as usual, suspected the worst. It took Pereira an hour to convince them there was no risk, telling them that it was they, not the Russians, who were guilty of duplicity. Bielobitski listened, unable to understand a word.

No, no, said the ambassadors – Pereira treats them as if they were a chorus, speaking in unison – we cannot let you go in case they take you hostage and force you to make conditions we cannot accept.

At this, Pereira burst out laughing. If the Russians did that, he said, they would brand themselves as 'barbarians, unworthy of human treatment'. After an hour of such arguments, he had an idea: what if only one went? They agreed, and decided on Gerbillon, so that if he vanished Pereira could take responsibility. Off they went. Pereira and his ambassadors settled down to wait for his return, while Pereira berated them yet again for threatening the treaty and for their lack of trust.

Time passed. No doubt many dozed, recovering from so much tension and lack of sleep. At one point, Songgotu, still immovably distrustful, suggested a wager to Pereira: 'If the treaty is signed, I'll give you a good horse. If not, you give me a clock.'

'I don't have a clock.'

'Well, pay me back when you get one.'

'A good horse,' said Pereira loudly, so that the crowd, which he guessed numbered over a hundred, could all be witnesses. 'One that is worthy of your status.'

Songgotu agreed. To a round of applause and laughter, he added, 'I would gladly lose.'

After a few hours, Gerbillon returned, to everyone's relief, with a list of conditions for the next meeting. Fears dissipated. Pereira apologised, humbly and at length, for berating his colleagues. And everyone happily made their way back to camp.

## NEGOTIATING A CONCLUSION

Next day, the twenty-ninth, Bielobitski appeared to discuss protocol, the main issue being the need for equality. Once that was agreed, other details took three more days to sort out. Then came a major question of geopolitics. The Russians wanted to discuss a mountain range about six hundred kilometres to the north-east, the Stanovoys. The only thing anyone knew about these mountains was that they divided rivers flowing north to the Arctic from those that flowed into the Amur basin and the Pacific, which made them a 'natural' part of China – for the Chinese. Not so for the Russians. They wrote a stern note: 'If you rise up against us, we, confident in the help of God and in the justice of our cause, shall defend ourselves to the limit of our energies.' The Chinese insisted. They had more troops, and Russia had no stomach for yet more arguing. Besides, the Chinese had a point – Manchuria was the homeland of China's Manchu rulers, and its minorities (Daur, Ewenki, Tungus and Mongol) already paid tribute to Beijing. The Russians relented. The Chinese got their way. They would hold on to areas north of the Amur, including the much-contested Albazin.

By now, both sides saw the end in sight. The two priests and Bielobitski spent four days and nights almost without sleep, 'translating at night what was conceded by day'. Both sides saw them as 'angels of peace'. One last back-and-forth, applauded by their guards as if they were finishing a marathon, and the deal was done. On 6 September, 'the whole night was spent in merrymaking', with lights and lanterns burning in the camp.

Well, not *quite* done. Next day, even as the Chinese delegation approached Nerchinsk for the signing, the Russians dithered over the final versions and the number of copies and who should sign which ones and in what order. It began to rain. Golovin sent the Chinese ambassadors a tent, with a polite apology. To Pereira, the delay was beyond belief. To quell any return of old suspicions, he broke away, ran to his team to urge patience, then ran back, resting to regain his breath, before reporting to Golovin. He was, he said, 'the doctor of two patients, one impatient, the other sickeningly slow'. A final sprint, and Pereira, panting and sweating, urged the Chinese forward, slowly, so that their approach would inspire the Russians to finish their last-minute fiddling.

Still, there was a question of seating. Knowing his people had been embarrassed by their wooden bench, Pereira suggested that the Russians too sit on a bench instead of their silken chairs. Golovin understood. To make all equal, he arranged a round, rug-covered table, with benches, and, at Pereira's suggestion, stepped outside to welcome the Chinese in. Two ambassadors, five officials and the two priests sat, with nine Russians.

Now that they saw the two copies – in Latin, the official version – another dispute arose, another delay. At the top were the names of the two rulers, Tsar (Peter the Great) and Emperor, in that order. It was surely an insult to place the Emperor in second place, muttered a Chinese official. No, said another, it's OK, because we all know our Emperor is in fact supreme.

Dusk was falling. Candles were lit. Then both copies were read out loud, to compare them, an exercise that went over the heads of most, since only three knew Latin.

At last, came the signatures, the Chinese first on their copy, the Russians first on theirs. In the treaty's hopeful words, it promised 'perpetual peace' between the two empires. As proof to all, it would be engraved in stone in Russian, Chinese, Manchu and Latin, 'which shall be placed as everlasting monuments on the frontiers of both empires'.

It was over. Servants brought plates of sweets, wine, vodka and, to the delight and amazement of the Chinese, 'a white loaf of sugar from the Island of Madeira', quickly finished as they all took a piece to show friends back in camp. The Russian band played, the Russians sang, ambassadors embraced and at midnight the Chinese, by candlelight, crossed the river for the last time.

Next day was for rest, with an exchange of presents: among them, four watches and the two silver cups from Golovin, silks and one of the Emperor's decorated saddles from the Chinese. Golovin invited the two priests for a farewell meal. On arrival they saw about a hundred Mongol prisoners, taken when the Russians put down the recent rebellion. That gave him an idea. China claimed many Mongols as subjects, and would claim many more in their newly acquired lands. A little generosity would act as good PR for Qing rule. Pereira asked Golovin to free them, a request to which he agreed. Pereira then did something extraordinary. He spotted a little Mongol orphan boy, and decided to adopt him. Again, Golovin agreed. Pereira gives no details, except to say he took the boy to Beijing, where he caught smallpox and died.

And now for the return. Songgotu sent a messenger ahead to tell the Emperor the good news and praise him for his wisdom in choosing the priests, 'to whom, we are not ashamed to say, we owe everything'. Praise, admiration and thanks rained down on them. Without them, there would probably have been no treaty, and what then? War, ignominy, ruin, disgrace.

The journey back was as hard as the coming. Crossing one river three men drowned, crossing another, no less than fourteen, with one 'unnoticed until his horse turned up rider-less'. A month later, they met the Emperor, who had come north to meet them. He was well prepared for them, with effusive thanks, holding a feast and even, in an unprecedented gesture, distributing food to the troops.

So to Beijing, a long debriefing for the two priests, and back to normal life with their Jesuit colleagues. The treaty was the high point of Pereira's career. His work was well rewarded in 1692 with an edict of toleration for the Jesuits. He worked on in China for another nineteen years until his death, and was given a splendid funeral by the Emperor.

The main result of the treaty was peace, but with many other consequences, some still with us today. It fixed a new frontier along the Erguna and Amur, handing Russia a slab of land the size of England to the west of the Erguna. This concession allowed Russia to continue colonising between Nerchinsk and the Amur, but banned her from the Amur itself and gave to China all Manchuria and all the land up to the Stanovoy mountains – an area the size of much of western Europe. What about those 'everlasting monuments', the quadrilingual stone engravings of the treaty supposed to be placed on the borders? Fine words, never instigated, soon forgotten. The Russian fort at Albazin was demolished, leaving the ruins that are still visible today.

The treaty also allowed China to focus on controlling the Mongols, particularly the Zungars. Their aggression against Mongolia in 1688 led Kangxi to invade, chase the Zungars out and extend Manchu rule to all Mongolia, in circumstances detailed below.

The treaty remained remarkably little known. In China, Kangxi, careful not to create opposition among his traditionalist officials, did not publish the text. No Manchu or Chinese secretaries took notes, so no accounts of the negotiations appeared in China. Kangxi's extraordinary flexibility did not influence his successors. China remained what it had always been: introverted, haughty, xenophobic. In Russia, the treaty was regarded as a defeat, best forgotten. Golovin wrote a report, but it has never been published. All this explains why there is so little written about the treaty and why its significance is not more widely appreciated.

But treaties are not easily forgotten. They lurk in their archives, until some ambitious leader wants to find a use for them. In this case, it would take two centuries for such a use to be found.

## How Mongolia gave itself away

Shortly after Nerchinsk, the Manchus acquired their next big slab of territory, Mongolia itself. This required no negotiations or force: it fell into Kangxi's lap.

As we know, a major problem for Emperor Kangxi was the advance of the Zungars, the last great independent nomadic power on the Central Asian steppe. Their ambitious leader Galdan aimed to build an empire to rival the Manchus and absorb Mongolia itself, divided as it was between three top khans and many lesser ones, united only by their Buddhist faith.

Buddhism had made spectacular advances from the early seventeenth century; Buddhism in its garish, gory Mongolian form, with its ferocious, corpse-trampling gods, its severed heads and flayed skins, not at all the gently pacifist Buddhism popular in the West. In a harsh world, prayers and propitiations offered the illusion of a way to the Pure Land of Shambhala, Mongolia's Shangri-La, from which the Universal King would emerge to slay all his enemies and bring a bloody peace. The growth of Buddhism resulted in a new institution headed by a Living Buddha, as in Tibet, a local equivalent to the Dalai Lama. His titles*

* His formal title was Jibzundamba (with various spellings, from the Tibetan meaning Reverend Noble One) Khytagt (Blessed One). He was the most senior 'incarnate lama', an 'emanation' (bodhisattva) of Vajrapani, protector of Buddha, as was Chinggis Khan, retrospectively.

are so complicated it is best just to call him the Bogd ('Holy') or Bogd Khan ('Holy King'). He and his seven successor incarnations, always 'discovered' in Tibet on the orders of the Manchu Emperors, acted as Mongolia's head of state. The people worshipped their Bogds, ignoring both their infamous immoralities and their prodigious wealth. In this unstable, borderless environment, the first Bogd became the social and political anchor, with a triple pre-eminence: the church conferred upon him fifteen pre-existences before his current incarnation; ordinary people believed he could work miracles; and he was honoured as a direct descendant of Chinggis Khan, the nation's founder.

Galdan's despotic rule and rapid expansion threatened everyone: the Manchus, the Russians advancing across Siberia and the Mongolians, mainly the élite – the Bogd, the lamas, and the lesser khans. It was the Zungar invasion of Mongolia in 1688 that impelled Emperor Kangxi to negotiate with the Russians at Nerchinsk. While letters went back and forth between Moscow and Beijing, Zungar armies raced into Mongolia, taking the only solid structure in the country, the great lamasery of Erdene Juu, the ruins of which are the most popular site for today's tourists. Even as the Manchus and Russians continued their negotiations, Mongol élite abandoned their tents, 'their vessels and tools, their horses, camels and sheep, and fled, night and day alike… they [the Zungars] have forced nobles to surrender, set fire to temples and destroyed scriptures and images'.[4] The survivors fled south over the Manchu border, eager for the Emperor's support.

With the Treaty of Nerchinsk successfully concluded, the Emperor now had the Mongol nobles at his mercy. In exchange for chasing the Zungars out of Mongolia, an alliance with – and control over – the all-too-eager Mongolian nobility was his for the asking.

At the end of May 1691, some 550 of them gathered at a grand assembly in the religious and trade centre of Duolun – Dolonnur ('Seven Lakes') in Mongolian – near Xanadu. They were joined by the forty-nine princes of the 'banners' (roughly the equivalent of counties) of Inner Mongolia, which were already under Manchu control. The Emperor arrived from Beijing, and received the submission of the nobles in a pavilion in front of the city gates. There followed four days of feasting, games and military exercises, after which the Emperor left.

That was it, the end of Mongolia's independence for the next 220 years.

By the Convention of Dolonnur, Mongolia fell completely under Manchu control. It was divided initially into thirty-four banners, all under one administrator, though the nobles all retained their titles and positions. All banners were responsible for their many festivals, like the annual Naadam, games at which the men competed at riding, wrestling and archery; the khans received lavish dispensations of impressive new Manchu titles; but in terms of real power, the nobles were impotent.

If you ask what happened in those 220 years, the answer is basically: sheep, horses and subservience. Most of the population of about half a million tended flocks, their only form of sustenance and wealth, though they did so on behalf of an overlord. The other main occupation – for young men – was soldiery. The Manchus kept Mongolia pickled socially and politically so that they could have an endless supply of soldiers for their army. Over the coming decades, tens of thousands were mobilised, animals by the hundred thousand were requisitioned. As Charles Bawden writes, Mongolia became

> a frontier province of the Manchu empire... organized on feudal-military lines, so as to constitute a reserve of mobile soldiery ruled by hereditary princes bound to the Manchu royal house by a system of hierarchical ranks and titles, by salaries and rewards, and by marriage alliances.[5]

For most Mongolians, cut off from Russia by a string of Manchu frontier posts, the major change was the presence of Manchu and Chinese traders. Despite an official policy to keep Mongolia for its herders, commercial interests ruled. 'Chinese merchant houses were able to overrun defenceless Mongolia to the extent that the whole country was in effect mortgaged to them during the two centuries of Manchu domination.'[6]

Two nationwide uprisings, in 1756 to 1757, were inspired by a desire for vengeance against Chinese shop-owners, not the nobles.

This was a deeply conservative society, the nobles on top and commoners below, underpinned by Buddhism, the dominant Yellow Hat sect of Tibetan Buddhism which enjoyed universal popularity. Some claim that the Manchus encouraged Buddhism to undermine the warlike tendencies of the Mongolians. Not so: Buddhism was popular enough without the Manchus. Young men who became lamas recited texts not in Mongolian but in Tibetan, as incomprehensible to most of them as Latin to Catholic countryfolk in medieval England. Many at all levels owned slaves: prisoners-of-war, the families of criminals, those in debt, daughters sold by poor families. No one talked politics, no one spoke of independence. In Europe and America, intellectuals were writing about science and debating revolution. Had any of them come to Mongolia, they would have despaired.

So much for the eighteenth century. The nineteenth wasn't any better. 'There can be few blanker pages in the history of the civilised world than the story of Mongolia in the nineteenth century,' writes Charles Bawden. 'Nothing of international significance occurred.'[7]

Significance would come only in the early twentieth century, in a blur of fast-moving events.

Plastic tanks keep watch over the Chinese side of the Khalkhin Gol battleground.

# PART IV

# AN AGE OF TURMOIL

*After Nerchinsk, for almost two centuries, the Russo-Chinese border seemed settled. Not so. As Manchu rule faltered, Russia advanced, seizing back lost lands and joining Western powers to rip China apart. In the early twentieth century, the new Soviet Union moved in on Mongolia, while Japan seized Manchuria, a step towards empire in the heart of Asia. In 1939, as world war loomed, Mongolia became the site of a crucial, but little-known battle in which a Russian and Mongolian army killed Japan's ambitions, with worldwide consequences. Mongolia, now a Soviet satellite, remained nominally Chinese, until it voted with one voice to reject its old master. That left the frontier to be stress-tested by the two superpowers, almost to the point of nuclear war. As its economy boomed in the 1980s, China began to tighten its hold on its northern minorities. Beside the Uighurs of Xinjiang, two other peoples, the Ewenki and the Mongols, endure enforced integration – one of many issues that may again threaten stability in this unstable region.*

*Nikolai V. Muraviev*

*Count Nikolai P. Ignatiev*

*Marshal Khorloogiin Choibalsan*

*These three – two Russians and a Mongolian – were responsible for depriving China of territory the size of western Europe.*

## CHAPTER 10

# How China lost half an empire

UNDER THE MANCHUS, CHINA'S EMPIRE WAS GROTESQUELY big, ballooning out in the late seventeenth century, when the Treaty of Nerchinsk and the Dolonnur Convention gave them about 2.5 million square kilometres of Inner Asia, half the size of all Europe if you exclude European Russia. Three hundred years later, they had lost what they had gained. This chapter explains how that happened.

### Losing the Amur watershed

Russia remained bitter over the loss of the territory between the Amur and the Stanovoys, a bitterness that led to another unexpected consequence of the Treaty of Nerchinsk. In 1839–42, in the first of two Opium Wars, Britain (or rather its proxy, the East India Company) forced the weakening Qing dynasty to sign the Treaty of Nanking, give up the port of Hong Kong and accept opium from India. Thereafter, foreign powers tore at China's flanks, seizing ports through which they could trade. Russia, Britain's great imperial rival, foresaw the opening of a new chapter in their struggle, focused on China. Britain's seizure of Hong Kong, along with other concessions, would give Britain a great advantage. British traders could and did get their products into Peking faster in sailing ships than the Russians using their painfully slow tracks across Siberia. The head of an Orthodox mission to China reported to Tsar Nicholas I that European goods were to be found in Peking 'in astonishing proportions', English cloth among them, of good quality, with prices cheaper every year.[1]

But in the far north, in 1844, Russia saw a chance to redress the imbalance. An expedition sent to study the permafrost ventured into the Amur basin, without seeking Qing permission. There were no objections, no Chinese garrison on the Amur. The river was apparently there for the taking, offering an intriguing prospect: a Russian fleet based on the Amur dominating the western Pacific, trading with America and cutting off British access to China.

Three years later, Tsar Nicholas I announced a new office of governor-general for Eastern Siberia, a role filled by a young major-general, Nikolai Muraviev, thirty-eight, a hot-tempered, gung-ho imperialist keen to lead his like-minded group, the 'Amurtsky', back to the Amur to reclaim all the lands held by Russia before the catastrophe of Nerchinsk. With his backing, a naval protégé sailed the length of the Amur without any Qing resistance and founded the town of Nikolaevsk, named after the Tsar. Muraviev proclaimed, 'Our destiny is down the Amur and into the Pacific,' where Russia would out-rival the British in the struggle to dominate China. He would realise Russia's imperial dream, in which the Amur would become the key to a new Far Eastern empire, a vast highway running from the heart of Asia to a Pacific fringed to the north by Russian-owned Alaska and on the far horizon by gold, in the form of a young and dynamic America. The Pacific coast, with the Amur as its gateway, would soon be the equivalent of America's far west. It was Russia's Manifest Destiny to rule from 'sea to shining sea', in Russia's case from the Baltic to the Pacific.

In 1854–6, Muraviev organised several squadrons – dozens of ships in each, including a steamer – bringing reinforcements to the mouth of the Amur, and also carrying several thousand colonists, the aim being to seize the whole area lost to China at Nerchinsk, ignoring or crushing objections from the Mongol, Nanai, Daur and Ewenki inhabitants.

In May 1858, Muraviev met Yishan, the Qing governor in Aigun, the port on the Amur that had been the base for the force that had attacked Albazin two centuries before. Speaking through a Manchu interpreter, Muraviev demanded a new treaty to hand back all the land taken by China in Nerchinsk. Yishan was not the best person to confront Muraviev. Born a Manchu royal, his princely jobs included the governorship of Canton (Guangzhou as it is now) during the First Opium War. Preferring parties to fighting and self-service to integrity, he surrendered the city and was downgraded, eventually ending up governing the backwater province of Black Dragon River ('Heilongjiang'), as the Amur is known in Chinese. In the event of trouble, he could expect no help from Beijing. These were hard times for the Qing, who were losing the Second Opium War (1856–60) against Britain and France, and simultaneously fighting to put down the Taiping Rebellion, a fifteen-year civil war in which millions died. So his objection to Muraviev's demand had no effect, except to make Muraviev lose his temper. The Russian gave Yishan twenty-four hours to accept, stormed off to his flagship and ordered a gunboat to fire mock fusillades throughout the night. Yishan turned to jelly, and signed the Treaty of Aigun the very next day, making the Amur the border and returning its whole northern watershed to Russia (including the future Khabarovsk, which had been the Manchu town of Boli for a century). The Qing government refused to ratify the treaty, but that turned out to be a minor problem. The Tsar was delighted and ennobled Muraviev by hyphenating to him the name of his acquisition, making him Count Muraviev-Amursky. The Tsar also celebrated his acquisition with the foundation of a new town at the confluence of the Amur and Zeya, named Blagoveshchensk: 'The City of Good News'.

Two years later, Moscow followed up with the next logical step – to complete the reversal of Nerchinsk by grabbing northern Manchuria, thereby giving Russia ownership of all lands to the Pacific. The man given this task was Major-General Nikolai Ignatiev, a fast-rising 28-year-old who had worked in the Russian embassy in London and was now, despite his youth, ambassador in Beijing. Here, among his diplomatic acquaintances, he included James Bruce, 8th Earl of Elgin (the son of the one who stole the Parthenon's marble statues), the British 'Ambassador Extraordinary', who had just arrived to conclude the Second Opium War by imposing terrible punishments on the Qing government, among them the burning and looting of the Old Summer Palace and the cession of Kowloon (part of Hong Kong). Ignatiev's chance came in October 1860, when Lord Elgin invited him to attend the signing of the treaty, known as the Convention of Peking, by Elgin, the French ambassador Baron Gros and the 27-year-old Manchu representative, Prince Gong, brother of the Emperor. After the signing, Ignatiev presented Prince Gong with a Supplementary Treaty applying to Russia alone. Overriding everything in the Treaty of Nerchinsk, it also gave Russia a part of Kazakhstan, allowed Russian traders into Urga (the Mongolian capital) and Kashgar (Xinjiang), agreed to consulates in both, and – crucially – handed 'Chinese' Manchuria to Russia. At the flourish of a princely pen, Aigun was ratified and Russia took over territory the size of much of western Europe. The original Russia-to-China transfer in Nerchinsk had been much more trouble. Never in the course of human history had so much been acquired so fast and so easily, and with no loss of life. Ignatiev allowed a minor concession: the Qing government could continue administering sixty-four Manchu villages to the east of the Amur, with consequences we will see shortly.

For Russians, the Amur and Manchuria were open. At the same time as American colonists were heading west, Russians headed east, to a rougher, tougher land than California. For a brief heyday, Nikolaevsk at the mouth of the Amur became the Paris, the San Francisco of the Pacific, where traders built grand houses and their wives bought French pâtés, only to fade again when the Amur's sandbanks and shallows and winter ice proved too much for most ships. But Russia was at least a permanent presence on the Pacific coast. With the influx of Russian colonists, a small Chinese town, Haishenwei ('Sea-cucumber Bay', after the sausage-like creature that is eaten worldwide) became the core of a new Russian port, Vladivostok ('Ruler of the East').

## A MASSACRE ON THE AMUR

But conquest imposed no peace. The threat of violence had been smouldering for four decades, since European powers, Russia among them, began seizing bits of China in the wake of Britain's easy victory in the Second Opium War. Russia, as ambitious as ever for more empire on the Pacific, leased the Liaodong Peninsula from China in 1895, giving them direct access to the Yellow Sea and another outlet to the Pacific. Fearing that Britain was about to seize it, they secured the peninsula for themselves in 1899 by agreeing with Britain that they, the Russians, could in effect do what they liked north of the Great Wall, which included completing the Chinese Eastern Railway across north-east China to Vladivostok. A Chinese diplomat decried this, with good reason, as the 'partition of China'. The result was a wave of pent-up fury from fanatical peasants, known as 'Boxers' by the British because, as part of their secret rituals, they performed calisthenics that would – so they believed – make them invulnerable to bullets. By late May 1900, they were in Beijing, aiming to kill 'the foreign devils' and destroy their property. They burned the Russian Orthodox Mission, murdered 220 Orthodox converts, turned one priest into a 'honeycomb' with their spears and tore the heart out of another. Joined by Qing government forces, they then besieged the British and other legations for two months before being driven off by an international brigade. Fifty-five foreign soldiers and thirteen 'foreign devils' died, along with an unknown number of Boxers. The story made international news.

It is told, with many inaccuracies, in a Hollywood movie, *Fifty-five Days in Peking* (1963).

The consequences in Manchuria were far worse, and far less known. In June,* the Boxers, backed by Qing army officers, seized some thirty Russians working on the Chinese Eastern Railway, and killed many of them, carving crosses on their chests in their anti-Russian, anti-Christian fervour. Qing soldiers ripped up tracks, hoping this would lead to the total destruction of the line. A Boxer-Qing force on the banks of the Amur opposite Blagoveshchensk bombarded the town with artillery for two weeks.

The attack provoked a brutal reprisal in the town. After it ended in a cross-river assault by Russian troops, the governor, Lieutenant General Konstantin Gribsky, gave orders for all of the Chinese 'north of the Amur' to be 'thrown across the river'. His forces rounded up at least 5,500, perhaps as many as 8,000, marched them five kilometres upriver to fast-flowing narrows some three hundred metres across and drove them at gunpoint and bayonet-point into the river, fully clothed, regardless of whether they could swim. Those who refused were killed with sabres and axes. One Russian officer later recorded, 'The execution of my orders made me almost sick, for it seemed as though I could have walked across the river on the bodies of the floating dead.' Only a few, less than two hundred, made it across. Gribsky's troops then turned on the sixty-four villages scattered over several miles to the east, and killed another seven thousand. Together with the five thousand possible deaths in the river, this was perhaps the grimmest example of ethnic cleansing before the First World War.

In Moscow, the government was jubilant at the opportunity the massacre offered. Three weeks later, a Russian army of 100,000, with reinforcements steaming east along the Trans-Siberian Railway, drove the Qing force over the border under the command of Pavel von Rennenkampf,

* The dating of these events is tricky, because sources vary in their use of Old Style (Julian) and New Style (Gregorian) calendars, which differ by eleven days. Here, I avoid the issue by not specifying dates.

a Baltic German by birth, with a genius for fast and brutal military actions. 'The smell of death and putrefaction filled heaven and earth,' wrote a Chinese eyewitness.[2] By the end of September, Manchuria was under Russian control (though not formally annexed). In Philip Snow's words, the 'Tsarist armies had finally sliced off the first panel of the great triptych of territories that constituted the Sino-Russian borderlands'. The occupation launched with high hopes and an influx of all things Russian, ground to a halt on the rocks of the Bolshevik Revolution, and sank (for thirteen years) when a newly expansionist Japan seized Manchuria in 1931.

Today, the Blagoveshchensk Massacre still festers, on both sides of the border, each with its own version. Colin Thubron describes the display in Blagoveshchensk's museum, where there is no hint of an atrocity, only a painting of Russian troops in staunch defence of their town, while 'local administrators have forbidden Chinese guides from delivering their own version'.[3] But in Aigun itself, now the town of Aihui, forty kilometres down the Amur from Blagoveshchensk, another museum recalls the massacre from a rather different point of view. Entry is by passport, for Russians are not allowed in. A gory diorama recalls the terrible events of July 1900 and a memorial records the names of all sixty-four villages east of the river.[4]

But outside the museums, lips are sealed. Chinese resentment and Russian satisfaction are both screened by the demands of trade, tourism and politics, with the massacre 'excluded [as Thubron says] from the dominant political narratives of Sino-Russian eternal friendship'.

## THE ROOTS OF MONGOLIAN (SEMI-)INDEPENDENCE

The Amur and Manchuria were only a part, under half, of the losses suffered by the Manchus. The other larger half – the third part in Snow's triptych – was Mongolia, where, if you recall Bawden's words, nothing of international significance had happened in a century. Now, suddenly, a great deal happened all at once – the collapse of the Manchus, independence (partial, twice), the Chinese out, the Russians in, all of these being local variations of the revolutions that were tearing the outside world apart.

Inside Mongolia, there had been changes, not for the better, so bad indeed that a political theorist might have predicted imminent revolution. Inequality increased, those without animals increased, banditry became more common. Vagrants gathered in poverty-stricken townships, doing odd jobs for Chinese merchants. Taxation, raised to pay the interest on exorbitant government loans, became punitive. The capital, Urga,* was a place of mean wooden houses and desolate *gers*. Near the centre were the only two large buildings, the Bogd's palace, the only two-storey house in the city, and the Gandan monastery, the focus for pilgrims from all over Buddhist Asia. It was a place without a hint of charm. Lamas roamed the streets ringing bells to attract anyone who would pay to hear a prayer. There were no sewers for the 25,000 inhabitants. Human waste was simply tossed into the earthen streets. In winter the shit froze solid, but from May to September the smell was execrable. Outside Urga was Beggars' Hill, where a poor lama known as the Boneman was employed to remove the bodies of those who starved to death.

Morally and materially, the lamaist church was 'the curse of Mongolia', in Bawden's words. All sense of spiritual vocation had long since vanished. Young men became lamas to avoid conscription and to live on charity. The 1,700 monasteries supported some 113,000 lamas in 1921, roughly one son per family, making the population slaves to their own piety and superstition. The costs were exorbitant. In 1820, it took 539 men and 1,600 horses to escort the fifth Incarnate Lama from Tibet, where all new incarnations had to be discovered. Venereal disease

* The Russian name, from the Mongolian *örgöö*, 'tent residence of a high-ranking person'. Mongolians called it Ikh Khuree, 'the Great Lamasery'. It became Ulaanbaatar ('Red Hero') in 1924.

affected practically every adult, according to Swedish nurses in 1924. (The population of Urga was predominantly male: lamas were all men and the Chinese merchants seldom brought their families, so prostitution flourished.) Lamas, who helped spread the disease despite being nominally celibate, said the scourge was due to sins that could only be cured by expensive and totally futile rites. They were of no help to the obese, syphilitic eighth Bogd, the Incarnate Lama at the top of this diseased society. Religious festivals brought a surge of pilgrims and traditions: *gers* by the hundred, dancers with skull-masks and demon-masks, the smallpox god with a face of buboes, plays in which monk-actors became battling demons. But masks, dances and chanting monks could do little to disguise the grimness of lives under a foreign power, a rapacious priesthood and a hidebound élite.

How in these dire circumstances could Mongolia ever find freedom? She couldn't, not yet.

## YEARS OF HORROR

An opportunity for change came at last from the troubles facing Mongolia's masters. The Qing were heading towards collapse. An attempted comeback by the Qing in Inner Mongolia, involving a plan for massive colonisation, succeeded only in inspiring large-scale resistance. In Mongolia itself, a new administrator ('amban') proposed opening new mines and brought in troops, planning to import tens of thousands of colonists to take over five thousand square kilometres, make Mongolia part of China and prevent Russian advances. The Bogd asked the Russians to back Mongolian independence, but they were not yet ready for such a bold step.

On 1 December 1911, the Bogd took action on his own account, throwing out the amban and declaring independence with himself as leader. Mongolia became a theocracy, a state with a religious head. The

Bogd Khan, 'dual ruler of religion and state' as he now styled himself, was enthroned almost a month later along with his consort, as the 'mother of the nation'. The ceremony was in a vast *ger* covered with imperial-yellow silk and blue designs to recall the Mongol deity, the Blue Sky. A new age seemed to be dawning. Qing soldiers and merchants fled. In China, Nationalists drove the Manchus out and proclaimed a new republic on 1 January 1912. The last Qing Emperor abdicated a month later, and China sank into a decade of anarchy, with warlord rivalling warlord and clique against clique.

This should have – might have – marked the beginning of real change in Mongolia. It didn't, because it was initiated by the élite, not the common people. Society remained as it had been, without effective medicine, without schooling, without industry and with Buddhism reinforced. No other nation recognised Mongolia.

Independence receded further in 1915, when Russia, China and Mongolia met in the border town of Kyakhta – Buddhist temples on one side, Orthodox churches on the other, between them low wooden houses – and, under Russian pressure, agreed that Mongolia – *Outer* Mongolia, that is, with Inner Mongolia handed to China – should be granted nothing more than autonomy under Chinese suzerainty. With the outbreak of the Russian Revolution in 1917, the final hope of Russian support vanished. The only 'support' forthcoming would be from either the Bolsheviks or the counter-revolutionary Whites in the ensuing civil war.

China's dominant party, usually referred to as a 'clique' because it had no democratic mandate, saw an opportunity. A diminutive Japanese-trained warlord named Xu Shuzheng, known as 'Little' Xu to distinguish him from 'Big' Xu, China's president Xu Shichang, led a private army of two thousand into Mongolia, aiming to re-annex it. On 15 November 1919, under duress from Little Xu, parliament 'requested' the revocation of autonomy and Little Xu became the country's supreme leader. On 19 February 1920, the Bogd Khan and his officials swore humiliating allegiance to the Republic of China, kowtowing to Little Xu, a portrait of Big Xu and the Chinese flag. A nine-year experiment was over: China was back. Had it all been for nothing?

For a while, even worse than nothing; that same year, a ruler from hell appeared to challenge Little Xu. Baron Roman von Ungern-Sternberg – the Mad Baron, as he was known – was a psychotic, anti-Semitic, anti-Bolshevik Estonian aristocrat with a drooping moustache and staring eyes. How he came to be involved in Mongolia is a long story, one that explains much about Mongolia's escape from China's grasp and her fall into that of the Soviets.

The baron was as eccentric as his German name, which means 'unwilling star-mountain'. In fact, the 'Ungern' – as he is widely known – derives from 'Ungarn' (Hungary), one of his family's several homelands.[5] A citizen of the Russian Empire, to which he was fanatically dedicated, he was what we would now call a conspiracy theorist, for whom the world order – aristocrats above, peasantry below – was threatened by occult forces, in particular the Jews. Having graduated from a military academy, he joined the Cossacks, who were bandits in the service of the Tsar guarding the borders of the region occupied by the Buryat Mongols. But Ungern was too prone to drunken rages for a career as an officer. A scar on his forehead was from one of his many duels. Out of a job, almost destitute, relying on hand-outs from his family, he was saved by the First World War. He enlisted, and was sent to the Eastern Front, where he fought the Germans with death-defying ferocity. Tens of thousands of Russians died, but he survived unscathed, a hero with several medals. Violence, brutality, cruelty and many other evils: for him, these were virtues. After two months in a military prison for assault, he was transferred east, to Manchuria. By 1918, Tsar Nicholas II was history, and the Bolsheviks – the 'Reds' – were seizing power nationwide in a brutal civil war against their enemies, the 'Whites', several disparate groups of monarchists, anti-semites, republicans, social democrats, nationalists and numerous eccentrics, united only by their virulent anti-Bolshevism.

Travel was by train, along the Trans-Siberian Railway, which divided on the Manchurian border, one line skirting the nominally Chinese territory to the north, the other crossing it directly. The railway was a major piece in a kaleidoscope of rival factions that, besides the Bolsheviks and their White enemies, included Japanese (colonising Manchuria), Czechs (ex-prisoners-of-war heading east, on a slow, epic journey homeward bound around the world), and Americans and British debarking in Vladivostok, aiming to help the Czechs and crush the Bolsheviks. Trains were mobile cities, with hospitals, brothels, theatres and opulent restaurants all run by ex-Tsarist employees, now available for the right price. Generals commissioned armoured trains with guns on their roofs. Prisoners were unwanted dross – shoved into railway cars, shunted into sidings and forgotten.

Based in Manzhouli, today's main crossing point between Russia and China, Ungern was close friends with a half-Buryat officer named Grigorii Semyonov, with whom he planned to raise a regiment of Buryats to destroy Bolshevism, restore the monarchy and see the return of a Greater Mongolia uniting all Mongols. In August 1918, they set up a new HQ in Chita, some three hundred kilometres east of Lake Baikal and two hundred kilometres north of the Mongolian border. With Japanese support, Semyonov became in effect 'Dictator of Trans-Baikal'.

Ungern, aged thirty-two, was his second-in-command, based three hundred kilometres down the track in Dauria, a station with a scatter of buildings named after the local Daur Mongols. He and his men looked after themselves by robbing Chinese merchants and acting as executioners of trainloads of 'Bolshevik' prisoners sent by Semyonov, turning the surrounding steppe into a butcher's yard of decaying corpses. Ungern was popular with his men. They liked his disdain for officers, his dirty clothes, his willingness to share loot without enriching himself. He took to opium, but was otherwise an ascetic, very different from Semyonov who had a dozen mistresses and turned a railway carriage into a harem, financing his dissolute ways with plunder. Semyonov tolerated Jews; Ungern wanted to exterminate them all. The two were drifting apart. Ungern was soon operating independently, with his own troops, which he called the Asian Cavalry Division.

It was not just these two who were drifting apart. Every anti-Bolshevik seemed set on division. Western Siberia was another would-be White nation under an ex-Tsarist admiral, Alexander Kolchak, whose army was holding back the advancing Bolshevik forces. He and Semyonov had much in common, but they loathed each other. And although both Semyonov and Ungern backed the idea of a pan-Mongol state, they disagreed on its nature: democratic (Semyonov) versus dictatorial (Ungern). Mongolians too were divided. A conference in early 1919 to promote pan-Mongolism in Dauria included Semyonov's people, Mongols from all areas and some Japanese backers, but it collapsed into violence, with Semyonov murdering the commander he himself had appointed. Though a failure, this outburst of nationalism would infect Soviet and Chinese agendas in Mongolia for decades to come.

By the summer of 1920, the Reds were near victory, the Whites doomed. Kolchak had fled to Irkutsk, and would be shot in February 1921. Semyonov could not hold out for long, but he later found sanctuary in Japan, remaining active in Japan's mainland colony of Manchukuo, until captured and executed by the Soviets in 1946. Faced by defeat in Russia, Ungern led his 1,500 horse-borne thugs into Mongolia, sending a secret message to the Bogd promising to defend him from Little Xu and restore the empire of Chinggis Khan. With Little Xu's troops alienating Mongols in an orgy of looting, murders and rapes, the baron looked like a saviour. To foil his plan, Little Xu placed the Bogd under house arrest in his European-style palace. Ungern's first approach failed to drive the Chinese from their stockaded base just outside Urga, and he retreated some three hundred kilometres east into Chinggis's homeland, the Khentii mountains for the onset of winter. He was back in late January, planning to take Urga and lay the foundations for a renewed Holy Asian Empire with the Bogd as its monarch. The first task, therefore, was to rescue the Bogd from house arrest in his palace, where he was guarded by 150 Chinese. This was done at night by a commando of fifty Tibetans, who crept through virgin forest on the nearby Holy Mountain – a strictly protected area since the eighteenth century – killed or scared off the guards and led away the Bogd, who was by now so obese he had to be supported on his horse by two sturdy Tibetans riding on either side. They took him to safety in one of his own monasteries, Manzushir, on the far side of the Holy Mountain, fifteen kilometres away (as the vulture flies, but forty-five by road).

That sealed Little Xu's fate. The next day, the Chinese officers fled, on horseback and in any of the few cars they could requisition, leaving the rank-and-file, some two thousand of them, in their poorly defended base at the mercy of Ungern's bloodthirsty troops. There was no mercy, only killing and looting that scattered the survivors into the frozen countryside, where they were hunted down by Ungern's Cossacks and Tibetans. Corpses littered the steppes, frozen solid, food for wolves and dogs. Three days of this gave way to the slaughter of any suspected Bolsheviks and Urga's few hundred Jews.

On 21 February, an auspicious day at the beginning of the Lunar New Year, the festival known in Mongolia as White Month, Ungern and the Bogd Khan together arranged for the khan's restoration. Streets were cleaned, new uniforms made, and Ungern was declared a reincarnation, a prince and a state hero. Monks chanted in procession to the main temple, followed by a carriage bearing the immense bulk of the Bogd Khan, with Ungern on a white horse behind him, showing the cheering crowds who was the power behind the throne. For Ungern, it was the beginning of a new era, of Heaven-blessed monarchy restored, monarchy being the core of his incoherent mix of Christian and Buddhist mysticism. A glorious future beckoned, a Greater Mongolia, a restored Qing dynasty, an end to Jews and socialists. For Mongolians, at this moment, he was the fulfilment of prophecies of salvation from the north, even for some a living god. For a few weeks, it seemed to work. Under his polyglot leadership – he spoke reasonable Mongolian and employed scribes to record his words in four languages (Mongolian, Chinese, Tibetan and Manchu) – Urga began to regain a semblance of normality.

But there was no normality. Ungern turned on Urga's few thousand Russians, any one of whom might be a Bolshevik. He set up a Bureau of

Political Intelligence under an alcoholic psychopath named Sipailov, who killed for pleasure and greed, enriching himself with the possessions of victims. No supplies came in from Russia and China. Down-and-outs of many nationalities lived by pillage, while Ungern stockpiled cash – Tsarist roubles, silver thalers left by the fleeing Chinese – and requisitioned animals by the ten thousand. By the summer, his popularity was down to zero, and he was consulting oracles about his future. 'I see the God of War,' muttered one little gypsy woman. 'His life runs out… Beyond darkness … I see nothing… the God of War has disappeared.'[6]

That June, he chose to challenge Fate with a new campaign, to confront the thirty-fifth Division of the Red Army at Kyakhta, straddling the border, two hundred kilometres north. It was the start of a long march to a miserable end. Ungern's four thousand ragged troops faced eight thousand hardened and victorious professionals. Ambushed in a ravine, his troops were scythed down by artillery and machine-gun fire. While Ungern tried to rally survivors, the Soviets, ten thousand of them, marched on to Urga, preceded by armoured cars and reconnaissance planes, where relieved crowds gave them a heartfelt reception.

Ungern and two thousand remnants fled south to the site of the old Mongol imperial capital, Karakorum, and sheltered in the nearby hills and swamps. Though he still terrorised his men with maniacal punishments, beating some to death, making others spend nights at the top of trees, he retained enough authority to lead his men north again, over the border, intending to rejoin Semyonov and start all over again. Along the way, they burned villages and slew any remaining inhabitants in case they were 'Reds'. They won a minor victory when they stumbled on another body of Soviet troops at an imposing monastery near Lake Gusinoye, just south of Lake Baikal, taking four hundred prisoners, of whom Ungern selected a hundred, randomly, as 'Reds' and had them shot. But ahead and above, in planes, were more Soviet forces. He saw that a further advance was useless, and turned with just five hundred exhausted survivors to make a slow ride back into Mongolia. What was left to them? Ungern declared they would head on south, magically avoid all Reds, cross the Gobi Desert and find sanctuary in the mountains of Tibet, a place of mystery where, he believed, old beliefs and practices survived.

This was too much. That night, a conspiracy of Russians formed, intent on killing him. The plan was to call him out of his tent and shoot him, but in the dark they got the wrong tent. When Ungern appeared from another tent, he assumed the conspirators were Reds, dodged a burst of inaccurate fire and vanished into the forest, leaving the conspirators to kill Ungern's two chief executioners. Meanwhile, Ungern retrieved his white horse, and found his way towards the conspirators, huddled in the dark, guns ready, scared witless by their own plans, muttering 'The Baron! The Baron!' at the sound of his approaching hooves. When he appeared, they were too paralysed by fear to act. He started to harangue them, yelling that Tibet was the only possible destination. Still, no one moved. The clouds parted, the moon revealed Ungern's wild features, and that broke the spell. One of them fired, followed by others, and all of them missed. Ungern spurred his horse away, stumbling at dawn upon a band of previously loyal Mongolians. Not loyal now: they bound his arms, put him on the baggage cart and set off, only to run into a contingent of Red cavalry. One of them asked the unshaven wreck in a filthy Mongolian *deel* who he was. 'I am Baron von Ungern-Sternberg,' he replied, deadpan. 'Commander of the Asian Cavalry Division.'

That was on 23 August.* A week later, Leon Trotsky, the war minister, announced his capture to the Moscow Soviet. Ungern, treated well as a vital element in Soviet victory, was taken by train to what is now Novosibirsk for trial. Journalists interviewed him. Crowds gathered at each stop to stare. In court, he made no excuses for his actions, since, as he had always said, his atrocities had all been sanctioned by military necessity and God.

* By the new Gregorian calendar, introduced in 1918.

The trial, held in a theatre in the city centre, handed down a sentence preordained by Lenin. The Baron faced a firing squad on the evening of the verdict, dying with no regrets.

## REAL CHANGE AT LAST

In hindsight, these grim events, though seared into the collective memory of Mongolians, were incidental to others that would define Mongolia's history from 1921 onwards. Here at last come the people and events that placed Mongolia in the Soviet sphere of interest and ended two centuries of Manchu-Chinese rule.

The people involved were not naturally Communist, for Mongolia, with its herding economy and lack of industrial development, was totally unsuited to a Communist revolution in conventional Marxist terms. No books on Communism appeared in Mongolian until 1925. These members of 'revolutionary clubs' were nationalists, from humble backgrounds. This is how radical they were: in a poster suggesting elections, they humbly addressed their demands to their oppressor, 'His Excellency Xu, who is endowed with all skill and wisdom'.

One of these amateur revolutionaries was a typesetter named Sükhbaatar, twenty-seven, who would become the greatest hero of the revolution and die at thirty. Another was Choibalsan, twenty-five, the son of a poor, devout and foul-tempered woman living in eastern Mongolia. As a teenager he ran away from a lamasery school and joined the Russian-Mongolian Translators School, later improving his Russian in Irkutsk.

On the advice of a Soviet agent, the conspirators formed the Mongol People's Party, a tiny Urga-based group that claimed to speak for the whole nation. They contacted the Red Army, which had just reached Irkutsk. In July 1920, with Little Xu and his thugs in control, the Bogd gave the party an appeal to Soviet authorities in Irkutsk. In it, he asked that the Russians drop the clause in the Treaty of Kyakhta stating that Mongolia was part of China and agree to send military and economic aid to help re-establish independence. This was a dangerous business, because they risked arrest by Chinese guards and the discovery of their treachery. In an incident soon to become legendary, Sükhbaatar hid the Bogd's letter in the handle of his whip (now in pride of place in the History Museum). Despite a thorough search by border guards, the letter was not found and he crossed the frontier with three others. Choibalsan and several more travelled separately. All journeyed on to Irkutsk in August, met Soviet officials and asked for aid. The top official, Gapon, asked them to write down what sort of a government they planned to establish. Sükhbaatar drafted an agenda: recover independence, make the Bogd a constitutional monarch, destroy the oligarchs. Three delegates were then chosen to go to Moscow to discuss Soviet assistance. Sükhbaatar and Choibalsan remained in Irkutsk to keep talking to Soviet officials and officers, while in Urga the Baron pursued his deranged dreams.

Meanwhile, plans for revolution advanced in Kyakhta, a town cut in two by the border, where Sükhbaatar arrived in November. His agenda was to raise an army and invade, recruiting more followers as he went. In just a few hectic weeks, he and his co-revolutionaries raised their army, staged the first party congress, set up a provisional government, defeated Little Xu's much larger (though demoralised) Chinese army fleeing from Urga and occupied the Mongolian part of Kyakhta, the first bit of Mongolian territory to be liberated in March 1921. Volunteers joined Sükhbaatar and attacked Chinese units. Red Army troops came in, mainly to crush White forces, but also to help the small Mongolian units take Urga in July. The baron was gone, hunted down, captured and executed. In September, the prime minister, Bodo, formally announced Mongolia's renewed independence, and two months later the new parliament declared Mongolia a republic.

Except that no one took any notice. China continued to see Mongolia as a rebellious province even as the Soviet Union tightened its control.

In 1924, when China recognised Soviet Russia, it was in exchange for the Soviets' recognition of Chinese sovereignty over Mongolia, a purely nominal statement that bore no relation to reality. In 1928, under Soviet pressure, Mongolia renounced any relations with the non-Soviet world, diplomatic, economic and cultural. Her isolation seemed as absolute as under the Manchus.

Soviet control visited upon Mongolia a new sort of hell, beyond anything she had experienced in the hell of 1920–1. The devil was now one of the authors of 'independence', Choibalsan, Stalin's creature, backed by the Soviet army and the KGB, eager to do his bidding. In the 1930s, fear of Japan, its influence seeping west and north from its semi-independent offshoot, Manchukuo, rose to a sort of hysteria. Choibalsan proved himself as ruthless as his master, eliminating all rivals in show trials that mirrored those in the Soviet Union. His main co-conspirator Sükhbaatar had died in 1923, possibly poisoned, possibly of liver disease, but anyway retaining in death his heroic status, as proclaimed by his horse-borne statue in Ulaanbaatar's central square. (The new Parliament blocks the square's north end, with its statue of Chinggis Khan enthroned in majesty. The square was once named after Sükhbaatar, but is now after Chinggis, hero of heroes.) Claiming to be the saviour of the nation in the face of the Japanese menace, Choibalsan unleashed a Stalinist Great Purge (1937–9), in which all eleven members of the praesidium died (two from natural causes, but denounced as traitors; the rest executed). From July 1937, with the help of Soviet security agents, Choibalsan turned on officials, lamas, Buryat Mongols, Inner Mongolians, 'pan-Mongolists' and 'Japanese spies', who were 'found' by means of torture and forced confessions. Over twenty thousand 'counter-revolutionaries' were executed, monasteries by the hundred flattened. Compared to Choibalsan, Ungern-Sternberg was an amateur. Almost none of the old guard from 1921 survived; almost all of the nation's top people died. At the heart of it all was Choibalsan's loyalty to Stalin, indeed his adoration, as exemplified by a saccharine ode sent in 1941: 'Thanks to Stalin's concern… into an uncultured land there penetrated the light of culture; black-eyed children made friends with pencil and paper; rosy-cheeked girls went to school. The high sky – our father; the vast world – our mother; the father of the people – Stalin.' Choibalsan and his Soviet aides ruled supreme, through the war, until his death from liver cancer in 1952, by which time Mongolia had cut its last formal ties to China in very odd circumstances, which we will get to at the end of the next chapter.

*Eastern Mongolia, August 1939: Choibalsan* (centre) *confers with Zhukov* (right) *before the battle. On the left is Grigori Shtern, Zhukov's No. 2, 'purged' by Stalin two years later.*

# CHAPTER 11

# THE MOST IMPORTANT BATTLE YOU'VE NEVER HEARD OF

## SIGNIFICANT, BUT LITTLE KNOWN

ONE SUMMER'S DAY IN 2009, I WAS IN MONGOLIA'S CAPITAL, Ulaanbaatar, in the crowded lobby of the grand, Socialist-era Ulaanbaatar Hotel, when the buzz faded to a sudden hush. Military men and police ushered the public back against the walls. In came the Russian president, Dmitry Medvedev (Putin having kindly allowed a four-year interregnum). He and his entourage immediately turned to a bench along a wall opposite, where half a dozen ancient men sat, dressed in loosely fitting uniforms, their chests laden with medals. Medvedev shook them each by the hand, tenderly, with obvious respect. Why? Aged about ninety, they were the last few survivors of a battle that was one of the most important but least known of the last century. That summer of 2009 marked the battle's seventieth anniversary.

Medvedev and the old men had gathered to commemorate the victory of Russian and Mongolian forces over Japan, or rather a Japanese army from the neighbouring puppet state of Manchukuo. It was the opening skirmish in the Second World War, and a very big deal for both Russia and Mongolia. For the eightieth anniversary in 2019, Putin himself came. *That* big a deal, and rightly so because it affected everything that followed in Asia and Europe. It is named in China and Japan after a nearby village, Nomonhan, and known in Mongolia as Khalkhin Gol (Khalkha River), after the river that runs north nearby.

Despite its significance, which I will spell out in a moment, it is remarkably under-appreciated in China and the West. One reason is that, for Westerners, it happened in a remote area at the wrong time – in the summer of 1939, which from the European and American perspective places it just outside the chronology of the Second World War. Second, for China, the site is a reminder that in the 1930s Manchuria, now part of China, was under Japanese control. Russians and Mongolians were fighting on the Chinese border, without Chinese participation. Until recently, this was considered an embarrassment, best ignored.

The site is still remote, more for adventure tourists than sun-lovers. But it has a major drawback: it is cut in half by the barbed wire and no-man's-land of the Sino-Mongolian border. The Mongolian half attracts groups of Japanese tourists and the occasional Westerner, drawn by a new museum and displays of military hardware. You could in theory explore the site in a day. In practice, travelling between the two would be such a nightmare I wonder if anyone has ever done it. You could take a northerly dogleg for four hundred kilometres along the frontier to the Russian border, cross into Russia, enter China via Manzhouli, then head south-east around Lake Hulun, assuming you have your visas in order; if not, you will have to go back to Ulaanbaatar (one thousand kilometres away) and take a direct flight to Hailar, if there is one, or possibly go to Hailar via Beijing. Once in Hailar, you drive 165 kilometres south-west, turn off the main road and head towards the border with Mongolia. A strange archway appears – two pillars in the form of immense rifles support a lintel of two model planes and a mock landing-strip. An electric bus takes visitors to a central area, with a dozen tanks, apparently real but in fact made of plastic, a huge bell hanging from concrete arches and a vast cubic building that when I was there looked like a morgue, but was going to become a museum. The Chinese, it seemed, were about to take the battle seriously.

Here is why they should:

1. It was the first major fight between all four elements of modern warfare – infantry, tanks, artillery and aircraft. It foreshadowed what was to come in Europe. Nothing on this scale had been seen before – no air battle like it until the Battle of Britain, no tank battle like it until Kursk in July 1943.
2. The Russian campaign was the brainchild of Georgii Zhukov, who later used his experience to engineer the defence of Moscow, Leningrad and Stalingrad, and ultimate Russian victory in 1945.
3. In the east, the battle put a permanent end to Japanese interest in securing a land empire in Central Asia, an empire that would have meant an end to Soviet control of Siberia and Mongolia.
4. Consequently, it turned Japanese attention to building an empire in south-east Asia. You could argue that the Russo-Mongolian victory at Khalkhin Gol explains why Japan bombed Pearl Harbor in December 1941, thereby opening world war in the Pacific.

Another way to understand its significance is to imagine the consequences if Japan had won. There were many disputes between Tokyo and local commanders in Manchukuo, for the so-called Kwantung Army in Manchukuo was a law unto itself. Its agenda was to take over Inner Mongolia (underpinned by control over the relics of Chinggis Khan), crack open Russian defences in Mongolia, break through to Siberia and advance until it could 'plant the Japanese flag on the Urals'. Supposing this had happened in 1939–40, imagine what might have occurred – no Soviet resistance to the Nazi invasion of Russia, the two great empires of Germany and Japan shaking hands across the Urals, the destruction and division of the Soviet Union, and a possible advance by Germany or Japan or both into British India. This speculation formed the heart of a fake document known as the Tanaka Memorial, supposedly authored by Prime Minister of Japan, Tanaka Giichi, in 1927. In fact, no Japanese original has been found. It first appeared anonymously in China, in

Chinese, in 1929 and then in English in 1931. Elaborating brilliantly on the agendas of Manchukuo leaders, it was taken seriously by many, and is still seen by some as a prediction that might have come true.

Other speculations come easily. We are dealing with one of the great what-ifs of recent history. With no Pearl Harbor to drag America into the war, it is easy to imagine events cascading into a different world: America staying out, the Japanese remaining on the Asian mainland, no atomic bomb to bring them to their knees, Chairman Mao failing to counter either the Japanese or his Nationalist rivals. Whatever alternative outcomes you imagine, a Japanese victory in August 1939 would have made the post-war world a completely different place.

## THE ROOTS OF STRIFE

To set the scene: these were chaotic times in Central Asia. No frontier was fixed. The various elements at play make three-dimensional chess look simple – Japan, its proxy Manchukuo, Mongolia, Mongolians in China, Russia, Uighurs in Russian-dominated Xinjiang, Nationalists versus Communists in China.

Here is a summary:

Japan had long-eyed Manchuria. This huge area – 1,200 kilometres wide and 1,500 kilometres from north to south; that is,1.8 million square kilometres, the size of France, Germany, Spain and Italy – had been Chinese, but with a strong Russian presence, which was replaced by Japan after Japan defeated Russia in 1904–5. Japan, busy building its industries and eager for a place among the world's great powers, wanted an overseas empire, both as a proof of status and as a source of minerals to fuel its new industries. Manchuria served both needs. Japan took it in 1931. The following year, the local Kwantung Army staged a coup and turned Manchuria into a separate state, Manchukuo ('Manchu-country'), often called a 'puppet state', though it acted almost independently of its nominal masters. Local officers had ambitions beyond anything contemplated by Tokyo, looking to expand into Inner Mongolia, Mongolia itself, Siberia, even the borders of Europe. Inspired by delusions of racial superiority and dreams of future conquest, Manchukuo was a clear threat to its neighbours: China, Russia and Russia's compliant ally, Mongolia.

In the second half of 1937, Japan used Manchukuo as a base to invade southwards, taking Beijing, Nanjing (with infamous brutality), Shanghai and Guangzhou, seizing much of Inner Mongolia and proclaiming a new 'Mongol Federation' in the name of Chinggis Khan. A local prince was to be made king. On the whole, Mongols liked the idea, welcoming the Japanese as liberators from Chinese rule. With China part-occupied, the rest remained contested by Mao's Communists and Chiang Kai-shek's Nationalists.

China's north-east was just one of several regions competing for Russian attention, Europe being one and China's north-west being another. There, in Xinjiang, Muslims had revolted under a twenty-year-old cavalry officer, Ma Zhongying, nicknamed Big Horse, who wanted to create an independent Muslim state. He was not alone. In 1933, other Muslims set up an independent Eastern Turkestan Republic, based in southern Xinjiang. Amid rumours that Japan was behind these independence movements, Russia was worried. If Japan took control, they would threaten Russia's Central Asian republics (Kazakhstan and the other -stans), perhaps even the oilfields of the Caspian Sea. Stalin struck, sending in two brigades of OGPU (secret police) troops, who crushed both independence movements – but promised to help them if they fought the Japanese. Two more uprisings – anti-Chinese and therefore possibly pro-Japan – were crushed by five thousand Red Army troops. With three hundred advisers in place to ensure access to Xinjiang's oil and minerals, Russian schools were set up and Cyrillic replaced the Turkic script. By mid-1935 Xinjiang was effectively a Russian colony.

In the east, the threat was obvious to Stalin. As he put it later, if a foreign power 'were to attack through Mongolia and the Trans-Siberian Railway, the USSR would be finished'.[1] His aim, therefore, was to build up Mongolia as a buffer-state against Manchukuo. A small force of two thousand Russian troops arrived in 1935. Two years later, he engineered a carefully stage-managed drama. On 24 August, a large Soviet delegation arrived in Ulaanbaatar unannounced. The next day the Mongolian government, which was totally subservient to Stalin, issued an 'invitation' to the USSR to station troops in Mongolia. By that time, the first of thirty thousand Soviet troops had already crossed the border, among them two mechanised motor brigades, artillery, vehicles, and a cavalry brigade.

In Mongolia, power was in the hands of the interior minister, Marshal Choibalsan, co-architect of the Mongolian Revolution in 1921 and chosen by Stalin as dictator in 1936 at the age of forty. In September 1937 – a month after the arrival of Russian troops en masse – he initiated the execution of some twenty thousand 'counter-revolutionaries', as detailed in the previous chapter. His brutality solved a problem: Japan, being against China, Mongolia's old imperial master, was actually quite popular in Mongolia, providing Choibalsan with an excuse for his excesses; to be accused of 'spying for Japan' was a common reason for a death sentence during the Purge. Despite being under Stalin's thumb, and despite his murderous record, Choibalsan is still admired today by many Mongolians, because his compliance won Stalin's confidence and assured the preservation of Mongolia's nominal 'independence'. In the town named after him – old-style Bayan Tumen, which plays a major role in the events that follow – a statue put up in 2005 marks the 110th anniversary of his birth. Its plaque reads: 'May Mongolian independence last for ever!'

On both the Russo-Mongolian and Japanese sides, attention focused on the area where the Khalkha River bends westwards away from today's frontier. In 1939, there was no physical frontier. Standing on the battle site today, you can see how it was back then – undulating dunes and grassland well-watered by the river, with good winter pasture on the eastern side. In winter, herders from Mongolia crossed back and forth over the frozen river with their flocks.

The Japanese saw the incursions as trespassing by Russian allies. They wanted a fixed frontier. But where? Traditionally the Russians and

Mongolians had drawn it up to twenty-five kilometres east of the river. The Japanese General Staff wanted it to be along the river itself. After all, the word *khalkh* means 'shield, protection or gateway', implying that the river is a natural border, which indeed it is for much of its length. But there was no proof that it had ever been considered a *political* border. Suspicions grew. Russia feared Japanese expansion into Mongolia and Siberia, Japan feared (correctly) that Russia wanted to spread revolution in China. A few border skirmishes occurred, and one two-week clash, in August 1938. In the battle, both sides lost several hundred men, while the Soviets lost dozens of tanks (the reported losses varied wildly). Despite the Soviets having a three-to-one advantage, the fighting was inconclusive and ended in a truce. Both sides continued to build up their forces and probe the other, with incursions, kidnappings, demands to remove observation posts and occupation of disputed sites. Neither side, however, foresaw a major clash.

For Stalin, dangers multiplied. In Europe, Hitler was arming Nazi Germany, intent on conquering what he called *Lebensraum* ('space for living') in Russia. In the east, Manchukuo threatened. In addition, Germany and Japan were allies. The Soviet Union was only twenty years old, and its very existence was at stake. It looked as if Russia faced war on two fronts simultaneously, against two allied powers. And they did not have enough tanks and planes to counter a German invasion. The prospect was a nightmare. Stalin needed time. He won it by proposing a non-aggression pact with Germany, which would allow him to deal with Japan, while building up enough armour in the west to deter or counter a German invasion. In March 1939, secret talks started with Germany. But there could be no official pact until the Manchurian Front was settled.

## THE COMING STORM

Both sides continued to build up their forces. The twenty-third Division, arriving from semi-tropical Kyushu in southern Japan in November

1938, had no experience of a Hulunbuir winter, no battle experience, only old weapons and not enough of them, and few vehicles suitable for the grasslands. Under their commander, Lieutenant General Michitarō Komatsubara, they would not be ready for action for many months. But action was needed, because in early 1939 the Russians and Mongolians built a bridge across the Khalkha, strengthening their forces on both sides of the river. On 11 May, the Japanese reoccupied the east bank of the Khalkha, and two weeks later the Russians expelled them again. By the end of May, the Russians had 700 infantry, 260 cavalry, 409 armoured cars, 60 machine guns, and 20 heavy guns. In reserve, east of Lake Baikal, were between 20 and 39 infantry divisions, 2,500 tanks and 2,500 aircraft.

This far outclassed the Japanese. They lacked information, despised the Mongol military and overestimated the effects of Stalin's purges on Russian leadership. In addition, Tokyo was more interested in their war in China. The Kwantung Army had one arm tied behind its back. Their plan was to sit tight and wait for a Russian assault. If it came – though few thought that these little border skirmishes would amount to anything much – they believed their counterattack would inevitably be successful, because Japanese 'spirit' was superior.

May 1939 saw the beginning of four months of escalating warfare. The conflict spread to the skies, where scout planes wheeled and fighters raided border posts. A small Russian force of 1,400 set up east of the river. To Komatsubara, it looked an easy target. What he did not know was that, some seventy kilometres west, there was a Russian rapid reaction force of over seventy trucks, five tanks and a dozen anti-tank guns.

Early on 28 May, two thousand Japanese in six units set out to encircle the Russians. Each would advance separately, then attack jointly. They expected an easy victory. But the operation demanded tight coordination by units that had never fought together.

It was a disaster, as survivors later reported. Radios failed, and one reconnaissance unit of 220 men under Lieutenant Colonel Azuma Yaozō dug itself in, only to find itself surrounded and the target of mortars fired from the west bank. The units failed to join up. By midday, Azuma's unit was trapped, pounded by artillery, low on ammunition, their weapons clogged by wind-blown sand. A messenger sent out on horseback failed to find help. That night, as the numbers of dead and wounded rose, Azuma's men fought off a Soviet assault, but at dawn Russian howitzers, field pieces, mortars and anti-tank guns began to pound them. By the afternoon, they were down to twenty-five men, and clearly doomed. One brave second lieutenant leaped aboard a Soviet tank, was hit by Russian fire and killed himself rather than be captured. Azuma died in a final, fruitless charge. Russian scout planes above reported that Japanese trucks were bringing reinforcements, and the Russians and Mongolians pulled back, ending the action.

If the Japanese leaders were shocked by the fight, so too were the Russians. Two days later, the new foreign affairs commissar, Vyacheslav Molotov, told the Supreme Soviet in Moscow that 'in virtue of our treaty with Mongolia, we shall defend its frontiers as energetically as our own'. In Minsk, the following day, the deputy commander of the Military District, Georgii Zhukov, was summoned to Moscow, where Marshal Kliment Voroshilov told him, 'I think the Japanese have started a big military gamble,' and ordered Zhukov to go to the Khalkha River border and assume command.

Some argue that history is the product of great forces, others that it is made by great personalities. Zhukov should really count as both. He became a national hero in the war, fell out with his bosses, but regained his heroic stature by the time of his death in 1974. Master of the art of mass warfare, one of the century's greatest soldiers, pre-eminent architect of Soviet victory: he has attracted these and countess other tributes. He was also callous, brutal, coarse, egotistical and rude. Perhaps these were the very qualities that he needed to succeed, given his poverty-stricken origins. Adopted by a peasant woman, raised in one-room shack, apprenticed to a furrier in Moscow, conscripted in the First World War, promoted for bravery, Georgii Zhukov became a cavalry commander and, in 1938, commander of the Sixth Cossack Corps in Belorussia, where he made a name promoting the idea of combined operations – cavalry, tanks, motorised infantry, bombers and fighters. As he says in his memoirs, 'I worked assiduously on operational and strategic questions... reading war chronicles and classical works on the art of war.' By June 1939, aged forty-three, burly as a wrestler with a jaw like a bulldog, he was the acknowledged expert in his field. This was his big chance to put his ideas into practice.

He arrived by air in eastern Mongolia on 5 June, sweating in his cavalry boots and coarse uniform. It was high summer, with daytime temperatures up to 40°C. He joined his Mongolian allies, most notably Choibalsan, now commander-in-chief.

Within hours, Zhukov saw the main problems: the Russian-Mongolian base was 120 kilometres from the front and did not even have any buildings; only one of the commanders had actually been to the front; and reconnaissance was bad. Zhukov concluded that Japan planned further action, and had to be stopped by reclaiming the bridgehead over the river and building reserves: more planes, more tanks, more guns, more manpower, more of everything.

Within a day, Moscow agreed. The supply base was Borzya, on the Trans-Siberian Railway, with another six hundred kilometres to go to Tamsag Bulag ('Tamsag Spring'), a small collection of buildings and tents that quickly evolved into the Russian-Mongolian base. In June alone, this line, with a newly built second track, brought in a tank brigade (including the formidable fourteen-tonne BT-7 tanks, with their three-man crews), three mechanised brigades, a motorised rifle division, heavy artillery, a Mongolian cavalry division and one hundred planes with twenty-one top-class pilots, who were already Heroes of the Soviet Union. One of them, Yakov Smuthkevich, had received his award for fighting German planes in the Spanish Civil War. Just recovered from appalling injuries sustained in an air crash, and still limping because one leg was shorter than the other, he was the air force commander. He would become a Hero again for his exploits in Mongolia – the only man ever to receive the award twice – before being falsely accused of treachery and executed without trial in 1941. Such was the madness of the times.

The air war intensified through June, with scores of planes engaging in dogfights, though reports on the effects varied wildly. Japanese planes were not allowed to penetrate Mongolian air space in order to avoid all-out war, but that changed on 22 June, when the Japanese made an unauthorised air-raid – technically, an act of war against a sovereign state, Mongolia. That day, according to Russian sources, Soviet planes shot down thirty-one Japanese aircraft, a quarter of their local air force, for the loss of twelve of their own planes, while Japanese sources claim their pilots downed forty-nine Soviet planes (on top of sixty-nine 'kills' in the previous four weeks).

That engagement convinced the Japanese high command to allow aerial attacks on Russian bases inside Mongolia. On 27 June came the first official air-raid into enemy territory – a dozen reconnaissance planes helped thirty bombers and eighty fighters (the figures are approximate) to raid the main base in the Tamsag area, with some planes going on to Bayan Tumen two hundred kilometres further. It was judged a triumph – over a hundred Russian planes destroyed for the loss of a heavy bomber, two fighters and a scout plane, and seven men killed, all in half an hour of fighting. But Tokyo was not pleased by the escalation, and saw it as another example of irresponsible warmongering by the Kwantung Army. Local officers complained that they faced two enemies – the Russians and their own high command.

By now, Zhukov knew what he was up against, thanks to intelligence from the Soviet spy Richard Sorge, who was based in Tokyo in the guise of a Nazi journalist. He was forty-three, handsome, a notorious womaniser, and – since Germany was Japan's ally – had high-level access to Japan's plans. Not only did he pass on Manchukuo's military strength – thirteen infantry battalions, one hundred anti-tank guns, five hundred vehicles, two hundred planes – but also the fact that Tokyo was more interested in China than empire in Inner Asia.

Zhukov needed victory, fast. His country's future – probably his own life – depended on it. For victory, he needed overwhelming force and he didn't have it yet. By comparison with Manchukuo, Russia had virtually unlimited resources – drawing on some two million men-at-arms and approaching ten thousand tanks – but not yet enough in eastern Mongolia to break the stalemate. Skirmishing continued through early July, with scout planes, fighters and bombers filling the sky. Horses hauled guns and wagons as if they were re-enacting nineteenth-century battles. Each side sought some advantage by seizing this or that mole-hill of slightly higher ground, mostly in appalling heat, sometimes in rain that trapped trucks in mud, and always in swarming clouds of mosquitoes and flies.

For example, on 3 July, a Japanese infantry battalion on the west bank of the Khalkha attacked Russian tanks with fire-bottles, now known as 'Molotov cocktails', soft-drink bottles filled with sand and petrol. These spread fire into the Russian tanks, exploding bullets and driving the crew to scramble out to be shot or bayoneted by the Japanese. But the Japanese infantry had no back up from artillery. The 150 tanks of the Eleventh Tank Brigade with the Mongolian Eighth Armoured Battalion drove some nineteen thousand Japanese from a little rise with a pile of stones on top, an *ovoo*, which often mark high spots in Mongolia. This little shrine was called Bayan Tsagaan ('Rich White') Ovoo. As Zhukov wrote in his *Memoirs*, the armour was 'our trump card… the battle [of Bayan Tsagaan Ovoo] showed that tank and motorised troops cooperating skilfully with the air force and mobile artillery are a foolproof means of carrying out swift, decisive operations'. The Japanese soldiers – their 'fire-bottles' used up, tormented by mosquitoes, trying to retreat across a single narrow pontoon bridge, hauling corpses and body-bags – were left to make useless, ineffectual sword and bayonet charges on Russian tanks. The Soviets and Mongolians lost some three hundred vehicles, but those losses were outweighed by Japanese losses – guns, mortars and vehicles littering the steppe, forty-five planes downed – and infantry deaths, exacerbated by thirst, exhaustion and lack of support.

Zhukov's hard-won victory justified his tactics: infantry, armour, artillery and airpower all working together. These were perfect conditions for tanks, which could range freely over the steppe. The Japanese had no shortage of samurai spirit, self-belief and do-or-die heroism. They were terrific at hand-to-hand fighting with cold steel. But that was not enough. They lacked information, food, fuel, water, maps, ammunition, tanks and artillery, and no amount of wishful thinking or battle cries of '*Banzai!*' could make up for those lacks.

Crucially, Zhukov still had not achieved the overwhelming force that he demanded, his superiors agreed and reinforcements poured in. Zhukov lists the supplies that rolled in over 650 kilometres of steppe: 18,000 tonnes of artillery ammunition, 6,500 tonnes of aircraft ammunition, 15,000 tonnes of fuel, 4,000 tonnes of food. By late July, Zhukov had some 70,000 men, and 2,600 trucks, with more forces arriving all the time by rail and truck.

The Japanese abandoned their attacks, and dug in with trenches and log bunkers. Three minor Soviet assaults designed to probe Japanese defences showed Zhukov that he still needed more troops and weaponry. But with war in the west imminent, Russian forces would also be needed in Europe. Whatever resources he got would have to be released again as soon as possible, in no more than a month.

## THE STORM BREAKS

Zhukov planned his major offensive for 20 August, by which time he commanded something like 100,000 men (against 70,000 Japanese), 4,000 trucks, 500 tanks, 200 heavy guns, 2,000 machine guns, and 550 fighters and bombers. Bombers took on fuel and artillery prepared for a pre-dawn offensive. Transmitters broadcast false information. Tanks with their tracks removed ran silently on wheels to hide in the willow-beds of the Khalkha, ready for a minutely timed assault.

At 05.45 that day, Soviet artillery opened fire, focusing on anti-aircraft and machine-gun posts. It was this little-known action, not Germany's invasion of Poland on 1 September 1939, that was the real opening battle of the Second World War. Forty-five minutes later, the guns fell silent, and 150 bombers and 200 fighters launched the world's first fighter-bomber offensive,* a foretaste of a tactic that would be refined against civilian populations in the war, in London, Hamburg, Dresden, Berlin and Tokyo. At 08.15, with the planes back on the ground, the artillery opened up again for fifteen minutes, pausing for the planes to resume their assault. In Zhukov's words: 'The strike of aircraft and artillery was so powerful and successful that the enemy was morally and physically suppressed, and during the first hour and a half could not even open artillery fire.' Finally, at 08.45, red signal rockets told the ground forces to advance fifteen minutes later. At 09.00, some fifty thousand Russians and Mongolians – with another fifty thousand in reserve – crossed the river to engage the Japanese centre. Trenches collapsed, bunkers fell apart, the few hand-dug wells filled with earth. In the 40°C-plus heat, men blotted up dew with cloths and sucked on them. By nightfall, Russian tanks had crossed the whole disputed zone.

Over the next three days, armoured units swept around the Japanese flanks to meet up at the village of Nomonhan, trapping most of the Japanese twenty-third Division. The action also involved many other units, in a fast-moving and complex story.

Here are a few telling details from the Japanese perspective:

There was little the Japanese could do but suffer. Of the twenty-third Division, all died except for four hundred. In grass blazing from flame-throwers, some tried to dig shelter with their bare hands. Wounded soldiers stopped ambulances already packed with casualties by throwing themselves in front of the vehicles. Survivors later recalled hearing what sounded like birds chirping, which was in fact the sound of machine-gun

---

* This was the first against *military* targets. German bombers of the Condor Legion had proved how effective massed bombers could be when twenty-four of them struck the undefended Basque town of Guernica during the Spanish Civil War on 26 April 1937. Deaths numbered between 150 and 1,600, a vague and much-disputed estimate. This was not the only lesson from Spain. General Dmitry Pavlov, who commanded a Soviet tank brigade on the Republican (anti-Franco) side, was made a Hero of the Soviet Union and was in Nomonhan advising Zhukov.

bullets passing overhead. At one command post, bodies were stacked up like cordwood. An attempted counterattack failed and reinforcements were trivial. Colonel Morita Toru, of the seventy-first Regiment, apparently believing himself to be immune to bullets, stood in full view until cut down by a burst of machine-gun fire. One officer, having lost eighty percent of his battalion, exhorted his men to die like 'beautifully falling cherry blossoms' then shot the wounded at their own request. One group, surrounded by sixty armoured cars and Russian-Mongolian riflemen, and bombarded by heavy guns, with every officer dead, made a last bayonet charge while the wounded committed suicide. A gunner reported hearing Japanese soldiers singing the national anthem and cheering the Emperor, a prelude to mass suicide.

It took three more days for the twenty-third and other units to die. Russian snipers took a terrible toll, and gained a fearful reputation for accuracy. They had many easy targets, because young Japanese officers showed their bravery by standing rather than crawling. Another reason for the snipers' success had to do with the plague of summer flies. In certain areas of the Mongolian grassland, the flies are a constant pest. Unless you have nets, the only way to deal with them is by retreating into a tent and building a smoky fire. I remember one summer's day in the Khentii mountains, speaking to a guide at a tourist camp on the Kherlen River. As we talked, we constantly waved flies away from our faces. From a few metres away, it must have looked as if we were communicating by semaphore. For the surrounded twenty-third, there were no nets and no smoking fires, just their hands. Many officers were still wearing their formal white gloves, covering skin that would otherwise have been exposed to horseflies. Imagine an officer waving away flies with his white-gloved hands. The sniper zooms in on the gloves as they pass in front of the officer's face, and the shot hits the target right between the eyes. That's how Russian snipers got their reputation for seemingly magical accuracy.

By 31 August, it was all over. After countless acts of heroism, thousands of dead lay scattered over the steppe, and the battlefield fell silent, because – as Alvin Coox puts it in his unrivalled account[2] – 'the Soviet-MPRA [Mongolian People's Republic Army] command had achieved precisely what they had set out to do'.

## AFTERMATH

At what cost? Estimates of both strengths and losses vary wildly. Estimates of Soviet strength locally range from 61,000 to 100,000, Japanese strength from 30,000 to 75,000. Japanese losses lie somewhere between 8,000 (claimed by Japanese sources) to 50,000 (according to Zhukov). Losses for the devastated twenty-third Division range from thirty percent to seventy-five percent. Frankly, in terms of manpower, no one knows how many Japanese died – probably something between 16,000 and 25,000. Soviet and Mongol losses were about 28,000. The scale of the losses also applies to the hardware.* What is clear is that Soviet losses exceeded Japanese losses, but that the Soviet forces could afford it, because they had so much more on site and in reserve.

The Mongolian contribution, by the way, was minute: thirty-nine planes, seven armoured vehicles and about 2,000 cavalry, of whom 297 were killed.[3] Ironically, they were thrown into battle against cavalrymen recruited from Inner Mongolia into the Japanese army, and so had to fight against men of their own ethnicity.

Within days, the consequences, like well-struck billiard balls, knocked Europe into war. With the eastern frontier secure, Stalin could proceed with his plans in the west. The Treaty of Non-Aggression – officially, the Molotov–Ribbentrop Pact – with Nazi Germany was signed on 23 August 1939, by which the two powers agreed to divide Poland between them. The next day, Britain and Poland signed a treaty of mutual assistance. A

---

* For example, with Soviet losses first: tanks: 250 (50%) v. 30 (41%); aircraft: 200 (21%) v. 160 (40%).

week later, on 1 September, Hitler's advance eastwards into Poland meant that, on 3 September, Britain and France declared war on Germany.

Locally, after a few small skirmishes as some Japanese tried to regain ground, peace came. Tokyo was keen to prevent a Russian and Mongolian drive into the heart of Manchukuo and the German–Russian non-aggression pact had apparently shown that their ambitions could no longer rely on a German threat to the USSR. By imperial command, all operations were stopped on 6 September.

Ten days later, with a bitter wind announcing the start of winter, Soviet and Japanese officers met in a tent to agree terms for exchanging and burying bodies. They confirmed that all the disputed zone would be part of Mongolia, as it is today (official demarcation of the whole frontier was not complete until May 1942). There followed the consumption of much vodka. Over the next ten days, about a thousand Japanese soldiers, their mouths and noses covered against the stench, found and buried several thousand corpses. In the prisoner exchanges, which continued throughout the winter, the Japanese prisoners were disgraced by their capture and would face court martials back home. The officers were reassigned, the troops left, eastern Mongolia returned to obscurity.

Stalin was now free to seize his prize in the west, and on 17 September he took over the eastern part of Poland. The lessons of Nomonhan – overwhelming force, mobile tank units, coordinated elements – were reinforced by Germany's invasion of France in May–June 1940. In due course, Nomonhan allowed Stalin to move troops westwards to reinforce Moscow, Leningrad and Stalingrad, where they would be needed when Germany broke the terms of the Treaty of Non-Aggression and invaded the Soviet Union on 22 June 1941. Perhaps the battle's greatest claim to significance was that it catapulted Zhukov into a position of supreme authority. As Marshal, he masterminded Russia's defence and then its advance to Berlin and final victory in 1945.

For Asia, and eventually the wider world, the consequences were equally wide-ranging With Mongolia and Siberia now closed to them, Japan's only possible empire lay in south-east Asia. To achieve mastery there, the main enemy became not the Soviet Union but America (other nations and outposts of the British Empire would prove easy targets). Almost exactly two years after their defeat on the borders of eastern Mongolia, Japanese forces bombed Pearl Harbor. A village and a river in an obscure part of an obscure country had been the focus of a battle that lit the fuse for worldwide war.

And still the world does not fully appreciate the battle. Yes, those few visitors who make it to the site, whether in eastern Mongolia or China's north-east, can see museums and photographs and weapons and some real and replica tanks. But great battles need great memorials. Would it be too much to hope that Russia, Mongolia, China and Japan will one day create a Special Tourist Zone of the complete battleground and speak of a moment when the world teetered on the brink of an alternative reality?

## A PLEBISCITE: FARCICAL BUT VITAL

With Japan's defeat in 1945, the Manchurian borders of China, Mongolia and the Soviet Union settled into their pre-war fuzziness, not yet agreed to the metre, with consequences to be described in Chapter 13. That left Mongolia in a legal limbo, *de facto* in the Soviet empire, *de jure* part of China. At the war's end, a solution seemed possible. In February 1945, at the Yalta Conference designed to sort out spheres of influence in the post-war world, Stalin had persuaded his wartime allies, the United States (Roosevelt) and the United Kingdom (Churchill), to consent to Mongolia maintaining its 'status quo' after the war.

A few months later it became clear that by 'status quo' Stalin meant 'Soviet satellite, with no Chinese suzerainty'. Mongolia was strategically important to the USSR, as a buffer state against China and as a base for Soviet armies. Stalin told the Chinese to recognise Mongolia's independence. He had a secret weapon to force China's hand: pan-Mongolism, the movement that would, if unleashed, bring all Mongolians together, including those in Inner Mongolia and the Buryats around Lake Baikal, which would tear China and Russia apart. In the course of tough talks in Moscow, Stalin warned the head of the Chinese Nationalist team, Yuan T.V. Soong, 'If this [China's recognition] does not happen Outer Mongolia will be a rallying point for all Mongolians. It's to the detriment of China and us.' With northern and north-east China poised to be overrun by Soviet troops on the point of entering war against Japan, China had no choice. China's leader Chiang Kai-shek gave in.

The deal was that Stalin would abandon his support for the Chinese Communist Party and the Uighur independence movement in Xinjiang, while China promised to recognise Mongolia's independence – but only after a plebiscite. The two powers signed the Sino-Soviet Treaty of Friendship and Alliance on 14 August 1945. Both sides realised, of course, that the referendum was for show – Mongolians would never *willingly* forgo independence – but Chiang wanted to use the results of the plebiscite to sell the 'loss' of Mongolia to his people. Stalin was happy to oblige.

The plebiscite would serve them both, strengthening Soviet control by asserting Mongolia's formal 'independence', or at least freedom from China. From 3 October 1945, the Mongolian People's Revolutionary Party held hundreds of political meetings in which tens of thousands of participants were told what was at stake and who to thank. In the words of a Russian report on the plebiscite, 'There were hundreds of statements expressing gratitude to the Soviet Union… and gratitude and best wishes to comrade Stalin, as teacher, leader and friend of the Mongolian people.' The actual day of voting, 20 October, 'turned into a spontaneous, genuinely all-people festivity', as crowds dressed in colourful *deels* celebrated with horse racing, wrestling and archery. The best horsemen delivered the results to regional centres.

In view of the advance propaganda and festivities on the day, the result was never in doubt: 98.6% of eligible voters took part, everyone except the 1.4% who were too sick or ancient to appear. Of the 487,409 votes cast *every single vote was for independence, one hundred percent, with precisely zero votes against.* It was the most overwhelming result in the history not just of plebiscites but of all elections anywhere. Even Iraq's dictator, Saddam Hussein, in his plebiscite of October 1995, managed only 99.96% of the votes cast. In their referenda, demagogues need a majority to vote, and a majority of that majority to say 'yes', but this was ridiculous. It was done – as the Soviet observers reported – at incredible speed, for Choibalsan wanted the result in hours, which led to the cutting of many corners. Officials voted on behalf of participants, forged signatures, allowed foreigners to vote (ninety-eight of those), and often did not actually count the votes, but guessed. Never mind: the Soviet observers, in their secret report to Soviet foreign minister Vyacheslav Molotov and Chinese foreign minister Wang Shijie, judged the whole thing a terrific success, confirming 'government authority among the wide masses'.

Not that the nation was cheated, as usually happens when dictators forbid opponents from voting. In this case, the vote would have been overwhelming anyway. The Party, namely Choibalsan, simply wanted ever greater success to feed his personality cult. No one objected, for no one would have dared disobey orders or dispute such a cheerful expression of national sentiment. Faked or not, Mongolia was at last legally free of its hated imperial masters. The state founded by Chinggis Khan in 1206 had once again become free, sort of.

But legal freedom was not real freedom. Mongolia had fallen from a Chinese frying-pan into a Soviet fire as a Cold War Soviet satellite, one of the USSR's eleven-nation Council for Mutual Economic Assistance (Comecon), dependent on Soviet aid, tanks, planes and troops. So it would remain for another forty-five years. Mongolia was not to achieve full independence until the collapse of Communism in 1992, when the fifty thousand troops and two thousand tanks withdrew in vast columns. Driving over the grasslands and the Gobi today, you can still see the ruins of abandoned apartment blocks and runways of reinforced concrete.

Peace descended on these much-disputed borderlands, and held firm when in 1949 Mao's Communists forced their Nationalist rivals to flee to Taiwan and welcomed aid from their Soviet mentors. But ancient rivalries lurked beneath the surface, and the borders were still unsurveyed. 'Good fences make good neighbours,' wrote the poet Robert Frost, quoting his dour New England neighbour, but between Asia's vast and prickly neighbours it would take more than a few years of peace to build a proper fence.

*Maria, the matriarch.*

# CHAPTER 12

# The Ewenki: Life, Death and Survival

## On to the Grasslands

HANGING ABOVE MY DESK IS A GOOD-LUCK CHARM – A CIRCLE of reindeer hair surrounding two circles of yellow beads. It is an image of the sun, the deity of the Ewenki* reindeer people, personified in stories as the Sungirl. She has been good luck for me so far, less so for the Ewenki. They are one of those minority cultures that until the seventeenth century peopled what would become the Russo-Chinese borderlands.** Until a few decades ago, the Ewenki kept themselves to themselves, separate from encroaching Mongols, Russians, Japanese and Chinese. That was then. Today, they are more and more part of modern China. But the memories remain of what they once were, and the effect

* In Russian, they are spelled Evenki, but Chinese lacks a *v* sound, so the *w* is now equally common.

** To list the main ones: Mongol subgroups (Buryat, Barga, Horchin, Daur and Khamnigan); Tugusic-speakers (Manchu, Ewenki, Nanai – called Ulch in Russia – Hezhe, Oroch, Oroqen, Negidal and Udege; and Koreans, who are nineteenth-century incomers. Many of these were assigned their own territories, but contact with Russians and Chinese, intermarriage, migrations, uprisings, warfare and deportations have turned them into an ever-shifting mosaic, made even more complex in Russia by groups applying for 'small peoples' status, of which there are now forty-five. See Billé and Humphrey, Chapter 4 and p. 300.

of the change has brought fame to one small group of them – the last of the Reindeer Ewenki.

I learned about them from an Ewenki anthropologist, Ilana, a woman with big round glasses: studious, dignified, passionate about her tribe and one of the most cosmopolitan people you could imagine. She was married to a Han Chinese, with a six-year-old son who was about to go to school in Ulaanbaatar. She was fluent in Ewenki, Chinese, Mongolian and English (learned in Hong Kong). 'My name is Yilina in Chinese,' she said in soft, almost accent-free English when we met in the provincial capital, Hailar. 'But actually, Ilana is an Ewenki name. It means "Sunshine".'

There are about thirty thousand Ewenki in China, she said, and another thirty thousand in Russia, west of Lake Baikal, which is where those in China originally came from. She was currently working with the Russian group for a master's degree, so she was also learning Russian. Once, the Ewenki had been more widespread, living right across eastern Siberia, even as far north as the Bering Straits that divide Russia from Alaska. 'Did you know that the word "Alaska" is actually Ewenki? It comes from our phrase *alash-ka*, which means "waiting for you". That's what our ancestors said after they crossed to America.' She laughed gently. 'Well, that's what we say. It's a legend, so maybe is not true.'

In China, there are three main Ewenki branches: the Solon (twenty thousand), who immigrated in the eighteenth century, the Tungus,* who came a century later, and the Yakuts, who were the last arrivals about a hundred years ago. Links with Russia remained close: many were baptised into the Russian Orthodox Church. In 1958, the government set up the Ewenki Autonomous Region, the idea being to eradicate links with Russia, create ethnic unity and impose new, pro-Chinese loyalties (though the naming of a region after an ethnic group does not confer

* The Tungus are sometimes called Khamnigan, a Russian name. But how exactly to define Khamnigan is controversial. In China, among the Ewenki, it has a derogatory sense of 'intruder', because some Khamnigan have been known to claim Ewenki status in order to access benefits.

land-rights; Han are free to buy land, as happened across all Inner Mongolia over the last two centuries). The last arrivals, the Yakuts, were the true reindeer people, hunting and herding in the depths of the Khingan forests. There were never more than about three hundred of them, yet they are the ones who have attracted most attention because of their recent forced assimilation into Chinese culture.

'I am a Solon Ewenki,' Ilana went on, pushing her glasses up her nose. 'My people are mainly herders, living quite close to here. We can visit them if you like.'

A few days later, we were off to see Ilana's relatives. We were a party of five: Mr Jiang the Chinese driver, Alatan, me, Ilana and a Polish social anthropologist named Katarzynka, who spoke Polish, Chinese, Mongolian and English, all with astonishing speed. Her Ewenki sounded pretty impressive as well. In anthropology, language is the key to culture. In the case of the Ewenki, it is almost all they have left. It *is* the culture.

'They have their language from their parents, at home,' Ilana explained. 'You see, our language is not written, and it is not taught in the schools. It is tragic that we do not have writing. One day, I hope to introduce a script.'

'Cyrillic?'

'Not now some of us are in China.'

'Why did you leave?'

'We were living as reindeer herders near Lake Baikal, close to the Buryat Mongols. Why we came is not very certain. Perhaps because the Russians wanted too many furs from us. We always lived, how to say' – she paused a moment – 'in the *deep* forest, not interacting with others, just living our own lives, so we had never been involved with wars. I think maybe this is to do with the personality of the Ewenki.'

They settled along the Nen River, which forms the border between Heilongjiang, in China's north-east, and Hulunbuir. In 1732, to secure the Erguna–Amur frontier against Russian intrusion, the Manchu (Qing) government ordered the Solon to move some 450 kilometres westwards, from the hills and forests of the Khingan to the grasslands near Hailar.

This meant that they could no longer herd reindeer. Instead, they became herders of the 'five animals', like the Mongols.

She had said her people came here to escape war, but in fact they proved good fighters when necessary. When the Solon Ewenki were moved en masse to Hulunbuir, three thousand of them joined the Qing army to fight in Xinjiang. They are remembered locally because the survivors founded today's capital, Hailar. Outside the Ewenki museum in Hailar is a statue of an Ewenki general, Hailancha (1740–1793) – 'our hero', as Ilana called him – who fought for the Qing in Taiwan and south China.

'But you said you didn't like war.'

'We don't. We just used to run away deeper and deeper into the forest. But, if we have to, we are good fighters. The point is we don't want to fight. An Ewenki says, "If you really want this place, take it, and I will go somewhere else, because I have excellent survival skills, so I can survive anywhere." '

Now we were sixty kilometres south-west of Hailar, far from towns and forests. The roads got ever smaller, until we were down to a ribbon of tarmac running over a vast expanse of grassland, flat as a windless sea. We came to a turn-off that led to a locked gate. Perhaps they were not keen on visitors. Yet a few metres beyond was a wooden platform three metres high, set up apparently to give visitors a 360-degree view. Grass ran from below our feet to the horizon, sharp in the pure, clear air. The only sign of life was a herd of sheep in the middle distance and, in the vastness of the sky, half a dozen storm clouds blurred with rain. We were in Ilana's home territory, Hoi Sum, one of five *sums* in an infinity of grassland, the Ewenki Autonomous Banner (well, nineteen thousand square kilometres, almost the size of Wales). Ilana's *sum*, four thousand square kilometres, has a population of only three thousand, divided into eleven *gacha* ('villages').

'That's a large amount of land for so few people.'

'Not large enough,' said Ilana. 'We need this for our animals. And we have to protect the grassland. This platform is not for tourists. It's for the government environmental people to oversee this area.' That explained the locked gate. 'This is a fragile place. The river down there is good for sheep, but settlements upset the balance of chemicals.'

A few kilometres further across the sea of grass, we came to a house belonging to Ilana's sister, Nerin, meaning 'early morning light'. It was a simple five-room, single-storey house, the base of a herding economy: Nerin owned thirty cows, thirty horses and fifty sheep on three thousand *mu* (two hundred hectares). A tent served as extra space and a kitchen. Amid a clatter of pots and pans, Nerin and her aunt Tsitsintoya prepared dark, Russian-style bread and plum jam (though this 'wild plum' was actually a sort of cherry).

Nerin had been to college, yet here she was living a herder's harsh life. Why had she chosen it? I imagined she would talk about the joys of country living and the need to sustain her culture.

Not so. 'In my second year at university, my uncle died, and I chose to come home and take care of the family. So I never graduated.'

She married, and had a daughter, now aged four.

'Would you choose this way of life for her?'

'No! I want my daughter to have a high level of education and live in the city. You know, a herder's life is hard and most of the time it's boring.'

But they had a rich social life and a strong sense of community. They needed it, to hold on to their identity. For instance, said Ilana, to get a passport you needed a family name, and Ewenki named themselves after their clan, a sort of extended family. 'In our passport, my family name is just three Xs, XXX.' I drew a sharp breath in surprise. 'Yes, so bad! I could give my clan name, Idugdat, but it is eighty families. We get together every year to sacrifice a sheep or a cow at our clan *ovoo*.'

The most fundamental issue is that of language. How could anyone be Ewenki without speaking Ewenki? How could it be preserved, this unwritten language that is not taught in schools and can only be learned from parents? It is a delicate plant. To advance in China and the wider world, Ewenkis need other languages as well. The aunt, a teacher of Korean, was going to retire and teach Mongol to Ewenki children.

'They speak Ewenki in the home,' she said. 'Then they learn Mongol. Then Mandarin Chinese. Actually, they are keen to learn Chinese first, because they find it easier to speak than Mongolian.' Reading and writing come later. By the time they are teenagers, Ewenki children have three languages and three writing systems (Mongolian vertical script, Chinese and pinyin, the Latinised transliteration system), which must surely guarantee a good facility with languages, but is no guarantee that Ewenki itself will survive. All I can say is that it has powerful advocates.

One is Ilana's uncle, Doklar Dorji. We were at supper with a dozen others celebrating a book launch for several volumes on Ewenki themes. At eighty-three, he displayed astonishing skill as a singer, and then equally astonishing powers as an orator. Yet, because not everyone present spoke Ewenki, he spoke in Chinese, and sang in Mongolian. The song – 'I was born by the side of the Yiming River', which runs through Hailar – was a 'long song', made long by the holding of many notes and the addition of vocal flourishes, ending on a high note drawn out longer than seemed possible and a leap into a falsetto that would have made an operatic soprano proud.

His speech was a powerful and moving plea – in Chinese – to save his language, for it is the usual fate of threatened languages to give way to a dominant one. This is a shortened version. After asking visiting scholars for help in inspiring the young, he went on:

> I love my people. I would not like to see the Ewenki language and culture vanish. I have studied both for almost fifty years. Our language is only oral and we have already lost many of our stories. We need to do better. We have done much, but it is only a beginning. Language is so important. If we can master the skills of writing we can record our culture and our history. Not just ours. Many place names in Russia, our ancient homeland, and in *The Secret History of the Mongols* [Mongolia's foundation epic, remember] are Ewenki. We cannot do without it. You visitors from England and Poland, please join our friends in Japan, Korea, Canada and Switzerland, and help us.

## THE AMAZING 'LINDA GREEN'

Before the Reindeer Ewenki started to attract attention, there were not many visitors, and fewer still who wrote of their experiences. One who did was a woman of whom I first heard in Kanjur Monastery, about two hundred kilometres south-west of Hailar. The guide mentioned a scholar from Cambridge called 'Linda Green' – that was how he pronounced the name on the basis of the Chinese characters. I was intrigued, more so when I saw a photograph of the same monastery taken by 'Linda Green'. A collection of her photos taken in 1929–32 had apparently been sent by Cambridge University. 'Linda Green' – Cambridge – a date – photographs: that's all I had to go on. The Museum of Archaeology and Anthropology in Cambridge solved the mystery. They had sent a collection of photos taken in Hulunbuir in 1929, not by 'Linda Green', but by a scientist called Lindgren. The same four characters, with two different transliterations.

Ethel Lindgren is worth a diversion. Her son John told me about her. At the age of eighty-nine, he was still living in his mother's wooden Scandinavian-style house outside Cambridge. She was exceptional in many ways. Here are two. Her middle name was John, which seems to mark her out as remarkable from birth. And she was extremely tall – almost two metres – which gave her a presence as commanding as her personality.

Born in America, she was the daughter of a Swedish banker and an Irish-English mother. Her father died when she was eleven, leaving her enough to fund a life of research and adventure. When she was fifteen, and already unusually tall, her mother and a new partner, a top-class violinist with a passion for Asian music, took her to China. A trip to Kalgan (today's Zhangjiakou), the old gateway between China and Mongolia, opened her eyes to the wild charms of the Mongolian Plateau, and she promised herself she would return. Back in the US, during a year at the all-women Smith University, a teacher told her that the only education worth having was in Cambridge, England. So she applied, and was accepted by the women's college, Girton. She studied

Chinese, completing the first two years of her degree in one year, then switching to psychology. She graduated with first-class honours at the age of twenty-two.

Almost at once she took a boat to China, travelling from Shanghai to Beijing, Harbin and finally to Mongolia's capital Urga (today's Ulaanbaatar). Mongolia at the time was under its new revolutionary Communist government and she might have stayed, studying Russian, but in that year the government was taken over by 'leftists', who collectivised the pastoral-nomadic economy, persecuted Buddhists and expelled foreigners who were not Russian. A brilliant young writer, Byambyn Rinchen (1905–1979), who would later become Mongolia's greatest scholar, advised her to go to Manchuria and study the Ewenki.

Hitching a lift in a truck, she returned to Beijing, trying to plan her trip to the Ewenki. A Danish friend suggested she contact a Norwegian trader and photographer called Oscar Mamen. His business with Urga had collapsed, so he was free, and keen to be involved. They were not well suited. He was a practical outdoors man, she an intellectual, but she was also a formidable personality who could pay the costs of the trip. The two teamed up, and journeyed to Hailar, where they planned their first trip to the reindeer people. Today you can cover that distance in a few hours, but at that time it took months, from April to October 1929.

Oscar organised a cart, horses and a Mongol assistant called Haisan, and off they went to the Erguna (one hundred kilometres), upriver to Shiwei (another hundred kilometres), which was then the terminus for a steamer that travelled up- and down-stream to the Amur. Following the Erguna River northwards along the border between China and Russia, she was much struck by the beauty of the landscape.

> Beyond Shihwei [her version of Shiwei] the wooded foothills are in sight... they fall steeply into the river itself, and the whole region assumes the character of the Siberian taiga with its typical birch, larch, and pine. The carriage road gives place to random tracks that lead from the narrow marshy valley of one deep swift stream over precipitous rises to another. Indeed, from this

> point onwards means of communication by land may be said to be closed to all but the pedestrian with his pack on his back or the traveller who can afford to risk his horse's legs at every turn.

She was a severely practical person, hard on herself as well as others, and with little interest in poetry. And yet, in her eyes, 'the wild beauty of the scenery grew in proportion to the difficulties of the trail. From the hilltops wide vistas opened out against a background of darkly wooded mountains.'

At a small outpost, they persuaded a local Cossack to forget his worries about bogs and mosquitoes, and become their guide. After another hundred kilometres they turned east to a branch of the Bistraya River, hoping to find the Ewenki (who she calls Tungus, meaning the Tungus Ewenki from east of Lake Baikal). As it happened, the Ewenki found them:

> It was our good fortune that perhaps the most enterprising member of the tribe, while on the trail of a bear, saw the smoke from our fire, and approaching nearer and gave the *halloo*, which is a sort of a password between the natives and the Russians who trade with them... He was gradually reassured by our cordiality... and consented to our visiting his wigwam on the following day. The first sight of a herd of reindeer among the birch and evergreens and the hospitable reception given us by the Tungus [Ewenki] amply rewarded us for our journey.

For several weeks, she and Oscar shared the Ewenki way of life. After eighty years of contact, they all spoke Russian and depended on Russian traders for flour, tobacco, tea and vodka. Their culture, though dying, was not yet dead. 'When we see the hunter setting out for the chase, with rifle and pack, flourishing his "palma", a long knife used to cut down branches in the path, the real Tungus emerges.' Their winter shoes and dress were of deerskin. The women did the home work, tending the reindeer and cooking, making birch-bark and deer-skin boxes, loading packs on to the reindeer when they moved camp, and boiling and sewing strips of birch-bark to cover the tents (exchanged for deerskin in winter). Russian unleavened bread had become part of their diet. The reindeer were milked three times a day, producing milk that was 'delicious, and as thick as cream'. In summer, they travelled only at dusk to avoid the mosquitoes, which were kept at bay with fire-smoke, made pungent by burning a bush called *Ledum palustre* (also known as Labrador tea, 杜香 *du xiang*). 'The Tungus never fail to cleanse of any evil influence any object bought from the Russians or Chinese by holding it in the smoke.' It was also used to stem bleeding when reindeer shed their antlers.

Ethel and Oscar would have stayed, but there was no game and fishing was ruined by floods. Hunger drove them out. After five days of travel, 'we were overjoyed to come across a gay company of Cossack haymakers… They laid down their work, the women soon had the kettle boiling for tea, and all stood about asking questions and smiling indulgently while we devoured the bread, cream and salted mushrooms which they heaped before us.'

Back in Beijing, Ethel wanted to return to Cambridge, and – as her son John put it – 'Oscar wanted to go back to Norway, and I was on the way! I was the cause of the marriage.' They married in Norway, and in April 1930, aged twenty-five and five months pregnant, Ethel gave a lecture about her trip to the Royal Geographical Society in London,[1] the second youngest woman ever to lecture there, then journeyed to the United States, where in August she gave birth to John.

'In October she and Oscar were off to China again, renting a house in Beijing, leaving me in the care of my grandmother. Her aim was to do a PhD on the Reindeer Ewenki. She and Oscar made two more trips to Hulunbuir, including a very cold one to the reindeer people in winter 1931.' On this winter trip, Ethel became good friends with a shamaness, Olga, who provided many more details of daily life, and especially the lives of women. A female ethnographer, a female informant – unheard of in an age of male researchers mainly interested in males. Oscar took thousands of pictures, including those that first introduced me to

Ethel. Their last trip was in summer 1932. The Japanese had set up their Manchurian colony, often intruding on the Ewenki, making further work impossible.

Then, John continued, 'she went back to her family in the US in September 1932 to arrange my future. My grandmother had died and I was in the care of a French nanny. Back in Cambridge, she met Miss Lavém, a Swedish physiotherapist who ran a gym, and had built this house. Hence its Swedish style. She said, "What will you do with young Johnny when he comes over? You better stay here." So, my mother, being sensible, moved in here with me in 1933. She was very work driven; he was an outdoors man, not an academic. The marriage fell apart quickly. She never went back to the Far East.' She was still only twenty-eight, and had a life of scholarship ahead of her.

I went in her footsteps, not literally, because she was on horseback or a cart, on tracks winding over the steppe, relying on canoes to cross rivers, and I was on expressways and paved roads in an air-conditioned 4x4. But the features are the same – the Hulun and Buir lakes that give the region its name, the sweeping grasslands that she found so beautiful, the forests of the Great Khingan, the Erguna River that Mongols claim as their original homeland and the reindeer people, or what was left of them.

## AMONG THE REINDEERS

In the UK, reindeers are the animals that pull Father Christmas across the sky, so we tend to think of them as big and docile and horse-like. Not at all, as tourists discover in the Erguna Birch Forest, a place entirely devoted to slender, white trunks that spread out in every direction, like an infinity of spears in a hall of mirrors. They grow in small groups, often in pairs, which is why, in folklore, birches symbolise loving couples. A big sign spells out 'LOVE', in English, and a noticeboard calls the forest 'the Love Mecca of North China.'

A walkway leads to a reindeer enclosure, where dozens mill round anyone who pauses to offer a handful of moss and lichen, their only food. They are much smaller and stronger and altogether feistier than I expected. One approached me, eager for a fluffy mouthful. He was the size of a Shetland pony. With quick movements of his rubbery lips, he snatched the food from my hand, and when I tried to hold a fur-covered antler to pat his flank, he jerked his head away impatiently. I should have known. Reindeer live outside through bitter winters, in temperatures down to minus 40°C and below. Their toughness made them good partners for the forest dwellers I had come to meet, in Aoluguya, in north-central Hulunbuir, 270 kilometres from Hailar.

Reindeer herders never had an easy life. In the early years of the twentieth century, few outsiders contacted them. A Chinese expedition in 1910 picked up a guide who led them through swamps and trackless forests to meet a few. The expedition leader wrote that they 'resembled dogs or horses, but had nothing in common with the race of men'. When Ethel Lindgren visited them in 1929, she reported: 'Essentially a peaceful people, asking only to be left to wander undisturbed through the forests, they prefer to travel over hundreds of miles rather than be brought into closer contact with their neighbours, to say nothing of being forced into open conflict or permanent subjection… The tribe numbers less than 250, and they are undoubtedly dying out.' Yet they were still there. I wondered what remained of their way of life.

Half an hour from Aoluguya, the road took us into forest, mainly firs with a few scattered birches. We had been told that there was an Ewenki forester's camp here, so I had a vague expectation of a busy reindeer farm, with people tending, feeding, milking, maybe even skinning reindeer carcasses. Turning off the road on to a muddy track, our four-wheel drive lurched past a sign announcing that there was a campsite here and urging us all, in one of Chairman Mao's slogans, to 'Go to the Mountains!' An array of solar panels showed that this outpost of the Ewenki hunting culture was in fact a part of the modern world, with power for lighting and a radio. The sound of pop music came faintly through the firs.

Leaving the car, we picked our way over boggy ground towards three wigwams covered in green canvas, two timber sheds, a rough wooden stockade, a wire fence and a tractor. Beyond the wire, half a dozen reindeer, many without antlers, trotted forward to greet these new arrivals. The floor of the whole camp was bare earth. A tree stump had been used as a chopping block, leaving a scattering of splinters.

A man in his late thirties, wearing a check shirt and jeans, sat at a table with four visitors, three young women and a man. The shed was a little shop selling toy guns and pots of powdered reindeer horn. The man in the check shirt was offering sunflower seeds to a small zoo of tame animals – little birds, two chipmunks and two rabbits. Occasionally, he used a catapult to shoot small stones at mice scouting for seeds under the shed floor. This was not a working community of reindeer herders, more a summer camp where a few adventure tourists could experience the forest for an hour or two. The shadowy light, the damp soil, the tinny radio, the low voices: I felt an overcast of melancholy.

His name was Gashka, and he had once been a hunter. 'Moose, red deer, roe deer. But going hunting does not mean we hunted everything. We never killed pregnant animals. We did not destroy the balance of nature. We needed our guns, not just for hunting but for self-protection. Not that I was ever in danger, but my brother met a bear once, and it slashed him across the face.' He tucked some snuff under his lower lip. 'But in 2008, the year of the [Beijing] Olympics, the government took away our guns.'

That was the final nail in the coffin for a culture that had been dying for years. In the 1960s, the reindeer herding had been collectivised, with the state buying pelts and antlers and putting the herders on a salary. That meant a loss of individual freedom, but at least left the economy intact.

The final change started in 2003. With the aim of protecting the forest, the government banned hunting and relocated the Reindeer Ewenki by moving them out of the forest into Aoluguya, where they were given free housing, free utilities and free medicine. State intervention was relaxed, part-privatising reindeer herding and the antler industry. The policies were justified as being part of a nationwide 'green-for-gain' campaign, in which local interests had to be sacrificed for the national interest. In this case, the national interest was best served by the conservation of China's largest forested zone, the Great Khingan mountains, the zone's main purpose being ecological – it was a 'green barrier' protecting agricultural lands to the south and east from the icy winds of Siberia, and should remain untouched.

There was also an ideological argument in favour of relocating the Reindeer Ewenki. In Marxist thinking, human societies were ranked, from hunter-gatherer to industrialised and socialist. On the scale of primitive to civilised, reindeer herders needed a helping hand to become more 'civilised' – meaning more Chinese – and take their proper place as members of an advanced economy.

From the Ewenki point of view, the ban on guns hurt as much as the ban on hunting. Once upon a time, they had used bows and arrows, until guns became part of their hunting culture in the eighteenth century. Guns provided food, protection and security, for oneself and for herds. Forbidden to hunt, deprived of their guns, their traditional life was over.

These events, life-changing for the Reindeer Ewenki, have implications far beyond them and their homeland. They raise fundamental questions about the protection of forests and grasslands, about gun control, about the effect of both on the nation, its cultures and its minority subcultures.

'Yes, I miss that way of life,' Gashka said, 'and so do my parents. They live in the city, but they are not used to city life. If my father had a rifle, he would still go hunting.'

I glanced at the canvas-covered tent. 'Does anyone still make tents in the old way, with birch bark?'

'We used skins when I was young. But we can't do that anymore, because we can't hunt.'

This was beginning to sound like a lament for a lost way of life. That was the agenda adopted by journalists and filmmakers who came to document the changes. They contrasted the old ways – sturdy independence, ancient wisdom – with the new: city dwelling, depression and drunken despair.

So, did Gashka want to turn the clock back? It wasn't that simple. Firstly, as he said, no one really wanted a return to the old ways. 'The younger generation, they hire people to help raise reindeer. They are not used to living in the forest. The state gives us the solar panels so we have power here, and anyway we're close to the city, so there are no large animals round here.'

Secondly, he had coped. Since he could no longer hunt, he had two businesses. The first was acting as host to some 4,500 tourists over the course of the summer months. The other was trading in reindeer antlers, which were turned into medicine, either as powder or in thin slices.

'We cut the antlers in May, to get the new growth. In November, the base falls off and new ones grow in the spring. The antlers sell to retailers for 3,600 RMB (about £360) per kilo, or 36 RMB per gram.' He had fifteen reindeer – some of which still had their antler stubs, this being mid-August – which brought him enough to live on. It was not an easy life. He had a pile of cut wood behind him, from fallen branches, because he was not allowed to cut down trees, and the forest administration didn't like him living in the forest. They thought he presented a 'fire hazard', despite the fact that forest Ewenki had never been known to cause fires.

Gashka cleared his throat and burst into song, a mournful Ewenki tune in praise of the forest. Three dogs I had not noticed, tied up among the trees, started to bark in chorus. An outsider might say he was yearning for the past. But it seemed to me he had accepted that the old ways had gone. He was a survivor, building on the ruins of the past.

## A CURE FOR EVERYTHING, A CURE FOR NOTHING

An hour later, we were back in Gun He, the suburb of Aoluguya where the Reindeer Ewenki now live. The government, well aware that the ban on guns would undermine their way of life, had provided for them, not just with free housing and electricity but also cash aid of 190 RMB (£19) per month.

For many ex-forest dwellers, it was not enough. What can replace a traditional way of life? Some fell into depression, some took to alcohol; journalists and filmmakers came to record what seemed a classic case of authoritarian meddling, with tragic and entirely negative results. An example is a prize-winning documentary made by Gu Tao, *The Last Moose of Aoluguya*, a moving, powerful and sad portrait of a lost generation of Ewenki forest dwellers. An ex-hunter named Weijia mourns, his words slurred by alcohol: 'Before in the old settlement, before we moved, we didn't have problems with drinking. We didn't really drink much. Then, the guns were gone. After we moved, there was nothing to do, so we started drinking. So, I drink. I have to work, so I am still alive. If I didn't have any work to do, I'd be dead too. It's like those Japanese samurai.' He makes a gesture of plunging a sword into his stomach. 'Let me just say it straight.' He comes close to the camera. 'If you lose your culture, it's like losing everything. So we begin to wither away. Drink! Just drink yourself to death! ... Is there any chance for us? No! It hurts to say it.' He drops his head in silent despair.

But this was not the whole truth, as Gashka showed. Yes, the Reindeer Ewenki have lost their world, with tragic consequences for some individuals. But there are other considerations. Few would wish to return to the tough life of a forest hunter, few would choose to live without medicines, few would wish to have no access to education (all points reinforced in my meeting later with the 'Ewenki matriarch', Maria). And even among the generation affected most strongly, some like Gashka adapt to a changing world.

I wondered what happened to the antlers he sold. An answer came from the tourist shop in Aoluguya, which stocked tangles of antlers, hanging from racks, a collection of reindeer hides and many boxes of antler medicine. The shopkeeper, a Han Chinese named Zhang Nailin, explained. He reached into a fridge, took out a plastic box and opened it to reveal twenty or thirty slices of antler. They looked like biscuits or potato crisps, and felt as light as polystyrene.

'It's like ginseng,' said Zhang. 'It improves your immune system. Try some.'

I did, and grimaced. Yes, polystyrene.

'You can also grind it into powder. For old people, it improves the brain.'

'In that case I better have a lot.'

'And for new-born babies, it helps to heal their heads when their skulls are still soft.'

Was there any truth in this? Certainly, reindeer antler, like antler velvet, has been used medicinally in China for centuries. Here is what an online review claims: deer antler base is 'anti-cancer, anti-fatigue, anti-osteoporosis, anti-inflammatory, analgesic, anti-bacterial, anti-viral, anti-stress, antioxidant, hypoglycaemic, haematopoietic modulatory, with therapeutic effect on mammary hyperplasia'. Well, anyone can make claims, and traditional medicine may be beneficial, but often isn't. After all, rhinoceros horn is sold as an aphrodisiac, on the basis of no evidence at all. Other papers are full of 'perhaps' and 'might', with nothing conclusive other than the fact that reindeer antler is harmless. In brief, it is a long-established placebo.

And quite a lucrative one. At 20,000 RMB (£2,200) per kilo, I would not be buying much, however diseased my brain.

'But you only take two or three grams a day,' said Zhang. That meant that each of the slices in the box cost about fifty RMB. 'You get about ten slices to each prong of an antler. The better slices come from the tip, but they are thicker, because they are more tender.'

Once, the state used to collect the antlers from the herders free of charge, but now, with privatisation, Zhang dealt directly. He bought antlers at 3,600 RMB per kilo, and he sold at 20,000 RMB per kilo. That's a profit of 550%: not a bad business, assuming the tourists kept buying. So far, so good. He had been here for twenty years.

He weighed a slice. It came to four grams, which would have cost eighty RMB, but he generously gave me a deal – two slices for a hundred RMB, a bargain that crumbled to dust in my backpack.

## THE MATRIARCH

I had heard that the reindeer people had a matriarch, an old lady who simply by her age was considered the most important survivor from the old days. Her name was Maria. She was amazingly old, they said, over a hundred. I imagined her as the last of her kind, a forest dweller who until recently had had no contact with the outside world, full of stories and folk-wisdom. I had seen pictures of her in the forest, in tepees, tending reindeer, and had been told that was where I would find her. Not so: she was right there in Aoluguya, in her daughter's apartment. Our local contact, Dai Guangyin, had arranged for me to see her. Water Xu would translate.

We drove to a back street, bought gifts of milk and fruit, entered a drab apartment block and climbed shadowy stairs to the first floor, to be greeted by Maria's middle-aged daughter, Dekesha. Her mother, Maria, was on a sofa, looking the very image of wisdom, her face gnarled as a walnut, silent and still. She spoke only Ewenki, so the talk flowed around her like water round a rock. Was she bored by yet another visitor, or baffled by talk in a language she did not understand? I could not tell, and apologised for the intrusion. After a few minutes it became clear that her silence was down to age and deafness. Her daughter did the talking.*

'You don't have to apologise,' said Dekesha. 'It is important that the outside world get to know about our endangered culture. No matter who

---

* Like most interviews, this one jumped back and forth between subjects. In addition, it was conducted in Ewenki, Chinese and English. I have edited it into chronological order to focus on Maria's story.

comes here, no matter where they come from, it is our responsibility – our mission – to preserve and promote our culture.'

I asked about Maria's youth, hoping that she herself would tell me. But when Dekesha spoke into her mother's ear, all she got in reply was a little 'Mm'. Dekesha spoke for her, with great sensitivity.

'My grandparents, my mother's parents, they lived on the Amur, and spoke Russian. We are the Amur-jo clan of Ewenkis. Before 1949, we used to cross the border all the time. I spoke Russian as a child, but I have forgotten most of it. Russians came hunting over here a lot, but after 1950 troops were stationed along the border, and we could not cross any more, and began to learn Chinese. By then my mother was twenty. She was born in the forest in 1930.'

So that made her not one hundred, but only eighty-nine. She looked older, showing the effects not so much of old age as the harshness of her life.

'Maria,' I said, though it comes out as Maliya in Chinese, with an *l*. 'Is that an Ewenki name?'

'No. It was given to her by the Russian Orthodox Church.'

*What?* Outside influences had reached her after all.

'Yes, she was taken to the church in… I forget… 'Oñi, where was it?' Dekesha spoke into her mother's ear, and Maria replied so quietly I could hardly hear: 'Toboi.'

'That's it. She was baptised in Toboi. I don't know if the church is still there.' (Or even the place. I could find no trace of it.)

'So,' I said, 'Maria, Maliya – that was her Russian name. She had another name before? An Ewenki name?

'Yes.'

'And that was?'

Another query from Dekesha to her mother, and the old lady said, 'Nököö.'

Around the time of her birth there had been another contact with the outside world. The indomitable ethnologist Ethel Lindgren had come with her companion and future husband, Oscar Mamen, with his camera. They were there three times between 1929 and 1932. Perhaps among the nineteen thousand photographs is one of Maria's parents, even Maria herself as a one- or two-year-old.

Her childhood was spent in the forest. 'There were two important things to say about life as my mother was growing up,' Dekesha went on. 'The first thing is that life for children was rather boring and simple. She used to go fishing and catch butterflies. She was taught about how to survive in harsh conditions by her parents, how to use a rifle to protect herself. It was a tough life, especially in winter when children and old people needed the hides of small bears to keep warm. They were very precious, those hides. And now you see models wearing them in fashion shows! There were stories, of course, stories about the Sungirl. So many stories! That was what her life was like for her before schooling started.'

Another surprise. For some reason I had assumed she was a child of the forest, and therefore had never been to school.

'When she was eight, the Japanese came, and she went to a Japanese school for two summers, in a camp in Erguna.'

'What was it like?' The Japanese, ruling in Manchukuo and intending to extend their empire into Central Asia, were such archetypal enemies that – as Dekesha spoke into her mother's ear – I expected Maria to say how terrible the experience had been. Not at all.

'Good!' she said, emphatically.

'It was a hard life, but was it also dangerous?'

'Well, we had guns, so we could protect ourselves. If you were unlucky, you might come across a bear with its prey. But normally, if you saw a bear, if you stayed calm and just looked at it, the bear would go away. The most dangerous thing was illness. We easily caught tuberculosis, and we needed medicine. Traditional medicine was not enough. We needed Western medicine. I had six brothers and sisters, but now only me and a brother survive. Five died from disease and accidents. This gentleman's father' – she nodded to Dai, sitting quietly to one side – 'Dai Yingshou, he devoted his life to bringing us medicine, travelling four or five days without sleep. He helped us for over thirty years. When we got sick, we would send reindeer to carry him into the forest. He saved many lives. And when the animals got sick, we turned to him. We have much respect for him.'

'Did you use reindeer antlers for medicine?'

'When my mother was young, they didn't cut off the antlers. Each family had about a dozen reindeer, but then life got better, and the numbers increased. In the 1980s, our groups of families had about four hundred reindeer. Only then did the state take over, and we started to trade in antlers.'

'Was it a big shock when guns were banned?'

'That was in 2008, and we weren't using guns so much anymore. But naturally guns were part of our lives. We loved using rifles. But we became educated in ways to protect the environment and the animals. There was a farewell ceremony, when young people kissed goodbye to their guns and handed them over to the government.'

'How did she feel about it now? How do young people feel?'

'The younger generation, they live on the internet. How would they get that in the forest? Yes, we need to protect traditional culture, but on the other hand it's important for the kids to get a higher education. Personally, I would not encourage my daughter to go into the forest. It's a contradiction.'

'Will the language and culture survive?'

'Well, the official language is Mandarin Chinese. That's what you need if you want to find a job. As long as there are reindeer, there will be people who raise reindeer. But they may no longer be Ewenki.'

As we said our goodbyes, I realised Maria and her daughter had revealed my ignorance. A way of life had vanished, but it had not been quite the loss I had imagined. Far from being totally isolated in the forest, Maria and her people had always had a working relationship with the outside world, and were, it seemed to me, better prepared for change than naïve outsiders imagined. I had assumed that Aologuya would be a place of depressive drunks, bitter at the government for taking away their guns and their hunting culture. But what was the alternative?

Government policy on gun control is nationwide. It could not easily allow for exceptions. And if it did, what then?

When we met again, even Ilana, though passionate about her people and their culture, had no answer. Yes, as she said, 'the suicide rate was serious, because people had been robbed of their culture. They took away everything. They took away our dreams.'

I hesitated. 'The government recognise this?'

'Yes. That's why they provide nice houses, electricity, water, everything. But still people feel empty.'

But again: what was the alternative? Ilana shook her head. 'Maybe there could be guns in the future… but that would lead to other social problems. Robberies, perhaps murders. And after all we have our autonomous banner, we have our leaders.'

In the end, it seemed that Dekesha had the best response: acceptance that the past was gone, acceptance of change, hopes for future generations. I was lucky to have had a brief insight into their Ewenki past. A few years from now, it will be too late.

*Postscript: Maria died on 20 August 2022. According to her daughter, she was aged 93, though journalists said she was 101.*

*Before it all went wrong: a propaganda poster from about 1950 shows Marx, Engels, Lenin, Stalin and Mao as the indivisible Communist pantheon. The slogan reads: 'Long live the invincible Marxism-Leninism and Mao Zedong Thought!' It didn't last much longer.*

CHAPTER 13

# THE WAR THAT NEVER WAS

## A SPLIT, AND BORDER CLASHES

IN SOME OTHER UNIVERSE, IN ONE OF THE INFINITE VERSIONS of earthly events that must in theory exist in an infinity of universes, a fallen candle did not burn down London, an archduke's murder did not start a world war, and a small battle on an insignificant river-island in Manchuria led to a nuclear holocaust. Well, in the world we know, events turned out differently, but in the last case it was a close-run thing. In the end, the crisis shocked the world's three major powers – America, Soviet Russia and China – into a new balance that would last for twenty years, and a fuzzy frontier was finally fixed.

Let's start with a name. In the spring of 1888, Stanislav Damansky, a Russian engineer, was with a team in Manchuria surveying a possible route for this section of the Trans-Siberian Railway. It was to join Khabarovsk on the Amur to Vladivostok on the Pacific coast, 750 kilometres to the south. The line would run parallel to the broad, meandering Ussuri River, which was the border with China, a few kilometres the other side of a line of hills.

After guiding their horses down through marshy forest to the river bank, Damansky and two soldiers set out in a boat to map one of the many islands formed and re-formed by the restless river. This one was a couple of kilometres long and five hundred metres across, with some grass and a scattering of trees. The map held by the Russians was one based on the 1860 Treaty of Peking, which drew the border down the Chinese side of the river, so they would not have known they were about to intrude on territory claimed by China. Something happened in mid-stream, and all three were drowned. Several days later, the river cast up Damansky's body on the island he had been about to survey. In his memory, his team gave the island his name.

But the island already had a name, not that Damansky and his colleagues could have known. In Chinese, it is called Zhenbao (zhēnbǎo 珍宝) Island, Treasure Island, because the local shepherds and fishermen said it looked like a traditional bowl-shaped golden coin.

Damansky/Zhenbao Island was utterly insignificant, along with over three hundred other islands in the Ussuri, until, almost a century later, it became the focus of worldwide attention, in a conflict that almost sparked nuclear war between the Soviet Union and China. The dispute, an Asian equivalent of the 1962 Cuban Missile Crisis, highlights both the geopolitics of the day and the dangers that are with us still: the precarious balance of great powers, egotistical autocrats and the adulation of their followers. It also revealed the need to fix the ill-defined Russo-Chinese border once and for all.

In the mid-1950s, that border should have been peaceful. Both nations were Communist, both worshipped the gods of Communism, Marx, Lenin and Stalin. In theory, they were good neighbours. But both had erratic leaders with giant egos – Joseph Stalin and then Nikita Khrushchev in the USSR, Mao Zedong in China – who were determined to impose impossible economic goals on their suffering populations.

China's fate depended on Mao's relationship with Stalin. The Soviet dictator had distrusted Mao, and in China's civil war (1927–1949) he had courted both sides. But after 1949 Stalin was the prime source of financial, ideological and practical support. Mao had no choice but to be the resentful junior, until Stalin's death in 1953 offered an opportunity to seize the leadership of the Communist world. To achieve this, Mao wrapped himself in Stalin's mantle. So Mao was appalled when

Stalin's heir, Nikita Khrushchev, denounced Stalin at the Twentieth Party Congress in 1956 and announced a new policy of peaceful co-existence with Europe and America, in the hope of a worldwide transition to socialism. This, he said, would bring affluence, 'a plate of goulash for everyone'. Mao struck back crudely, playing on the sound of the Russian word in Chinese. 'Every Russian,' he said, 'would get a plate of *gou la shi* [dog shit].'

In 1958, Mao pronounced that China would make a Great Leap Forward, in which his impoverished country would use its peasant population to overtake all capitalist countries in a single bound and dominate the world. This was to be achieved by ordering everyone to smelt steel and at the same time to multiply their harvests many fold. Of many mad orders, these were the maddest, and the cruellest. In the ensuing famine (1959–62), whole regions were reduced to calorie levels equal to those of prisoners in Auschwitz. Cannibalism was common. In one village in Gansu, a couple killed and ate their eight-year-old son. An official report from Linxia, south of Lanzhou, listed other cases, this among them: 'Manner of crime: Hacked to death. Cooked and eaten. Reason: Livelihood issues.'[1] In a time of chaos, missing records and official lies, estimates of the dead range widely, with a 1979 analysis, arguably the best, putting the number at 45 million.[2] Society collapsed almost totally. In Frank Dikötter's words, survival 'came increasingly to depend on the ability to lie, charm, hide, steal, cheat, pilfer, forage, smuggle, trick, manipulate or otherwise outwit the state'. Indeed, these very evils were what kept anything at all running. Mao's Great Famine was the worst man-made disaster in history.

To help out their Communist brothers, the Soviet premier, Khrushchev, promised to fulfil Mao's long-held dream of acquiring an atom bomb, plus much technical aid. To reassure Mao that he had a free hand in the whole country, Khrushchev pulled all things Russian out of Russian-dominated Xinjiang. But Mao nursed his resentment over Khrushchev's denunciation of his hero, and also over the Unequal Treaties, by which Russia had seized large chunks of Siberia and Manchuria, backed

Mongolia's independence (detailed in Chapter 11), and taken control of several islands along the Amur and its tributaries. In April 1960, the Chinese Communists denounced the Russians as 'revisionists', traitors to the doctrines of Marx, Lenin and Stalin, a crime as heinous as 'Western imperialism'.

Khrushchev was incensed. Two months later, at a congress of the Romanian Communist Party in Bucharest, the Soviet delegation jeered the Chinese. 'Since you love Stalin so much,' said Khrushchev, 'why don't you take his corpse to Peking?' The following month, he withdrew all of Russia's 1,390 scientific and technical experts, and scrapped 441 science projects and industrial enterprises. The promised prototype atomic bomb was never sent.

Mao was unfazed, or pretended to be. He would ensure that China got the bomb anyway – and it did, in 1964. Nuclear war was coming, he told the new Soviet foreign minister Andrei Gromyko, but so what? 'You [Russia and the US] may well be wiped out. China too will suffer, but will still have 400 million people left over' – enough to spread Communism across all Asia and Africa. When, in the Cuban Missile Crisis of October 1962, Khrushchev agreed to withdraw Russian rockets from Cuba, his climb-down inspired diatribes from Mao, with a direct appeal to the Russian-dominated nations of eastern Europe for their support.

Meanwhile, the matter of the Unequal Treaties kept bubbling up, like a neurosis from the Chinese unconscious. It was there in 1943, when the Nationalists and Communists both claimed credit for the 'abolition' and 'termination' of the Unequal Treaties. Mongolia was also part of the problem, because China blamed Russia for ripping Mongolia from the Manchu Empire. Only in January 1946, three months after the plebiscite, did China recognise Mongolia as a nation-state. In the lives of many Chinese, therefore, Mongolia was in effect part of China. It was so for centuries in past times: under the Qin on and off, depending on relations with the Xiongnu; under the Mongols for a century (1262–1368); under the Manchus (1691–1912); and, in theory if not in practice, under Chinese Nationalist rule (1912–46). This was Chiang Kai-shek's view before Mao came to power and, as a result, the Nationalist government in Taiwan included Mongolia as part of China in its maps for many years after 1949. Mao shared the same opinion. He raised the issue with Stalin in February 1949 and again with Khrushchev after Stalin's death in 1953, suggestions that both Soviet leaders brushed away. On 8 March 1963 an editorial in the *People's Daily* made the first official mention of the Unequal Treaties, saying it was a problem that would have to be addressed. In July 1964, Mao told Japanese Socialist Party members that before Russia occupied all the Far East, much of it – including Mongolia – had been Chinese and 'We have not yet presented our account.'

Resentment bred resentment, on both sides. Clashes multiplied all along the unsurveyed border, with both parties blaming the other. In June 1960, local officials in Xinjiang ordered shepherds to drive fifteen thousand sheep across the border to back a claim that the land was China's. It took weeks for Soviet guards to usher them out. In the spring of 1962, Kazakhs started to flee China's famine to seek a better life in Soviet Kazakhstan. Soviet border guards created gaps in the fences for them and 62,000 Kazakhs made the crossing.

As for the Amur and Ussuri region, the Unequal Treaties were high on Mao's list of grievances. He pointed out that the nineteenth-century maps had been inadequate and that river-borders should run along the deepest part, as prescribed by international law. This would place many islands, including Damansky/Zhenbao, inside China.* The Soviet leaders were not totally intractable. In early 1964, a Russian delegation in Beijing to discuss the border disputes was ready to concede Mao's point, until Mao mentioned the land lost to Russia. His claims involved not only the length of the northern border and hundreds of islands, but also everything that had been part of the Manchu Empire and therefore by rights belonged to China. This was not negotiation. It was sabotage.

---

* Another example: at the junction of the Ussuri and the Amur, just west of Khabarovsk, the island of Great Ussuriisk (Black Bear Island to the Chinese) was in theory Chinese, but was seized by Russia in 1929. A new agreement in 2004 divided the island between both powers.

Positions hardened. When Khrushchev was pensioned off in 1964, his dour successor Leonid Brezhnev showed little interest in détente. Nor did Mao. In February 1965, Brezhnev's second-in-command, the mournful-looking premier Alexei Kosygin, came to Beijing on his way back from Vietnam, aiming to restore relations by getting Mao's agreement to forgo public polemics, to which Mao replied that he was happy to continue them for ten thousand years, though he would drop that to nine thousand in acknowledgment of Kosygin's visit.[3] A Soviet treaty with Mongolia on 15 January 1966 allowed for new Russian bases there, and over 100,000 troops, which rose by 1969 to twenty-seven divisions and an estimated 800,000 men.[4] Border guards clashed several times in 1967–8 – Russia claimed 2,000 border violations in 1967 alone, while China claimed 4,189 of them in 1964–9 – with tensions rising further after the Soviet invasion of Czechoslovakia in 1968. This was justified by the so-called Brezhnev Doctrine, proclaiming Moscow's right to intervene militarily wherever socialism was threatened – which might conceivably include China.

## ENGINEERING CHAOS

A major point of conflict was our old friend the Damansky/Zhenbao island. According to China, this useless crescent of sandy pasture was legally Chinese not only because it was on the Chinese side of what should be the border, but also because it had once been joined to the Chinese bank, before the river cut through. Indeed, at low water, in summer, you could walk across to it, as Chinese fishermen sometimes did to dry their nets. In winter, when the river froze solid, you could drive or walk across from both sides.

China claimed that Russians intruded on to the island numerous times in 1967–9, citing many well-documented abuses – ramming Chinese fishing boats, robbing nets, squirting fishermen with high-pressure hoses, kidnapping them, assaulting frontier guards, violating Chinese air space, and sending tanks and armoured cars into Chinese territory. Russia replied that they had often allowed Chinese on to this *Russian* soil to fish, herd livestock and cut hay, but that in no way conferred the right of ownership.

All this during the next catastrophe imposed by Mao on his unhappy people, the Cultural Revolution, a ten-year rampage by millions of young and impressionable Red Guards, who were unleashed to shore up Mao's shaky authority by humiliating and torturing 'capitalist roaders', 'revisionists' and other fictitious or vastly exaggerated dangers, driving many to death or suicide.

Among their targets were 'pan-Mongolists', who dreamed of a Greater Mongolia, linking Inner, Outer and Buryat Mongolians. To Mao, for whom national unity now trumped minority rights, Mongolian nationalism could tear China apart and restore the empire of Chinggis Khan, or at least its core. Prime suspect as would-be perpetrator was the man who ruled Inner Mongolia, Ulanhu, or Yun Ze as he was originally, before giving himself a Mongolian name meaning 'Red Son'. He is worth a digression,[5] because his career spotlights the tension between nationalisms, Chinese and Mongolian, and the agenda that brought China to the brink of war. A staunch Communist, colleague of Mao and anti-Japanese warrior, Ulanhu had ensured Inner Mongolian support for the Communists. His reward was high office – chairman of the Inner Mongolian government, the only minority Politburo member, and several other positions. But he was living with a paradox: Mao had once promised autonomy for oppressed minorities, including the Mongols, treating them as subjects colonised by the Manchu imperialists; yet now he said they were not oppressed after all, but Chinese citizens bound by the need for national unity. In brief: to support Mongols was to betray China. The 'Mongolian Khan' – as he was labelled – was accused, in early 1967, of plotting with the Soviets to join Inner to Outer Mongolia, of trying to turn himself into Chinggis Khan the Second. This ludicrous accusation, which sparked a riot in Inner Mongolia, was soon set aside. He went on to serve as vice president from 1983 to his death in 1988. In Inner Mongolia, he is still as close to royalty as you can get in China, and so are his descendants. His son, Buhe, also became Inner Mongolia's chairman, as did Buhe's daughter, Bu Xiaolin – the third generation to govern this vast estate. Ulanhu's Mongolian was poor, his granddaughter Madam Bu's non-existent, reflecting the shifting balance between minority rights and the demands of the state – now largely resolved in the state's favour, I'm sorry to say, as we shall see in the Epilogue.

To return to our subject, the dispute over that island in the Amur, the focal point for Mao's virulent nationalism.

Both sides sent more troops to the border. By the late 1960s, the Soviets had about 300,000 men, with reserves quickly available along the Trans-Siberian railway, and a massive superiority in tanks, artillery, armoured cars and aircraft. China had about 170,000 men in the Manchuria region, rising to the equivalent of forty divisions – some 500,000 men. But China's superiority in numbers would be quickly countered by Russian armour. The stage was set for a major confrontation, possibly all-out war.

Patrols on Damansky/Zhenbao clashed like rival street-gangs, using clubs and rifle-butts. In the bitter snows of February 1968, the Chinese organised loudspeakers and crowds shouting slogans and waving Mao's Little Red Book of quotations. 'A sharp command sounded from the amplifier,' recalled a Russian officer. 'The entire crowd numbering several hundred turned in our direction. I was scared. On the faces of the Chinese were grimaces of evil and hatred. They were all hysterically yelling, shaking their fists, slogans and posters.' In months of confrontation, troops and protesting crowds chased each other away from presumed borderlines, with both sides obeying orders not to be the first to open fire.

On 22 January 1969, the Russians, commanded by an officer called Ivan Strelnikov, a handsome senior lieutenant who was recovering from a leg injury (nick-named 'Captain Limpy' by the Chinese), released dogs and seized nine weapons, some loaded and ready to fire. 'Those bloody Russian dogs were ferocious,' recalled one Chinese participant. 'They took chunks off many of the lads... I still have the teeth marks in my thigh.'[6] A month later, in a more serious clash, the Russians fired six shots. All missed, but live fire raised the stakes. Mao decided on new tactics.

## THE FIRST BATTLE

The Ninth Party Congress was due in April, and Mao needed a foreign enemy to divert attention from the excesses of the Cultural Revolution and offer a symbol of triumph over that enemy. There would be a show-down, an ambush, in which the Russians would appear to be at fault. A special unit of three hundred men received automatic assault rifles and cold-weather gear. Thirty others would act as decoys, luring the Russians on to territory the Chinese claimed as their own. All the Russians would be killed, and with no witnesses China would act the innocent but brave victim.

On the night of 1 March, the ambush teams, armed with Kalashnikovs and with white capes over their shoulders, scattered into the dunes and ridges of Damansky Island, unravelling telephone lines. Fortified by rice vodka and biscuits, they spent a bitter, sleepless night on straw mats. Shortly after 8 a.m. that Sunday the decoys set off in two teams along the frozen Ussuri towards the southern tip of the island.

Around 10.40 a.m. they were spotted from a Soviet observation post. Senior Lieutenant Ivan Strelnikov set off over the ice with six others (including a photographer) in a staff car, followed by an armoured personnel carrier (APC) with fifteen men and a two-tonne vehicle-rescue truck with twelve men, which was underpowered and fell behind, luckily for one of the men inside.

At about 11.15, Strelnikov's group, carrying automatic rifles, parked on the ice and walked forward to confront the Chinese (as photographs taken by cameramen on both sides show). A second group peeled off to the island. The Chinese seemed not to be threatening, but at a signal – two shots in some memories, or a shout in others – everything changed.

In one version of events, the front rank of Chinese parted to reveal a second rank, who drew submachine guns from under their coats and opened fire. In another version, those hidden on the island opened up. Strelnikov and the six others died instantly (including the photographer Private Nikolai Petrov, who fell on his still camera, inadvertently hiding it when the Chinese searched his body later, preserving his pictures). The second Russian group, on the island itself one hundred metres away, returned fire, but all except one died.

The Chinese hidden on the island emerged, fired, advanced and finished off wounded Russians with bayonets – a war crime, denied by China, but attested by Russian photographs.

Only one Russian, Private Genady Serebrov, survived, relating what happened when he regained consciousness in hospital. Approaching from the now stationary tow-truck, he recalled: 'Private Yegupov as walking in front of me. Suddenly I saw Chinese lying in the snow behind the trees. They were aiming their rifles at us. Then we heard a loud shout, apparently the order to open fire. Bullets struck Yegupov and he fell on the snow. I immediately shot a long burst from the machine gun at the Chinese. They stood from their hiding places and came directly towards us, firing on the move. I attempted to take cover behind a tree, but felt a strong blow to my leg, above the knee, then a second, a third, and a feeling as if it was being torn to pieces, and then I lost consciousness.'

Meanwhile, the news of the Chinese 'incursion' had reached a Russian observation post some seventeen kilometres to the north and an APC with twenty-three men was advancing south on the ice. Arriving in the middle of the battle, the men inside got out and joined in. The APC started to circle the island, with its commander firing its heavy machine gun, taking out the Chinese command post, until fire from the Chinese bank knocked out his gun. Chinese soldiers from the ambush group, with no new orders from the shattered command post, made a ragged withdrawal back to the Chinese bank, dragging their wounded with them, but leaving one body behind.

By about midday, the battle was over. The Russians began to treat their wounded before frostbite set in, helped by local villagers with sleighs and a helicopter that had been on manoeuvres one hundred kilometres away. They lost fifteen wounded, and three vehicles; thirty-one died at the scene, while one, Private Pavel Akulov, was taken alive, but tortured to death; his body was exchanged for the Chinese body found on the battlefield and identified by his mother. The Chinese losses remain unknown, but were in the order of twenty to thirty dead and seventy wounded.

The same day, China's Foreign Ministry sent an amazingly deceptive and self-righteous note of protest to the Soviet ambassador. Soviet troops, it said, 'flagrantly intruded into the area of Zhenbao Island, which is indisputable Chinese territory, carried out blatant provocations… and were the first to open cannon and gun fire.'

In Moscow, the Soviet leaders were frantic at the failure of their intelligence. What if the Chinese attack was a prelude to all-out invasion? Brezhnev briefly considered a pre-emptive strike on Beijing, before settling for a limited response. Reinforcements rushed to the Ussuri – four companies of a motor-rifle regiment, artillery and most crucially nine T-62 tanks. These magnificent beasts, weighing thirty-seven tonnes each, had long gun-barrels designed to fire shells that would pierce the armour of new Western tanks, like the British Centurions. The four-man crew could drive them at forty kilometres per hour cross-country. China had nothing to match them.

Mao, though apparently willing to court nuclear war, had a more limited agenda. For the Ninth Party Congress in April, he planned to claim leadership in the spread of Communism worldwide and present the 'revisionist' Soviet Union as an aggressor, China as the victim. That was the message pumped out by the state-controlled media. Mobs high on outrage induced by propaganda gathered outside the Soviet embassy. In days, the protests spread nationwide. By 12 March, several hundred million had demonstrated in dozens of cities.

Mao needed more for his high-risk strategy to be complete – victory in a second, greater Battle for Damansky/Zhenbao Island, with more infantry, more artillery, more heavy machine-gun companies and anti-tank units and mines to deal with the T-62s. The tactics would be the same: to lure the Soviets into a fight on Chinese territory. The first plan was to engage on an island a few kilometres to the north, but it was less suitable for tanks, and the idea was for the world to see the Soviets in full force, tanks and all, brutally assaulting the heroic defenders of the Chinese homeland. By the evening of 14 March, with twelve anti-tank minefields newly laid, the Chinese were ready for action.

So were the Soviets. They planned a pincer assault from north and south with their tanks and a dozen APCs, in the company of infantry and backed by long-range artillery based on the Soviet bank.

## THE SECOND ROUND

Early on 15 March, Soviet APCs delivered forty-five soldiers to the middle of the island. They dug in. At 8 a.m., from loudspeakers on the Chinese shore, a woman speaking perfect Russian demanded that the Russians leave 'Chinese territory'. At 8.30, Chinese artillery and mortars opened up on the Russian APCs and infantry. Two APCs went up in flames. The Chinese sent two thousand men in a charge across the ice. Russian machine-gun fire felled many but failed to stop them. The Russians, now low on ammunition and under pressure from China's ten-to-one superiority in manpower, retreated, then counter-attacked with five tanks, twenty APCs carrying 180 men and multi-barrelled rocket launchers. The lead tank hit a mine, which blew off one of its tracks, and the crew abandoned it. The commander, D.V. Leonov, fell, shot through the heart. The Chinese kept on advancing in groups of two hundred, until it became clear that it would take a bombardment by Russian howitzers and 'Grad' rockets on a hill four to five kilometres away to knock out the Chinese guns.

But that would widen the battle. With the sun going down and the temperature dropping, time was short, but no one in the Soviet command post was ready to take responsibility for giving the order to use heavy artillery. Permission finally came through from Brezhnev himself. The batteries opened fire at about 17.00, for just ten minutes, with pinpoint accuracy, destroying the Chinese guns and leaving unknown numbers of dead. The barrage was followed up with two hundred soldiers in eighteen APCs and the surviving tanks.

The battle was over by 18.30, the island cleared of all Chinese. The Russians lost about sixty men, six APCs and a T-62 tank (which has its own story, as we will see later). Chinese deaths were probably several hundred, perhaps as many as eight hundred, a figure widely quoted but never proven, since most of the dead were buried in mass graves near the battle site. A memorial hall in the nearby town of Baiqing lists only sixty-eight names.

That evening, Moscow, in the self-righteous tone adopted by both sides, protested at 'this new, naked, armed aggression by Chinese authorities... Damansky Island is an integral part of Soviet territory... The borders of the Soviet Union are sacred and inviolable... all responsibility for possible serious consequences of similar reckless actions rests squarely on the Chinese.'

In China, the Party ramped up fear of an imminent invasion. Today the Cuban Missile Crisis is fading from living memory in the West. Younger generations can hardly comprehend the fear felt in the US and Europe, the sudden obsession with four-minute warnings and bomb shelters. In China, the fear amounted to nationwide hysteria. News reports, government policy and rumour combined to create an atmosphere of scarcely controlled panic. '*Brezhnev plans to attack China!*' people told each other. '*A million Soviet soldiers are ready to strike!*'

'I was a student at the time,' my friend and adviser Alatan remembered. 'We dug out shelters by hand, then to forget the fear we played hide-and-seek in them.'

## Reminders of the Great Fear

Alatan's words came alive in a park in north-east China, near the border. Busuli Fortress, said the placard at the entrance. A 'No Smoking' sign reminded us that we were in the depths of the Khingan forest, from which the place took its name, 'Busuli' being the word for 'dense forest' in the local language, Oroqen. We saw no hint of any fortress. But the past was not far away. Hills closed in the north, east and west, with a valley open to the south to bring in reinforcements or provide escape. A slogan from the late 1960s urged everyone to 'Get ready in case of starvation!' Military statues beside a line of shops reminded passers-by that this had once been a military base. Quite a base, the guide told us as our electric bus carried us past two lakes, the biggest base in north China – seventy-three square kilometres. It had once housed two thousand soldiers, who had lived here in secrecy, building the place up in case of war. We were off to see its heart, the key to survival in the event of a nuclear strike.

Our 'electric donkey', as it was called, turned on to a gravel-covered parade ground, in the lee of a steep, forest-covered hill, maybe 150 metres high. We stopped beside a wooden shed, from which park wardens produced green, padded army greatcoats. It was a sunny day in August, yet we were being prepared for winter, because (said the guide) inside the hill it was always winter. A stone-sided gully led to a tunnel with a metal door. It was the entrance to a different universe: ominous, grim and cold – the temperature dropped with every pace, down to three degrees Celsius, even on a hot day like this one.

In we went. Well-spaced bulbs turned the tunnel into pools of light, our shadows creeping from pool to pool as we stepped over pipes and past mysterious side-chambers full of containers. 'This was where they stored the fuel – the fuel – the fuel,' echoed the guide's voice. Small chambers held 100 tonnes, he said, larger ones 2,227 tonnes. How many tonnes were stored here? Couldn't tell, he replied, because this was one of nine tunnels, each with its own entrance, with thirty-six storage tanks in all. This whole line of hills had been hollowed out to house and sustain an army for six months.

I let the others go on ahead through another metal door, watching them fade into darkness like ghosts, and found myself in a set for a horror movie. Far-off voices echoed from the concrete walls. Light from scattered bulbs glinted on puddles, formed by drops from the damp walls. The cold began to eat into my hands and feet. Pipes ran underfoot and vanished into shadows. My imagination began to work overtime. What would it have been like down here, trapped by atomised ruins and radiation? What if the door, for no reason, clanged shut and the lights failed and I was alone in total darkness? I shivered, shrugged off the hint of claustrophobia, stepped through the doorway and hurried to catch up with the others.

Outside, we exchanged padded coats for sunshine. Further along the side of the hills, past another eleven entrances that led into the maze of hidden tunnels, was the command centre, four white single-storey buildings set into the steep, wooded slopes like cave-dwellings, a type of construction that helped with heating in the winter. Here were the remnants of that fear-filled world – austere dormitories, storerooms for food, a basic kitchen, a communication room with old radios, a weapons store and on the walls posters to remind officers of their duty to Marx, Lenin, Engels, Stalin and Mao. Everyday objects – washbowls, wickerwork helmets, blankets piled on wooden beds – recalled the basic lifestyle of the officers who supervised the work crews digging out the kilometres of tunnels. It took almost thirty years, during which time the locals had no idea what was happening inside the secret base. Only in 1997, five years after the collapse of the Soviet Union, did work on Busuli stop and the veil of secrecy was lifted.

Close to the commander's house was a dark green Russian tank, a T-62, set on a plinth. This was the park's prize exhibit, despite being a copy. The real thing has a story of its own.

## THE TAKING OF TANK 545

As the fighting ended on 15 March 1969, the wrecked T-62 stood in the snow, its left track broken, sixty metres from the river bank, on ice peppered by shellfire. Well aware that the Chinese would want to copy its advanced features, the Russians determined to destroy it, while the Chinese were equally determined to salvage it. For ten days, the two sides duelled, the Russians firing mortars and machine guns, the Chinese risking death clearing mines and laying barbed wire to deter Russians, but leaving a pathway for themselves to approach the tank.

On the twenty-eighth, a thirty-man team arrived with a steel cable and a winch. Actually, the team included a woman, a mechanical engineer named Xiong Kefang, who had been working on upgrading China's most up-to-date tank. Married, with a two-year-old son, she combined expertise with austere practicality and a cool head. 'When I was assigned the mission [on the T-62],' she recalled later, 'I left my son with a close relative and immediately hopped on a train without saying goodbye to my husband. All I did was leave a note on the kitchen table... [on arrival] all the men and I were in one tent. It was inconvenient, but I am used to roughing it.' Ignoring the risks from Russian mortars and sniper fire, she insisted she had to enter the tank before any attempt was made to tow it. With two guards to help her, working in twilight,

> I tried to board the tank, but one shell landed too close for comfort and I lost my footing on the caterpillar track. I fell backward into a shell-hole in the river. Luckily the soldiers held on to me, stopping me from being totally submerged in the freezing water. But my padded pants were wet. The soldiers asked me to go back and change, but... I am not a princess, and stepped into the tank, with a torch in hand. I felt around and discovered there was no bulkhead wall, and I could look into the engine compartment as well as put my hand in and have a good feel around.[7]

Spring was on its way, the temperature rising. Xiong's work came to an abrupt end a few days later, when the tank fell through the weakened ice into two metres of water. Muddy sediment held it fast, frustrating attempts to tow it out. On 12 April, four navy divers arrived with a stronger winch. Working in twilight to avoid Russian snipers and machine-gunners, the Chinese cut a channel in the ice. It took several attempts by the scuba divers to find the towing eyelet and attach the cable, only for a Russian shell to cut it. On the eighteenth, the weather improved more, and the ice began to break up, making further scuba diving impossible.

As spring advanced, hard-hat diving suits arrived. To hide operations from Russian spy planes and observers, tractors brought in shelters and used their engines to drown the noise of the work. Divers managed to attach a stronger cable and also remove the turret of the tank, lightening the body. Finally, on 30 April, before dawn, it was dragged ashore, a task made even more difficult because the wheels were locked in gear. On 2 May, with the wheels unlocked and the gun turret replaced, it was ready for display at an award ceremony safely clear of the battle zone. Weeks later, it was in the Military Museum in Beijing, where the newly introduced features – infrared night scope, gun stabiliser and details of the diesel engine – all proved useful for engineers working on a new generation of Chinese tanks.

## How Nixon saved Mao

Back in mid-March, tensions remained high. The only slight reassurance came on 21 March when Kosygin spoke to Zhou Enlai, and both agreed war was not about to break out. In an incident that soon became famous, they spoke only after Kosygin had tried to call Mao, a call which ended abruptly when the Chinese operator refused to put him through on the grounds that he was a 'revisionist', and cut him off.[8] Pending a long-term resolution, there were bound to be more confrontations like the one on the Ussuri, perhaps with even worse consequences.

The next one followed five months later. On the far side of China, in the arid semi-desert on the frontier with Soviet Kazakhstan, the border was nothing but a pencil line on a map, a place where shepherds had always crossed back and forth in search of pasture. Following the Ussuri incident, Soviet troops put up a wire fence, cutting across long-established migration routes. On 10 August, a Chinese guard went missing and was found dead, hanging on the wire, his body severely beaten. The Chinese, believing an assault was coming, planned a patrol to a border post named after the Terekti (Tielieketi) River, which flows into Kazakhstan, before evaporating in lowlands. Before dawn on 13 August, the Chinese border patrol started to dig in on high ground the Soviets claimed as theirs. Exchanges of fire killed twenty-eight Chinese and two Soviet soldiers. The *Washington Post* reported that Russia was considering a nuclear strike.

By now, however, Mao had reason to believe his high-risk gamble had paid off, thanks to an unexpected word from the man who he had once considered his greatest enemy: Richard Nixon, America's newly elected president.

This is the story as told to me by Alatan in the car as we left Busuli. It was apparently common knowledge in China, and has been backed up by subsequent accounts,[9] explaining Mao's actions and the stunning geopolitical change that followed in 1972.

This is how the story goes:

Nixon wins the American presidency in November 1968. It's the height of the Cold War, USA versus the USSR. The US believes that Communism, a monolithic ideology, will spread worldwide if given a chance: first Russia, then Mongolia, then China, with Vietnam next and beyond. This is the so-called Domino Theory. To stop Communism, America is fighting a war in Vietnam. Nixon inherits that war. It's a political and economic quagmire. He wants out, but how? China has split with the Soviets, who face two opponents, not one. Perhaps this division offers an opportunity.

From spies in the Kremlin, Nixon hears that Brezhnev may be planning nuclear war with China. If this comes to pass, it will turn the Soviet Union into a *super* superpower, undermining America's dominant position on the world stage. He must stop it. He opens secret lines of communication through the US embassies in Pakistan and Romania, and sends Mao a warning of the Soviet plans. Mao gambles that he can face down the Soviets: firstly, by seeming ready to survive nuclear war; secondly, by giving the Russians a bloody nose. Hence the orders for fall-out shelters and troops sent to the north-east border.

But now there is a new, triangular balance of power. America and China need each other, if not as allies, then as co-conspirators to keep the Soviets down. Mao can accept the idea because the US had never seized land in China, as European nations and Japan had done. Nixon is free to start talks about withdrawal from Vietnam.

Mao's gamble pays off. Russia, facing enemies on two fronts, is willing to talk peace. Zhou Enlai and Kosygin meet in September in Beijing and agree to hold border talks.

To preserve the new balance, Mao needs to keep Nixon on side. After Nixon's warning about Brezhnev's intentions, he trusts Nixon. In 1970, he tells his friend Edgar Snow, famous author of *Red Star Over China*, a history of the Communist Party, that Nixon would be welcome, either as a tourist or as US president. In February 1972, Nixon visits China, perhaps the greatest resetting of international affairs in the post-war world.

A reset for Sino-US relations, but not for Sino-Soviet ones. That would take another thirty years, which we will cover at speed to round off this chapter.

With the Soviets still ready for war in the east – a hundred submarines and sixty major warships in their Pacific ports, one million men deployed with 15,000 tanks and 1,125 aircraft and overwhelming superiority in nuclear weapons – border talks led nowhere. Trade was negligible. But at least, with America and China on the same side, a precarious peace held. Mao died, Deng Xiaoping opened the gates to capitalism, China boomed, even made peace with Japan, and still nothing shifted in Sino-Soviet relations, not for ten years.

Finally, the immense cost of its paranoia, combined with its disastrous occupation of Afghanistan (1979–89), drove the Soviet Union towards bankruptcy. As Russia sank, China rose. On the subject of the Unequal Treaties, the new and (relatively) youthful, reformist leader Mikhail Gorbachev conceded that China had a point. Tensions eased, Russian troops withdrew from Afghanistan, students began to visit each other's nations, with the unforeseen consequence that Chinese young people started to expect, and then demand, Russian-style reforms. Political and economic change affected each other at bewildering speed. Gorbachev was actually on a state visit in Beijing as student protests on Tiananmen Square rose to their catastrophic climax on 3–4 June 1989, when unknown numbers of troops massacred unknown hundreds of students and wounded unknown thousands more. (To this day, the Chinese government will do anything not to reveal the figures.)

This was lightning from the background thunder of an economic revolution. Russia, once the superior source of manufactured goods for her impoverished neighbour, became the source of raw materials for Chinese factories, the products being sold back with Chinese credits (totalling 1.5 billion Swiss francs). In 1989, Russia even asked China for aid – one symbol among many of an economic miracle to match those of Germany and Japan after the Second World War. The following year, the *New York Times* judged the Chinese economy to be about equal to the Russian,[10] on an inexorable thirty-year path to becoming the world's No. 1 or No. 2, depending on how you measure it.

In China, a new generation took office, among them several who had trained in Moscow, including Jiang Zemin, the Party's general secretary. He visited Moscow in May 1991, which is when the two empires sorted out most of their border issues. Of the 320 Ussuri islands, the two powers recognised 167 as Russian and 153 as Chinese, including Damansky/Zhenbao. Ideologies had dissipated like mist at dawn, and no one cared any more about a few hundred pinprick islands. But Gorbachev's *perestroika* (restructuring) and *glasnost* (transparency) – both terms became journalistic clichés – could not bring a return to solvency. The collapse of the USSR in December 1991 broke the empire into fifteen parts, sixteen if you include semi-colonised Mongolia, thrown into an independence it had not known since the fourteenth century. China now had to deal with three new neighbours – Kazakhstan, Kyrgyzstan and Tajikistan – as well as the Russian core of the Soviet empire. It took years, but to avoid upsetting its Muslim and Turkic peoples in the west, China needed stability more than desert, and after a decade of talks, agreed the western borders. One area remained in dispute: the fifty-kilometre stretch of islands on the Amur, upstream from Khabarovsk, capital of the Russian Far East. In October 2004, Putin visited China and the two nations agreed to divide the area half and half, bringing three hundred years of contention to an end* – for the time being.

* Yinling/Tabarov Island and the western half of Heixiazi (Great Bear) Island went to China, the eastern half of the same island (Bolshoi Ussuriiskii in Russian) to Russia, to act as a shield for Khabarovsk.

*This show,* The Mongol Khan, *has been a spectacular success internationally, but its preview in Inner Mongolia (part of China) was suppressed because it was in Mongolian.*

# Epilogue: Future Imperfect

## The 'Unequal Treaties'

FOR CHINA, THE LOSSES OF THE AMUR WATERSHED AND OUTER Manchuria were always skeleton-in-the-cupboard issues, shut away by the need for good diplomatic behaviour, but never out of mind. The treaties of Aigun and Peking are among the several Unequal Treaties imposed on China by foreign powers during the 'century of dishonour'. Scholars and diplomats cannot agree on what an Unequal Treaty is exactly, but there are at least twenty-one of them. The term refers not only to loss of territory, but also to enforced reparations, opening ports to trade, leasing territory and anything else that implies a humiliating loss of sovereignty. Since all the nations involved are now at peace with China, it is indelicate to mention them. But they remain as unpleasant reminders of unresolved tensions, on both sides of the border. Both sides have renamed regions and towns, over one thousand in Russia alone, as if suppressing the symptoms of a chronic disease. China's Suchan has become Russia's Partizansk; Russia's Khabarovsk is still Boli to the Chinese. Aigun itself has a new name, Aihui, as if that will help erase humiliation.

Still the disease festers. The bitterness of the 1960s is history, but even in 1989 Chinese leader Deng Xiaoping complained to the Americans that Stalin had 'severed' Mongolia from China. 'Those over fifty in China remember that the shape of China was like a maple leaf,' Deng told President George H.W. Bush. 'Now, if you look at a map, you see a huge chunk in the north cut away; the maple leaf has been nibbled away.'

Today, Russia and China are as much joined across the Amur as divided by it. At a local level, everyone, including members of Indigenous groups, is linked across international borders by mobile phone (though the internet and digital groups are monitored on both sides). 'These days, people can manage without running water... but cell phones, TVs and laptops are essentials.'[1] Russian tourists love to escape their drab hometowns for the bright lights and bars of Manzhouli; and former villages like Heihe (opposite Blagoveshchensk) and Fuyuan (sixty kilometres west of Khabarovsk) have become thriving towns. At a national level, Russia and China need each other: Russia to export her raw materials (timber, coal, soybeans, gold, oil, hydroelectricity, gas), China to provide the labour (and often the finance) to develop them and the population to consume them. In Manzhouli, besides the Russian tourists, or in Erlian, where the railway crosses from Mongolia to China, you see trainloads of Siberian tree trunks on their way to feed China's voracious wood-processing plants. In 2021, Putin approved a new $9.5 billion railway to deliver coal from northern Siberia to China. National rail networks interlink across a new bridge joining Tianjiang in China to the Jewish Autonomous Region.* Both sides have new gods to replace Marx and Lenin: Oil and Gas. That used to be a joke; now it's a truth. Siberia has more zillions of both than most of us can conceive. Just one of its half-dozen major fields, Kovikta north of Irkutsk, has 2.7 *trillion* cubic metres of gas – that's twelve zeroes, making 27,000 cubic kilometres. This one field alone plans to produce twenty-five cubic kilometres of gas per year for the next thirty years. That's just the current contract. It could go on at that rate for another thousand years, assuming they replace the four thousand kilometres of pipeline now and then. A spur pipeline, diving into tunnels under the Amur, will carry thirty-eight cubic kilometres of gas to China annually when completed. Similarly boggling amounts of oil and coal will also flow to China and out of Russia's Pacific ports, Sakhalin and Vladivostok. At a cost of hundreds of billions of dollars invested in infrastructure, Russia hopes to gain in the east enough to

* An odd name: it was set up in the 1920s as a 'homeland' for the Soviet Union's Jews, to offset the appeal of Zionism to Jews interested in founding the state of Israel. Few Jews remain. The name is an anachronism.

counter sanctions imposed in the west after Putin's invasion of Ukraine. Not everything goes Russia's way – like the fact that the Belt and Road linking China to the west runs through Kazakhstan not Siberia – but generally, for Russia, in 2024, China is more salvation than threat. So far, in the eyes of the two major partners, so good.

But locally problems loom. Russians are painfully, obsessively, fearfully aware that their Far East population of 6 (declining) million is dwarfed by the 110 (increasing) million in China's three Manchurian provinces. Old tropes of the Yellow Peril, common in Europe and America a century ago, resurface with local characteristics, for Russians and Chinese have little in common. Russians abandon decaying towns to industrious Chinese immigrants, bringing their 'cheap', 'shoddy' goods, 'taking our sacred land',[2] fuelling resentment and confirming prejudice. For their part, Chinese immigrants recall the inequality of the treaties of Aigun and Peking, and easily believe they are repossessing what is rightfully theirs. As an economic report on Russia's Far East concludes, 'the Chinese (both who live in the Russian Far East and who live in the border provinces of China) consider the Russian Far East to be historically Chinese'. If that attitude should ever justify a takeover, what, I wonder, would happen to Russian property, energy reserves and pipelines? Well, look at what happened to China after 1842, when Western powers moved in. It would be the beginning of 'a century of humiliation', in reverse.

## HUNTING THE DISSIDENTS

Further west, China's grip tightens. In pursuit of unity, China has turned against its minorities, notoriously the Uighurs of Xinjiang, and including the Mongolians of Inner Mongolia, because (says Beijing) they defend their culture, resist Han unity and harbour old dreams of pan-Mongolist independence. Today, 'pan-Mongolism' is a crime because it threatens

Unity, which, along with Gas and Oil, make up a new Trinity. Beijing's rationale is to deny the existence of indigenous groups – they are all supposed to be equal members of the Chinese family, with no special rights – and suppress their languages and cultures. 'Learn Chinese and become a civilised person,' runs the official slogan. Despite a constitution that claims to protect minority languages, a new language policy, approved in September 2020, declares that 'education in minority language is unconstitutional'.

Some Mongolians, mainly dissidents, choose to flee from what they call 'Southern Mongolia' into Mongolia itself.[3] One eighty-year-old writer named Lhamjab Borjigin (named, like many families, after Chinggis Khan's clan) did so in March 2023 after receiving a two-year prison sentence followed by indefinite surveillance. His crime: to have written a book entitled *China's Cultural Revolution*. He fled with the help of friends to Mongolia, where he planned to publish three more books detailing the oppression of Mongols in Inner Mongolia. From a temporary residence in Ulaanbaatar, he wrote:

> People like myself – branded as undesirable and blacklisted as reactionary – are under the authorities' strict control, monitored and followed round the clock... In schools, including kindergarten classes, all Mongolian teachers have been replaced by Chinese instructors hailing from the interior provinces... Mongolian textbooks have been removed from bookstores and libraries.

But, as Lhamjab discovered, Mongolia is not totally free of its old colonial masters. In April 2023, a month after he published his criticisms, family members told him that 'an army of police and security personnel are visiting [your] family and pressuring them to bring [you] back'. On 3 May, four Chinese policemen in two vehicles came to his apartment, arrested him and deported him to China.

In June 2022, a Mongolian human rights activist, Munkhbayar Chuluundorj, who had been in detention for four months after he criticised both China for abusing human rights in Inner Mongolia and his own government for its close ties to China, wrote an impassioned open letter 'to all Mongolians'. It was headed, 'Wake up, Mongolians, if you don't want to be wiped out!' In July of that year, after a trial in which he had been declared innocent for lack of evidence, he received a ten-year sentence in a second trial for 'collaborating with a foreign [unnamed] intelligence agency' against China. He had been in frequent contact with an unnamed human rights activist, called a 'spy' by the prosecution, without evidence. When his lawyer, Ms Baasan Geleg, asked which intelligence agency was involved, she was told, without evidence, that it was a department of the embassy of India. 'Mongolian intelligence authorities,' wrote Chuluundorj, 'are defending the interests of the People's Republic of China.' By implication, Beijing requested his arrest, and the Mongolian authorities complied. 'I am not just defending Chuluundorj,' Ms Geleg said, 'I am defending the sovereignty and independence of Mongolia. I am defending the entire Mongolian people from Chinese oppression.' On 11 January 2023, a former Mongolian president, Tsakhyiagiin Elbegdorj, nine other human rights activists and ninety-six human rights organisations signed a plea for Chuluundorj's release and for all charges to be dropped.

In brief, China often acts as if it still owns Mongolia, which is no surprise, because the two economies are intertwined. Mongolia's economy is small on the world stage (a GDP, in 2023, of $19.87 billion, ranking it 124 in the world, just below Jamaica, and a thousandth that of China), but it has vast unexploited mineral wealth and an eager market in China, which takes about ninety percent of all exports. Of the 25 million tonnes of coal produced in Mongolia every year, 15 million go to China. A huge gold and copper mine, Oyu Tolgoi ('Turquoise Hill'), in the Gobi almost on the southern border is the second biggest copper deposit in the world. It is controlled by Rio Tinto and the government, but exports approaching 500,000 tonnes annually to China via a new cross-border rail link. Chinese companies buy mining rights and property and use their own workers, who, being unpopular in Mongolia, keep themselves to themselves.

This is a marriage made in hell. The two despise each other, but are bound together by history, by the presence of six million Mongolians in China and by economic necessity. No wonder that many Mongolians suspect that China is creeping up on them, ready to take over, and ready also with historical justifications. In Chinese eyes, Mongols are really, deep-down, part of China. And if they are not right now, well, if they become so in the future, that will be a return to the natural order of things.

## TWO CULTURES, INTERWOVEN

Mongolia and China are so entangled it is hard to tease them apart. Look, for example, at the new town of Kangbashi.

In 1949, China had sixty-nine cities. It now has approaching seven hundred. Never has so much been built so fast. Not all will flourish. Some are ghost towns, others boom. Kangbashi is half and half. Lying a fifteen-minute car ride south of Ordos City, it was nothing but a small village at the start of this century. Kangbashi: a strange name with a story. Once upon a time, in the Qing court, there was a Mongolian adviser named Haya, a member of the Emperor's bodyguard, a fine warrior, and also a scholar. He came to Ordos as a teacher, a Bagsh ('teacher' in Mongolian). One day the place was attacked by bandits, and he sacrificed his life fighting them off. The locals named their village after him, Haya Bagsh, Haya the Teacher, which, for some reason to do with the local dialect, became Kangbashi. In the early 2000s came a vision of progress, dreamed up by the local Communist Party leader. The desert village would become a garden city. By 2009, after less than a decade of frantic building – at 'Ordos speed', as they like to say locally – the city was ready for take-off. Though still a place of empty apartment blocks, people come in their tens of thousands particularly summer tourists, for the centre is a work of art.

The square, actually a rectangle, is one of the biggest, if not the biggest, town square on the planet – two and a half kilometres long, half a kilometre wide – with giant displays of Mongolian wrestlers, five-metre-high Mongolian chess pieces, the world's highest fountain and, after dusk, constantly changing lights. On one side is its first building, its museum, created by the international master-architect Ma Yinsong. It looks like a giant unshelled peanut, all graceful curves, the essence of modernity, as unlikely in its original semi-desert setting as a spaceship, which is precisely what Ma intended. 'When I saw the landscape, suddenly one image came to my mind,' he explained to me. '*Star Wars* Episode 2, when this mirror reflector vessel lands on the desert.' He was referring to the Naboo Royal Starship, a sleek, silvery cross between a supersonic plane, a rocket and a shark. 'I was trying to create a reference to the local landscapes a thousand years ago, without a tree, without a flower.' No wonder Kangbashi is a four-star tourist attraction, not for any one element, but the whole town.

Considering the site was a desert not long ago, you might think history would not figure much. But just down the road is Chinggis's Mausoleum. His story is not far beneath the surface. The main square is named after him, and at its top end, in front of a grand sweep of government buildings, he is part of the present, in the form of five immense bronze statues that portray events and characters in the one-and-only Mongolian source for his rise to power, the *Secret History of the Mongols*. Fifty metres long, many tonnes in weight, they are like towering icons of a history unknown to most Chinese people.

These huge memorials are puzzling to outsiders, because the Mongols were, after all, conquerors from the 'barbaric' lands beyond the Great Wall, and Chinggis's invasions caused the deaths of millions. That's not the point. They are here because they represent something else entirely: Chinese unity. Chinggis's conquests opened the way for his grandson Kublai to take all China and to found the Yuan dynasty, which ruled all of present-day China, including Xinjiang, Tibet and Mongolia itself. That empire was restored and preserved by another borderland people, the

Manchus, and then at last by today's Han. Those who take their selfies beside the bronzes – solid-looking as stone during the day, glittering and spot-lit at night – absorb their message: the Mongols were not brutal conquerors from beyond China's edge, but part of China's extended family. Chinggis's story is China's story; his country is part of China. How does this adulation of Chinggis fit with the current policy of suppressing Mongolian culture? It's surreal, Orwellian. You have to work at what Orwell in his dystopian 1948 novel *1984* called double-think, the ability to hold two contradictory beliefs or attitudes at once.

## A SKIRMISH IN THE CULTURE WARS

One consequence being the following example:

In 2023, I was involved as translator in the London run of a Mongolian spectacular, *The Mongol Khan*. My wife, playwright Timberlake Wertenbaker, adapted the surtitles. The show originated in 1998 with a play, *The State without a Seal*, by Mongolia's leading playwright Lkhagvasuren Bavuu. It's a fine play: grand Shakespearean themes and soaring literary language. Set 2,000 years ago during the empire of the Hunnu (in Mongolian)/Xiongnu (in Chinese) – covered in Part I – it tells of a fictional khan deceived by his evil chancellor into accepting a sadistic, brain-damaged son as heir. The khan emerges from the ensuing mess as the selfless servant of his empire, which arises from decay and chaos, as today's Mongolia has arisen from her colonial past.

After the playwright's death in 2019, its director, 'Hero' Baatar, transformed the play, adding a seventy-strong chorus, and wonderful choreography, costumes and music to support the superb leading actors. In the words of the prime minister, Oyun-Erdene, this was more than a play – it was soft power on steroids, promoting Mongolian culture as the 'defence of our independence and our democracy.' Mongolians loved it. Baatar, with the bulk of a wrestler and the authority of a khan, is a man of towering ambition* and top-level contacts, being the elder half-brother of the prime minister. He arranged help-in-kind from his government and raised cash from investors to fund foreign productions, the first of which was to be in London's 2,500-seat Coliseum in November 2023. The play needed a new title, the old one being incomprehensible outside Mongolia. Though the Hunnu/Xiongnu predated the Mongols by 1,000 years, Mongolians see them as ancestors. Hence *The Mongol Khan*.

With the London show imminent, the company needed a space bigger than Ulaanbaatar's 550-seat state theatre to upgrade the production. Baatar approached the 1,300-seat Red Theatre in Inner Mongolia's capital, Hohhot. Contracts were signed, visas issued, tickets sold, the crew of 130 settled on the train south (including six Brits overseeing the sound and lighting, and filming a documentary about the show), three trucks of costumes, sets and lighting rigs dispatched across the Gobi.

Three days before the opening, with the trucks still *en route*, Inner Mongolia's government realised that the show was not a harmless bit of exoticism, but a powerful statement of cultural identity with irresistible appeal to the region's four million Mongolians, now a minority in their own homeland. Moreover, the show broke the new law forbidding the use of Mongolian in public. Officials came to the company's hotel and told Baatar: so sorry, the show's cancelled, because, by an unfortunate coincidence, there's to be a Communist Party conference at the same time in the very same theatre. Ticket holders were offered refunds. Nothing more was heard of the Party conference.

This preposterous breach of contract appalled both the company and the Mongolian government (headed, remember, by Baatar's half-brother). The foreign ministry protested to Beijing, to which the response was, very well, China would allow three productions in Ordos, that vast area of semi-desert south of the Yellow River, where the capital, Ordos City, has a fine new 1,400-seat theatre, named Edsen Khoroo (The Lord's

* And considerable skill as a self-publicist. His pseudonymous name – 'hero' in English plus his given name, 'hero' in Mongolian – makes him doubly heroic. His real family name is Bat-Ulzii.

Enclosure), after Chinggis's mausoleum a short drive away. Left with no choice, Baatar redirected the trucks 250 kilometres to the south. Clearly, the intention was to bury the production in the provinces, unnoticed.

Exactly the opposite happened. For Mongolians, Ordos has immense significance, conferred by the mausoleum, by their history, by those vast bronze statues of Chinggis, his family and friends standing nearby. To Mongolians, it was unmissable. The productions sold out in three days. Mongolians from all across their vast homeland and beyond, even several from Japan, began to arrive, an intolerable embarrassment for the Chinese authorities.

But what could they do to stop the show? Censor it? On September 18, a censor watched the dress rehearsal and then ordered cuts – including references to 'Hunnu/Xiongnu' and 'empire' – that were both ludicrous and impossible. The next day, on the afternoon of the first show, three dark-suited officials arrived 'to test the fire-fighting equipment'. One of them opened a hydraulic pump, which flooded the stage. Appalled but undeterred, the company spent two hours cleaning up with mops and buckets.

But some forty minutes before the start, with ticket-holders lined up at the doors, more officials arrived, claiming there was a problem with the electricity. Switches were examined. The lights died, plunging the theatre into semi-darkness, leaving just enough light for a forty-strong phalanx of dark suits and uniforms to usher everyone from the darkened theatre into the bright lights outside. This was sabotage, pure and simple. Outside, the 1,400 enraged ticket-holders yelled their frustration. When offered refunds, many refused, preferring to keep their tickets as souvenirs.

None of this made any impression. Back in the hotel, Baatar kept up the morale of his devastated, frightened company by organising a table-tennis competition and a day out to visit Chinggis's mausoleum, while rejecting black-suited demands for an immediate return to Mongolia by insisting that the costumes, lighting and sound gear had to be returned first. For an even worse catastrophe loomed: the equipment lost, professional lives ruined, and goodbye to London, let alone other international venues.

After a three-day stand-off, an agreement: the equipment rescued, and everyone ushered into three buses for a twelve-hour drive to the border town of Erlian. After a night in a hotel, there followed the blessed four-hour train journey to Ulaanbaatar. The equipment trundled back across the Gobi and flew on to London, where, under intense pressure, the company set up in the Coliseum and opened as planned on 17 November, to a rapturous reception and a sell-out two-week run.

Two months later, after a formal protest and a flurry of publicity – excellent for the show, not so for China – the Inner Mongolian government offered $2 million as compensation. This was the cost of under-estimating the power of live theatre to focus emotions – in this case, the mere threat of live theatre. This was what it cost China to kill a Mongolian-language show they had themselves contracted.

## HOW IT COULD ALL GO WRONG

OK. So the borders are fixed for the present. Putin and Xi are friends, each backs the other against the US, and both love despots. But China is warming, along with the rest of the globe. In 2005, Jared Diamond, in his book *Collapse*,[4] pointed out the looming problems for north China, in an apocalyptic list of overlapping causes and effects: highly variable rainfall, high winds, droughts, soil erosion, increases in the number and floor-area of households, increasing demand for meat, eggs and milk leading to increasing agricultural waste, pollution so bad that it forces city dwellers to wear face masks, soils destroyed by discharges and run-offs of fertilisers and pesticides, desertification due to overgrazing, excesses of industrial and domestic plastic trash, forests cut down (except for the far north-east), storms that carry dust from the Gobi to Beijing and on and on. Now, so far, the drawbacks do not outweigh the benefits of a high-ranking economy, but that equation is unlikely to last.

Two years after the publication of Diamond's book, James Lovelock, the British ecologist, predicted that heat would drive populations northwards across the northern hemisphere. After a lecture he had recently given in the US, he said, people were 'coming up to me asking where in Canada they should buy real estate because they believed me when I said much of the US will be uninhabitable… we should be scared stiff'. In north China, he predicted, 'people will press to live in a newly lush Siberia before the century is out'.[5] As I write, that was seventeen years ago. Mark his words; look out for the Great Siberian Property Boom.

Another problem may be the growing inequality between the two partners. They used to be master and pupil, then equals, and by 2024 China's economy was ten times Russia's, with many consequences, like the fact that China takes fifteen percent of Russia's foreign trade, yet Russia takes one percent of China's, or that China no longer wants Russian arms, just the technologies to make their own. Given these changes, would a declining Russia be able to withstand a Chinese tsunami eager to redress old inequalities beyond the Amur?

Siberia and Manchuria are not the only territories lost to China. There's also Mongolia, once part of Yuan Dynasty China (aka the Mongol Empire), and then, after a gap of three centuries, drawn into Qing Dynasty China like a star swallowed by a black hole. It could happen again, for China already absorbs most of the copper from Oyu Tolgoi, and Chinese mining companies seek licences to hunt for every mineral in Mongolia's subterranean treasure chest. Take lithium, for instance, vital for every car battery: Mongolia has over 600,000 tonnes of this 'white gold', enough for 75 million car batteries. Mongolia's coal darkens the skies of Ulaanbaatar in winter, but most of the rest lumbers south by rail and truck. Chinese loans and investments pump up Mongolia's economy and finance important parts of Xi Jinping's Belt and Road Initiative.[6] As we have seen earlier in this chapter, Chinese influence works its way into Mongolian society like water into a sponge. This is not the result of official policy, but the way a certain type of imperialism works, with its assumed superiority and often with apparent generosity.

In a few decades, who knows, Mongolia will be as dependent on Chinese whims as it once was on those of a Manchu Emperor. If so, it would be a final step in a slow and steady process for a cowed and corrupted Mongolian government to 'request' their southerly neighbour for 'help' in administering an economy that would by then be largely under Chinese control. For China, it would seem a natural step, righting the wrongs of the Unequal Treaties.

Here's a scenario: Imagine that over the course of decades, as China's central plains turn to desert, the post-Putin, post-Xi leaders fall out. Mineral wealth declines, the population ages, the birthrate falls, the economy falters. China is left with no alternative, for reasons of self-preservation, but to retake the areas once held by the Manchus. They tell themselves and the world that this accords with the treaty signed in Nerchinsk in 1689. Overwhelmed by the weight of numbers and armaments and cash payments and the lure of a vast marketplace, neither Mongolia nor Russia will resist.

Would the world? It would surely complain. Other nations would recall the result of failing to object to Russia's seizure of Crimea in 2014. 'Borders are sacrosanct!' they'd cry. That is the fundamental tenet of international relations! It has been so ever since the Peace of Westphalia ended the Thirty Years War in 1648!* That was the principle that underpinned the Treaty of Versailles in 1918–19, that justified opposition to Soviet takeovers of two dozen independent countries after 1917 and acceptance of their re-emergence in the 1990s, and the invasion of Kuwait by a 42-nation coalition to drive out Saddam Hussein's forces in 1990–1, and more examples of fine words than we can list. But what would the rest of the world actually *do*? My guess is not much. Nothing anyway to force a reversal, for who would want to trigger a world war over distant deserts, grasslands and forests? After all, we're talking about a fraction of a giant nation, not the whole thing. Who would risk losing the chance to share Russia's mineral wealth? Would America fight in defence of Russia

* Widely believed, much disputed.

or for the rights of a nation-state, most of whose resources will be going to China anyway? Would Russia, though humiliated, risk a nuclear war, or even a conventional one, given China's vast armed forces, her vast reserves of manpower, her sheer overwhelming vastness?

Besides, China will claim justification, for these lands were all once hers. Mongolia, the prodigal daughter, will return to the family, and will be forgiven for her century of absence. As for the rest, technically, as international lawyers will argue, the treaties of Nerchinsk and Peking will still be valid, specifying that the Amur watershed right up to the Stanovoy mountains and a large chunk of Manchuria were all Chinese. Every treaty since then (they will claim) was rendered invalid by the illegal, immoral rapacity of Russian imperialism. The cash may no longer be there to pay for Russia's oil, gas and coal, but China still needs them, and (she claims) has every right to them.

So yes. China swallows the rest of Manchuria, parts of Siberia, Mongolia, the lot.

The crisis passes. The two sides agree to share the energy and resources they both need. The border that once ran along the Great Wall settles 1,600 kilometres to the north. The Manchu Empire is restored. After two thousand years, peace comes to the once-disputed lands beyond the Wall.

All is quiet on the northern front.

APPENDIX I

# RULERS OF THE NORTH: MAJOR DYNASTIES AND STEPPE EMPIRES

| ***Native Chinese dynasties*** | ***Dynasties of foreign origin*** | ***Steppe entities/ peoples*** |
|---|---|---|
| Qin and Han (221 BCE–220 CE) | | Xiongnu (209 BCE–mid-2nd century CE) |
| | | Xianbei (130–180) |
| Three Dynasties (220–280) | Tuoba or Northern Wei (386–534) | |
| Period of Disunion (280–581) | | Rouran (c.500–552) |
| Sui (581–618) | | Turks (552–742) |
| Tang (618–907) | | Uighurs (744–840) |
| Five Dynasties, Ten Kingdoms (907–960) | | |
| Song (960–1279) | Liao (Khitan) (907–1125) | Mongol (1206–) |

| *Native Chinese dynasties* | *Dynasties of foreign origin* | *Steppe entities/ peoples* |
|---|---|---|
| | Western Xia (Tangut) (1028–1227) | |
| | Jin (Jürchen) (1125–1234) | |
| | Yuan (Mongol) (1271–1368) | Mongol (Yuan) (–1368) |
| Ming (1368–1644) | | Mongol (Northern Yuan) (1368–1691) |
| | Qing (Manchu) (1644–1912) | Zungars (1634–1755) |
| Nationalist (1912–1949) | | Mongols (under Chinese or Russian influence, 1921–1992) |
| Communist (1949–present) | | Mongols |

(Adapted from Thomas Barfield, *The Perilous Frontier*, p. 13.)

APPENDIX II

# WERE THE HUNS THE XIONGNU?

SOME TIME AFTER THEIR DEFEAT BY CHINA IN 89 CE, THE Xiongnu vanished into the heart of Asia, leaving evidence of their presence in their graves, in Chinese sources and in the DNA of modern Mongolians. In 376 CE, there emerged at the far end of Asia a tribe with a similar lifestyle – nomads, tent dwellers with wagons, mounted archers – and a vaguely similar name. The Huns, under their leader Attila, famously contributed to the fall of the Roman Empire in the fifth century, but their origins were a mystery. In 1748, the French orientalist Joseph de Guignes (1721–1800) proposed that the Huns must surely be the Xiongnu, reborn in poverty. Edward Gibbon in his six-volume *Decline and Fall of the Roman Empire* (published in 1776–89) turned theory into accepted truth with fine phrases. The Huns, he said, were descendants of the Xiongnu, made 'formidable by the matchless dexterity with which they managed their bows and their horses; by their hardy patience in supporting the inclemency of the weather; and by the incredible speed of their march'. For the next two centuries, Gibbon stood unchallenged until the 1930s, when scholars pointed out that there was absolutely no evidence to bridge the gap between the two. As Edward Thompson, one-time professor of classics at Nottingham University, wrote in his 1948 book on the Huns, 'This view has now been exploded and abandoned.'

But it has recently regained lost ground. The two tribes were briefly so close in time and space that it is hard to believe they were separate. Remnants of the Xiongnu, fleeing through southern Kazakhstan, reportedly reached the Syrdar'ya River by about 120 CE. In round figures, that's 2,800 kilometres in thirty years, or a mere 90 kilometres a year. In 160, the Greek polymath Ptolemy mentions the 'Khoinoi', with the initial *kh* pronounced like the *ch* in the Scottish *loch*, which makes them sound pretty much like 'Huns'. These people he placed between two other tribes, the most distant of which, the Roxolani, probably lived on the Don, thus putting the Huns just north of the Sea of Azov. The gap has narrowed to two thousand kilometres and forty years – a gap easily crossed at the slow pace of fifty kilometres a year.

There is *almost* hard evidence for the link. Both Huns and Xiongnu made iron cauldrons; but so did other groups, with varying designs that do not suggest an evolutionary sequence. Both Huns and Xiongnu occasionally elongated the skulls of children with bindings, but so did many other groups. The two shared bow designs, the upper limb being longer than the lower limb, for unknown reasons. But other groups also used asymmetrical bows, so that's no proof of a link.

What about folklore? Stories about ancestral origins can last centuries, as in Mongol culture. Indeed, Mongolians today refer to the Xiongnu as Huns, and in China 'Hunnu' is a common transliteration. But if there was a link, the Huns did not proclaim it. Attila had his bards, but no Roman or Greek visitors mentioned them singing of conquering forebears.

We get little help from language. Though Attila employed interpreters and secretaries, no one wrote in Hunnish, only Latin or Greek, the languages of the dominant cultures. No single word that is undoubtedly Hunnish has survived. Some Hun names suggest links back to Turkish. The name of Attila's uncle Octar seems to derive from Old Turkic (*öktör*, 'powerful'), as does that of his father Mundzuk ('Pearl' or 'Decoration'), among others. But there is nothing to link Turkish names with Xiongnu ones. Anyway, names have no necessary connection with the culture of their owners: my name John derives from the Hebrew meaning 'Yahweh is gracious', which doesn't explain much about being English.

Perhaps the most suggestive evidence is that of the name 'Hun' itself. An analysis by Christopher Atwood* lists dozens of versions of the name in many different languages. He suggests a multi-stage process. First, the Sanskrit and Greek terms for 'Hun' derived from the Chinese word 'Xiongnu' 'by the first century BCE', which argues for contact across Eurasia. Then, by around 350 CE, a core of Hun tribes arose in western Kazakhstan, incorporating remnants of the Xiongnu Empire. They would have been members of the many so-called 'Scythian' tribes that ranged across the Central Asian steppes, unrecorded except on the fringes of their world. Finally, subgroups of Huns fanned outwards, spreading the name in many languages. In 376 CE, one group came to the attention of the Roman Empire when they pushed the Goths across the Danube, the first step in a series of conquests that contributed to the fall of the Roman Empire four decades later.

These considerations would explain why there is no direct, incontrovertible evidence of the Xiongnu-Hun link. The Xiongnu could have become part of a mix of Hun tribes, swirling about in Central Asia, their patterns and language unrecorded by themselves or the outside world, and leaving few traces for modern archaeologists. The Xiongnu might have been – could have been, possibly were – the distant cousins of the Huns, but there's no proof. Yet.

The only firm conclusion is uncertainty. The Huns were *probably* of Turkic stock, *probably* spoke a Turkic language, which *may* have shared roots with Mongolian and Xiongnu. We await more evidence.

---

* Atwood, Christopher P., 'Huns and Xiōngnú: New Thoughts on an Old Problem' (see Bibliography).

APPENDIX III

# GENGHIS OR CHINGGIS: ON SPELLING AND PRONUNCIATION

'Genghis', with a soft *G* – a *dj*-sound, [dž], as it is in the International Phonetic Alphabet, as in 'George' – is the most common spelling and pronunciation in English, but both are wrong. He's pronounced 'Chinggis' in Mongolian, which is reason enough to call him Chinggis. But there's another reason that we'll get to shortly.

The *G* in English comes from the French orientalist, François Pétis de la Croix (1622–95) in his *Histoire du grand Genghizcan* (published by his son of the same name in 1710). De la Croix the father was a brilliant linguist (as was his son), and researched many sources in Persian, Turkish and Arabic. He would have known – as Marco Polo did over three centuries before – that Chinggis's name began with a *tsh* sound [tš]. But French has no equivalent. *Ch* in French is pronounced as *sh* [š], as in 'champagne'. His *G* was the best he could do, though the French pronounce it as an even softer *g* [ž], like the *s* in 'pleasure'. The *-can* ending is his version of 'khan', which is not part of the name – it just means 'king'.

The English translation of 1723, *The History of Genghizcan the Great* (London: J. Darby, et al.,) simply took over de la Croix's spelling, which

English readers pronounced with that soft *G* [*dž*]. The hard *g* [g], as in 'get', is even more wrong, and illogical: whoever heard of anyone called George addressed as 'Gorge'? It seems to have spread like a virus over the last century, occasionally made worse by an abominable misspelling, 'Ghenghis'. The *g* as in 'get' was even accepted by the BBC's Pronunciation Unit, because it 'reflects' usage rather than dictates it. Please, just *get it right*.

The translator, by the way, was a woman, Penelope Aubin (1679–1731), a popular but now almost-forgotten novelist, playwright, poet, and translator from French. She gets no credit in the book, unsurprisingly, given the position of women at the time, especially women writers.

Why *-e-* in second place rather than *-i-*? Because de la Croix was not working from Mongolian, but from Turkish, Arabic and Persian, which include vowels only as diacritics (accents), not as letters. He made a random choice that is with us still. The *-ng-* is a single letter in Mongolian vertical script, pronounced like the *–ng-* in 'angle or 'finger' [ŋg]. But in English, there is another -ng-, as in 'ringer' or 'singer', [ŋ] without the *g*. So we need the second g in Chinggis to avoid confusion. Luckily Russian has no [ŋ] sound, so the Cyrillic version of Chinggis (Чингис) is fine. The *-i-*' is correct, and so is the *-s*, as in 'this' (not *-iz*, which is used occasionally, e.g. by de la Croix and Marco Polo himself, suggesting that the former followed the latter, whose *Travels* had been available in French and Latin from the early fourteenth century).

# ACKNOWLEDGEMENTS

With thanks to: Alatan; the late Prof. Charles Bawden, who started it all; Batmunkh; Kerry Brown; Sam Carter, and all at Oneworld; Cheng Dalin and Cheng Yinong; Ding Ding; Diimajav Erdenebaatar; Ge Jian, Water Xu and all at Grasslands; Paul Godfrey; Matthew and Enkhee Henderson; Unurmaa Janchiv; Jorigt; Oliver King; Nachug; Benjamin Ren; Goyo Reston; the late Igor de Rachewiltz; Sharaldai; Sainjirgal; Colin Thubron; Tsagaan Törbat; Jack Weatherford; Roland Walters; Prof. Wei Jian; Doug Young; and Lijia Zhang.

# Bibliography


Allsen, Thomas T., 'The Rise of the Mongolian Empire', in Herbert Franke and Denis Twitchett (eds), *The Cambridge History of China*, Vol. 6: *Alien Regimes and Border States, 907–1368* (Cambridge: Cambridge University Press, 1994).

——— *Culture and Conquest in Mongol Eurasia* (Cambridge: Cambridge University Press, 2001).

Amitai-Preiss, Reuven, and David O. Morgan (eds), *The Mongol Empire and Its Legacy* (Leiden and Boston: Brill, 1999).

Atwood, Christopher P., 'Huns and Xiōngnú: New Thoughts on an Old Problem', in Brian J. Boeck, Russell E. Martin, and Daniel Rowland (eds), *Dubitando: Studies in History and Culture, in Honor of Donald Ostrowski* (Bloomington, Indiana: Slavica Publishers).

Atwood, Christopher P., *Encyclopedia of Mongolia and the Mongol Empire* (New York: Facts on File, 2004).

——— *The Secret History of the Mongols* (London: Penguin Random House, 2023).

Ban Gu, *The History of the Former Han Dynasty* (Baltimore: Waverly Press, 1938–1955).

Barfield, Thomas J., *The Perilous Frontier: Nomadic Empires and China, 221 BC to AD 1757* (Cambridge, Mass., and Oxford: Blackwell, 1989).

——— 'The Hsiung-nu Imperial Confederacy: Organization and Foreign Policy', *The Journal of Asian Studies*, Vol. 41, No. 1, November 1981.

Baumer, Christoph, *The History of Central Asia, Vol. II: The Age of the Silk Roads* (London and New York: I.B. Tauris, 2014).

Bawden, Charles, *The Modern History of Mongolia* (London and New York: Kegan Paul, 1968, revised 1989).

Bemmann, Jan, et al. (eds), *Current Archaeological Research in Mongolia, Bonn Contributions to Asian Archaeology*, Vol. 4 (Bonn: Rheinische Friedrich-Wilhelms-Universität, 2009).

Benjamin, Craig, *The Yuezhi: Origin, Migration and the Conquest of Northern Bactria* (Turnhout, Belgium: Brepols, 2007).

Billé, Franck, and Caroline Humphrey, *On the Edge: Life Along the Russia-China Border* (Cambridge, Mass, and London: Harvard University Press, 2021).

Bodde, Derk, *Statesman, Patriot and General in Ancient China* (trans. from Sima Qian's biographical essays on Lü Buwei, Jing Ke and Meng Tian, with a commentary) (Newhaven: American Oriental Society, 1940).

Brosseder, Ursula, and Bryan K. Miller (eds), *Xiongnu Archaeology: Multidisciplinary Perspectives of the First Steppe Empire in Inner Asia*, Bonn Contributions to Asian Archaeology (BCAA), Vol. 5 (Bonn: Rheinische Friedrich-Wilhelms-Universität, 2011).

Bulag, Uradyn E., *The Mongols at China's Edge: History and the Politics of National Unity* (Lanham, Maryland: Rowman & Littlefield, 2002).

Chimiddorj, Yeruul-Erdene, and Ikue Otani, 'The Chinese Inscription on the Lacquerware Unearthed from Tomb 20, Gol Mod Site 1, Mongolia', *The Silk Road*, Vol. 13, 2015.

Chubb, Edmund O., *China and Russia: The "Great Game"'* (New York: Columbia University Press, 1971).

Coox, Alvin D., *Nomonhan: Japan Against Russia, 1939* (Redwood City, California: Stanford University Press, 1990).

Cosmo, Nicola Di, *Ancient China and its Enemies: The Rise of Nomadic Power in East Asian History* (Cambridge: Cambridge University Press, 2002).

——— 'Han Frontiers: Toward an Integrated View', *Journal of the American Oriental Society*, Vol. 129, No. 2, April–June 2009.

Crespigny, Rafe de, *Northern Frontier: The Policies and Strategy of the Later Han Empire*, Australian National University Faculty of Asian Studies Monographs, New Series, No. 4, Canberra, 1984. (An edited version: *The Division and Destruction of the Xiongnu Confederacy in the First and Second Centuries* AD, available as an internet edition, 2004.)

Desroches, Jean-Paul, et al., *Mongolie: Le Premier Empire des Steppes* (Mission archéologique française, Paris: Actes Sud, 2003).

Diamond, Jared, *Collapse: How Societies Choose to Fail or Survive* (New York: Penguin, 2005).

Dikötter, Frank, *Mao's Great Famine* (London: Bloomsbury, 2010).

Erdenebaatar, Diimajav: *Хун Улсын Соёлын Өв/The Cultural Heritage of Xiongnu Empire* (Ulaanbaatar: Munkhiin Useg Publishing House, 2016).

Eregzen, Gelegdorj (ed.), *Хүннүгийн Өв/Treasures of the Xiongnu* (exhibition catalogue), National Museum of Mongolia, 2011.

Franke, Herbert, and Denis Twitchett (eds), *The Cambridge History of China, Vol. 6: Alien Regimes and Border States, 907–1368* (Cambridge: Cambridge University Press, 1994).

——— *From Tribal Chieftain to Universal Emperor and God: The Legitimation of the Yüan Dynasty* (Munich: Bayerische Akademie der Wissenschaft, 1978).

——— *China Under Mongol Rule* (Aldershot, Hants: Ashgate, 1994).

Giscard, Pierre-Henri, and Tsagaan Turbat (eds), *France-Mongolie: Découvertes Archéologiques – Vingt Ans de Partenariat* (exhibition catalogue), Institute of History and Archaeology, Ulaanbaatar, 2015.

Grousset, René, *The Empire of the Steppes* (New Brunswick and London: Rutgers University Press, 1970).

Han Feizi, *Basic Writings*, trans. Burton Watson (New York: Columbia University Press, 2003).

Hanks, Bryan, 'Archaeology of the Eurasian Steppes and Mongolia', *Annual Review of Anthropology*, Vol. 39, 2010.

Honeychurch, William, 'Alternative Complexities: The Archaeology of Pastoral Nomadic States', *Journal of Archaeological Research*, Vol. 22, No. 4, December 2014.

——— 'The Nomad as State Builder: Historical Theory and Material Evidence from Mongolia', *Journal of World Prehistory*, Vol. 26, No. 4, December 2013.

Impey, Lawrence, 'Shangtu, the Summer Capital of Kublai Khan,' *Geographical Review*, Vol. 15, No. 4, October 1925.

Kessler, Adam T., *Empires Beyond the Great Wall*, Natural History Museum of Los Angeles County, 1994. A shorter version: 'Beyond the Great Wall of China: Archaeological Treasures from Inner Mongolia', *Minerva*, Vol. 5, No. 3, May/June 1994.

Khazanov, Anatoly, *Nomads and the Outside World*, (Cambridge: Cambridge University Press, 1984).

Lai, Benjamin and Zhang Yiming, *When Brothers Fight: Chinese Eyewitness Accounts of the Sino-Soviet Border Battles, 1969* (Warwick, UK: Helion & Company, 2023).

Lattimore, Owen, *Inner Asian Frontiers of China* (New York: American Geographical Society, 1951).

——— *Studies in Frontier History* (Oxford: Oxford University Press, 1962).

Loades, Mike, *The Composite Bow* (Oxford: Osprey, 2016).

Lovell, Julia, *The Great Wall: China Against the World 1000 BC–AD 2000* (London: Atlantic Books, 2006).

Loewe, Michael, *Crisis and Conflict in Han China* (London: George Allen & Unwin, 1974).
——— *Records of Han Administration*, 2 vols (Cambridge: Cambridge University Press, 1967).
——— 'The Campaigns of Han Wu-ti', in Frank A. Kierman and John F. Fairbank (eds), *Chinese Ways in Warfare* (Cambridge, Mass: Harvard University Press, 1974).
Lüthi, Lawrence M., 'Restoring Chaos to History: Sino-Soviet-American Relations, 1969', *The China Quarterly*, No. 210, June 2012.
Maenchen-Helfen, Otto J., *The World of the Huns* (Berkeley, Los Angeles and London: University of California Press, 1973).
Man, John, *Gobi: Tracking the Desert* (London: Weidenfeld & Nicolson, 1997).
——— *Genghis Khan: Life, Death and Resurrection* (London: Bantam Press, 2004).
——— *Attila* (London: Bantam Press, 2006).
——— *The Terracotta Army: China's First Emperor and the Birth of a Nation* (London: Bantam Press, 2007).
——— *The Great Wall* (London: Bantam Press, 2008).
——— *Xanadu* (London: Bantam Press, 2009).
——— *Barbarians at the Wall* (London: Bantam Press, 2019).
Martin, H. Desmond, *The Rise of Chingis Khan and his Conquest of North China* (Baltimore: Johns Hopkins University Press, 1950).
Markley, Jonathan, *Peace and Peril: Sima Qian's Portrayal of Han–Xiongnu Relations* (Turnhout, Belgium: Brepols, 2011).
Miller, Bryan K., *Power Politics in the Xiongnu Empire*, University of Pennsylvania dissertation, published online at https://repository.upenn.edu/entities/publication/d7403e54-4819-44f8-9434-ccc93e630998.
Millward, James, *Eurasian Crossroads: A History of Xinjiang* (London: Hurst & Co., London, 2007).
Morgan, David, *The Mongols* (Oxford, UK and Malden, Mass.: Blackwell, 1986).
Mote, F. W., *Imperial China 900–1800* (Cambridge, Mass., and London: Harvard University Press, 1999).
——— 'The T'u-mu Incident of 1449', in Frank A. Kierman and John F. Fairbank (eds), *Chinese Ways in Warfare* (Cambridge, Mass.: Harvard University Press, 1974).
Okada, Hidehiro, 'China as a Successor State to the Mongol Empire', in Reuven Amitai-Preiss and David O. Morgan (eds), *The Mongol Empire and Its Legacy* (Leiden, Boston and Cologne: Brill, revised edition, 2000).

Ossendowski, Ferdinand, *Beasts, Men and Gods* (New York: Dutton, 1922).

Palmer, James, *The Bloody White Baron* (London: Faber & Faber, 2008).

Paludan, Ann, *Chinese Sculpture: A Great Tradition* (Enfield, Chicago: Serindia Publications, 2007).

Psarras, Sophia-Karin, 'Exploring the North: Non-Chinese Cultures of the Late Warring States and Han', *Monumenta Serica*, Vol. 42, 1994.

——— 'Han and Xiongnu: A Reexamination of Cultural and Political Relations', in two parts: (1) *Monumenta Serica*, Vol. 51, 2003, and (2) *Monumenta Serica*, Vol. 52, 2004.

Rachewiltz, Igor de (trans. and ed.), *The Secret History of the Mongols: A Mongolian Epic Chronicle of the Thirteenth Century,* 2 vols (Leiden, Boston and Cologne: Brill, 2004; supplementary vol., 2013).

Ratchnevsky, Paul, *Genghis Khan: His Life and Legacy*, trans. and ed. Thomas Haining (Oxford, UK, and Cambridge, Mass.: Blackwell, 1991).

Rogers, J. Daniel, 'Inner Asian States and Empires: Theories and Synthesis', *Journal of Archaeological Research*, Vol. 20, No. 3, September 2012.

Rossabi, Morris, *Khubilai Khan: His Life and Times* (Berkeley, Los Angeles and London: University of California Press, 1988).

Ryabushkin, Dmitry and Harold Orenstein, *The Sino-Soviet Border War of 1969*, Vols 1 & 2 (Warwick, UK: Helion & Company, 2021).

Seres, Joseph, *The Jesuits and the Sino-Russian Treaty of Nerchinsk (1689): The Diary of Thomas Pereira, SJ*, Bibliotheca Instituti Historici, Vol. XVIII, Rome, 1961.

Shang Yang, *The Book of Lord Shang*, with Sun Tzu: *The Art of War* (Ware, Herts: Wordsworth Editions, 1998).

Sima Qian, *Records of the Grand Historian: Qin Dynasty*, trans. Burton Watson (Hong Kong and New York: The Chinese University of Hong Kong and Columbia University Press, 1993).

Sinor, Denis, 'The Inner Asian Warriors', *Journal of the American Oriental Society*, Vol. 101, No. 2, April–June 1981.

Snow, Philip, *China and Russia: Four Centuries of Conflict and Concord* (New Haven and London: Yale University Press, 2023).

So, Jenny F., and Emma C. Bunker, *Traders and Raiders on China's Northern Frontier* (Washington: Smithsonian Institution, 1999).

Thompson, E. A., *The Huns* (revised by Peter Heather from original edition, *A History of Attila and the Huns* (Oxford: Oxford University Press, 1948; Blackwell, 1999).

Thubron, Colin, *The Amur River* (London: Chatto & Windus, 2021).
——— *In Siberia* (London: Chatto & Windus, 1999).

Törbat, Tsagaan, *Khunnugiin jiriin irgediin bulsh* (Ulaanbaatar: Mongolian State Educational University, 2004).

Trever, Camilla, *Excavations in Northern Mongolia (1924–1925)* (Leningrad: J. Fedorov Printing House, 1932).

Turchin, Peter, 'A Theory for Formation of Large Empires', *Journal of Global History*, Vol. 4, Issue 2, 2009.

Wakeman, Frederic, *The Great Enterprise: The Manchu Reconstruction of Imperial Order in 17th-Century China* (Berkeley and Los Angeles: University of California Press, 1985).

Waldron, Arthur, *The Great Wall of China: From History to Myth* (Cambridge: Cambridge University Press, 1990).

Watson, Burton, *Ssu-ma Ch'ien, Grand Historian of China* (New York and London: Columbia University Press, 1958).

Weatherford, Jack, *Genghis Khan and the Making of the Modern World* (New York: Crown, 2004).

Yang Haiying, *Genocide on the Mongol Steppe*, Vol. 1, trans. Enkhbatu Togochog (Tokyo: Iwanami Shoten, 2009).

Yap, Joseph P., *Wars with the Xiongnu: A Translation from Zizhi Tongjian* (Bloomington, Indiana: AuthorHouse, 2009).
——— *The Western Regions, Xiongnu and Han* (Joseph P. Yap, 2019).

Yetts, W. Perceval, 'Discoveries of the Kozlov Expedition', *The Burlington Magazine for Connoisseurs*, Vol. 48, No. 277, April 1906.

Yule, Henry, *The Travels of Marco Polo, The Complete Yule-Cordier Edition*, 2 Vols (New York: Dover Publications, 1993).

# Illustration List

18. Maria, the Ewenki matriarch. Author's Photograph.
19. A Chinese propaganda poster from c.1950 showing Marx, Engels, Lenin, Stalin and Mao as the indivisible Communist pantheon.
20. Poster for *The Mongol Khan* at the London Coliseum.

# Notes

## Preface

1 For a summary of them, see Appendix I.

## Prelude: The making of the borderlands

1 Changxing Shi, Luan Zhang, Jiaqiang Xu and Lipeng Guo, 'Sediment Load and Storage in the Lower Yellow River During the Late Holocene', *Geografiska Annaler. Series A, Physical Geography*, Vol. 92, No. 3 (2010), pp. 297–309; Laurie Winkless, 'London Has Been Putting On Weight, Thanks To Construction', *Forbes* magazine, November 2010.

## 1. Forging unity, twice

1 Quoted by Joseph P. Yap, *Wars with the Xiongn*, see Bibliography.
2 Joseph P. Yap, op cit.
3 Three other sources on the Xiongnu – by Sima Qian, Ban Gu and Fan Ye – have also been translated by Joseph P. Yap in *The Western Regions*. See Bibliography.
4 Both quotes from *Han Feizi: Basic Writings*, in Burton Watson's translation. See Bibliography.
5 These anecdotes are from Bodde's translation of Sima Qian, see Bibliography.
6 'Stateless Empire', in *Xiongnu Archaeology*, see Bibliography.
7 These details are estimates by Barfield, *The Perilous Frontier*, p. 47.
8 In 'Stateless Empire', *Xiongnu Archaeology*. As Kradin adds, 'A similar phenomenon happened time and again in history… ending with the developing of the New World by American pioneers.'
9 His account was a major source for Sima Guang in the eleventh century. Here, both sources are used.

## 2. A war to end the war

1 *Wars with the Xiongnu*, p 174.
2 Kovalev et al., 'The Shouxiangcheng Fortress' in *Xiongnu Archaeology*.

3 Amartüvshin et al., 'On the Walled Site of Mangasyn Khuree' in *Xiongnu Archaeology*. You can see both places on Google Earth (42.36/105.10.5 and 42.33.45/107.24.14).

### 3. The annihilation of the Xiongnu

1 Ursula Brosseder 2007, quoted in Miller, *Power Politics*. The Chinese knew about Afghanistan – Bactria or Da Xia – from the traveller Zhang Qian, so the Xiongnu would surely have known of it as well. There is a detailed chemical analysis of Gol Mod gold in Desroches et al., *Mongolie, Le Premier Empire des Steppes*.
2 Cologne Museum and Corning Museum, New York.
3 Chimiddorj and Otani, 'The Chinese Inscription…' See Bibliography. The inscription reveals the size of this operation and the complexity of the bureaucracy controlling it. For production, there was a production inspector, an assistant clerk, a workshop overseer, a head secretary and an executive officer. For overall inspection, a deputy director of the right, and a director, in this case a provisional director.
4 *Power Politics in the Xiongnu Empire*. See Bibliography.
5 Mostly. There are some remains of weapons, e.g. in Khudgiin Tolgoi. See Hyeung-Won Yun in *Current Archaeological Research in Mongolia.*
6 With thanks to Alatan for his translation.
7 Translation by Bryan Miller in *Power Politics.*

### 4. The Xianbei and their cave

1 Translation by Water Xu.
2 Paludan, p. 188.

### 5. Chinggis in China

1 From Atwood's 2023 translation, as are all quotations in this chapter, except one (noted on p.132).
2 Billé and Humphrey, p. 163.

### 6. In Xanadu

1 *Geographical Review*, 1925. See Bibliography.
2 On Google Earth: 42° 15′ 49″ N/ 115° 58′ 44″ E. And check the distance to Xanadu – 19.5 kilometres direct, a bit longer cross-country.
3 In The Art, Archaeology and Ancient World Library, Oxford.
4 Mu Qing Ge 睦清阁.

5 In the Yule-Cordier edition, without the brackets that include different versions of the *Travels*.

### 9. Two priests and the new frontier

1 Seres. See Bibliography.
2 Snow, *China and Russia*, p. 9.
3 *The Amur River: Between Russia and China*, p 101.
4 From Sh Natsagdorj's *Khalkhyn Tüükh* ('Khalkha History'). Bawden's translation in *The Modern History of Mongolia*, p. 76.
5 Bawden, *The Modern History of Mongolia*, p. 81.
6 Bawden, p. 83.
7 *The Modern History of Mongolia*, p. 135.

### 10. How China lost half an empire

1 Snow, p. 103.
2 Don C. Price, *Russia and the Roots of the Chinese Revolution, 1896–1911*, Harvard, Cambridge MA, quoted by Snow, p. 161.
3 Thubron, p. 132.
4 Billé and Humphrey, Chapter 5, 'Friends, Foes, and Kin Across the Border'.
5 My main source for what follows is James Palmer's *The Bloody White Baron*.
6 Ossendowski, *Beasts, Men and Gods*, a highly imaginative international bestseller. He claims he was an eyewitness to this incident.

### 11. The most important battle you've never heard of

1 In Chubb. See Bibliography.
2 Coox, *Nomonkhan*. See Bibliography.
3 Coox's figure. Other sources claim both more and less, but not much.

### 12. The Ewenki: Life, death and survival

1 Published as 'North-Western Manchuria and the Reindeer-Tungus' in *The Geographical Journal*, Vol. 75, No. 6 (Jun., 1930), from which the quotations were taken.

### 13. The war that never was

1 Dikötter, *Mao's Great Famine*, p. 322.
2 Dikötter, p. 325

3 Snow, p. 437.
4 Snow, p. 449.
5 For a good analysis, see Bulag: *The Mongols at China's Edge.*
6 The two sources for the quotations and details of the clashes are Lai and Yiming; and Ryabushkin and Orenstein. See Bibliography.
7 Benjamin Lai and Zhang Yiming, *When Brothers Fight*, p. 51.
8 A famous anecdote, told by many sources including Lüthi, 'Restoring Chaos to History', p. 384 and Snow p. 450.
9 Summarised by Lüthi, op. cit.
10 Snow, p. 483.

**Epilogue: Future imperfect**

1 Billé and Humphrey, p. 140.
2 Colin Thubron heard rumours that Chinese companies owned or rented twenty percent of the arable land north of the Amur. *The Amur River*, p. 139.
3 This case and many others are quoted on the website of the Sothern Mongolia Human Rights Information Centre (webmaster@smhric.org), based in New York.
4 Chapter 10, 'China, Lurching Giant'.
5 The *Guardian*, 15 March 2007, article by Stuart Jeffries.
6 Trade grew 'by 38 percent (US$2.8 billion) in 2021 compared to the previous year. Trade volume between China and Mongolia reached US$10.1 billion in 2021 with exports valued at US$7.64 billion and imports at US$2.49 billion.' (China Briefing, online, 2024).

# Index

*Note:* Page numbers in italics are illustrations.